The Evolution of Human Language

Advances in Consciousness Research

Advances in Consciousness Research provides a forum for scholars from different scientific disciplines and fields of knowledge who study consciousness in its multifaceted aspects. Thus the Series will include (but not be limited to) the various areas of cognitive science, including cognitive psychology, linguistics, brain science and philosophy. The orientation of the Series is toward developing new interdisciplinary and integrative approaches for the investigation, description and theory of consciousness, as well as the practical consequences of this research for the individual and society.

Series B: Research in progress. Experimental, descriptive and clinical research in consciousness.

Editor

Maxim I. Stamenov
Bulgarian Academy of Sciences

Editorial Board

David Chalmers
University of Arizona

Earl Mac Cormac
Duke University

Gordon G. Globus
University of California at Irvine

George Mandler
University of California at San Diego

Ray Jackendoff
Brandeis University

John R. Searle
University of California at Berkeley

Christof Koch
California Institute of Technology

Petra Stoerig
Universität Düsseldorf

Stephen Kosslyn
Harvard University

† Francisco Varela
C.R.E.A., Ecole Polytechnique, Paris

Volume 57

The Evolution of Human Language: Scenarios, principles, and cultural dynamics
by Wolfgang Wildgen

The Evolution of
Human Language

Scenarios, principles, and cultural dynamics

Wolfgang Wildgen

University of Bremen

John Benjamins Publishing Company

Amsterdam/Philadelphia

∞ ™ The paper used in this publication meets the minimum requirements of American National Standard for Information Sciences – Permanence of Paper for Printed Library Materials, ANSI Z39.48-1984.

Library of Congress Cataloging-in-Publication Data

Wildgen, Wolfgang
    The evolution of human language : scenarios, principles, and cultural
        dynamics / Wolfgang Wildgen.
            p.   cm. (Advances in Consciousness Research, ISSN 1381–589X ; v.
57)
    Includes bibliographical references and indexes.
        1. Language and languages--Origin. I. Title. II. Series.

    P116 .W55 2004
    401-dc22   2004045067
    ISBN 90 272 5193 2 (Eur.) / 1 58811 518 6 (US) (Hb; alk. paper)

John Benjamins Publishing Co. · P.O. Box 36224 · 1020 ME Amsterdam · The Netherlands
John Benjamins North America · P.O. Box 27519 · Philadelphia PA 19118-0519 · USA

In memoriam René Thom

I am convinced that language, this depository of ancestral knowledge in our species, contains in its structure the keys for the discovery of the universal structure of Being

René Thom (translation by the author)

Table of contents

Acknowledgments

The writing of this book began during my sabbatical semester in the winter 1998/1999, when I spent one month at the "Max Plank Institute of Psycholinguistics" in Nijmegen. I thank Wolfgang Klein for his invitation. In February 1999 I stayed one month at the "Konrad Lorenz Institute of Evolution and Cognition" in Altenberg (near Vienna). I thank Rupert Riedl for his invitation and the hospitality at his institute. On the basis of my research during the sabbatical 1998/99, an unpublished manuscript in German was written and some conferences (in English) were given in Aarhus (Denmark) and Urbino (Italy). I thank Per Aage Brandt for his invitations to the Winter Symposia in Aarhus and Pino Paioni and Fabio Frosini for their invitations to Urbino. In April 2000, I had the opportunity to give three lectures on "Evolutionary Semiotics" at the Institute of General Semiotics at Aarhus, which became the backbone of the present book. In April 2001 I spent a week at the University of Limoges (France); I thank Jacques Fontanille for his hospitality. In Limoges, I gave a paper on Cassirer's philosophy of symbolic forms and on Leonardo da Vinci's *Last Supper*, and I visited eight decorated caves in the area of South Western France (Périgord). In December 2001, I had the opportunity to present major results of my analysis of Paleolithic art at a workshop in Groningen (this was a first version of Chapter 5). I thank Barend van Heusden and Marcel Bax for discussions and suggestions. In March 2001 I contributed to a seminar on "Visual Semiotics" in Paris and in July to a workshop on the "Semiotics of the Image" in Kassel. I thank Martina Plümacher, Anne Beyaert and Stefania Caliandro for their cooperation. Since 1998 I was member of a team of philosophers and semioticians working on the topic "theory of representation" at the universities of Bremen and Groningen (Silja Freudenberger, Barend van Heusden, Arend Klaas Jagersma, Detlev Pätzold, Martina Plümacher, Hans Jörg Sandkühler, Wolfgang Wildgen). This group published in 2003 a handbook on Cassirer's philosophy (cf. Sandkühler & Pätzold 2003). Some of the philosophical ideas in the present book have been discussed in this context. During my sabbatical in summer 2002, I reorganized the materials of the planned book and elaborated on the text. In April, I spent ten days at the "Max Plank Institute of

Evolutionary Anthropology" (Leipzig) in order to complete my knowledge in evolutionary biology, paleontology and genetics. I thank Bernhard Comrie for his invitation and the hospitality in his department. I gave a talk on the topic of "protolanguage", which later became part of Chapter 8 of this book.

I thank Blossom Wrede, who corrected the text for English grammar and suggested many stylistic changes, and Victoria Tandecki, who did typewriting from the manuscript and checked the final version of the text.

CHAPTER 1

Introduction

Why should one believe that evolutionary aspects could bring new insights into linguistics, semiotics, and cognitive science? Saussure dismissed historical, and with them developmental, issues as secondary for our understanding of language, stating that all languages and all their developmental stages constitute self-contained entities in their purely conventional regularity. In cognitive science, the computational paradigm treated cognitive systems as closed, self-contained and auto-referential systems of rules. Now that psycholinguistics has already broken up this line of strict (static) structuralism, as has sociolinguistics, and developmental and socio-dynamic aspects are being admitted as arguments or even as explanatory factors, it seems urgent to continue this line and to advocate an overall dynamic view of language and cognition (cf. Wildgen 1994), which includes the evolution of language. One could object that hypotheses on the evolution of language seem to be so uncertain that one cannot hope for scientific clarity in any specific question of linguistic theory, e.g., in phonology, morphology or syntax. I think there is a basic dilemma here. On the one hand, the amount of contemporary data on languages and their grammars is growing quickly, so that the present quantity of data forms a stark contrast with our very limited knowledge of prehistoric languages and the role of language and other symbolic behavior in prehistoric societies. On the other hand, all existing languages are in a certain sense at the same level relative to an evolutionary time scale and it is only for their *historical* development that we have good, i.e., reliable (written) records which span a period of maximally 3 to 5 ky (ky = 1000 years); the problematic Nostratic family would cover maximally linguistic situations ca. 10 ky BP = before present). Typological studies of Amerindian and Australian languages may perhaps allow guesses about historically divergent lines, which spring off at a bifurcation point 40 to 20 ky ago, but they are not helpful in the reconstruction of a protolanguage because (phonological, lexical, syntactic) change is too quick. Moreover, it depends on social contexts, even if mixture, pidginization, creolization, and language contact were less influential before large civilizations arose.

Our concern in the present book is the whole field of linguistic and symbolic capacities and the (causal) links they have with the bodily evolution of human beings, with changes in the ecology of man and with the evolution of human societies. The method of inquisition is neither that of historical reconstruction, nor that of theoretical deduction. In Chapter 2 I sketch possible scenarios of the evolution of higher semiotic capacities in humans and human societies based on current evolutionary biology. In Chapter 3 I take a closer look at the transition between animal communication and human language with a focus on laughter and the evolution of the comical genre. Chapter 4 assesses the evolution of linguistic cognition starting from the human tools and technical skills. The first traces of symbolic thinking are artifacts like stone tools, sculptures, drawings on bones and rocks, cave paintings, etc. I follow the development of these symbolic manifestations until the rise of writing which is also the beginning of the documented history of languages (in Chapter 5). The evolution of art is already at the transition from biological to cultural dynamics and Chapter 6 will deal with the general problem of innovation in language, art (exemplified by the work of Leonardo, Turner and Moore) and science. Chapter 7 describes the implicit manifestations of evolutionary thinking in the lexicon. Chapter 8 considers questions of an evolutionary theory of language and tries to guess the form of a possible protolanguage and to establish some principles of an "evolutionary" grammar. Chapter 9 discusses the general classification of symbolic forms (or generalized media of communication) and the place of language in this context. The final Chapter 10 concludes with reflections on consciousness, language universals and a new methodology of linguistics.

Language is a developmental feature specific to humans, although under experimental conditions primates (i.e., apes near to the hominid line of evolution) can learn quasi-linguistic skills, which correspond roughly to the competence of a two-year-old child. Still, it is evident that a specific endowment for language is given to all humans independent from other physical differences, such as size, color, anatomic characteristics, etc. This language capacity allows for the attainment of a stable level of human communication even in the absence of many other skills or at a very low level of intelligence. As communicative skills are central for all elementary human acts, such as the selection of friends and partners, maintaining the family, the rearing of children, cooperation in the work place and all kinds of social and cultural processes, language is a capacity, which lies at the heart of the human condition. It is, therefore, plausible that specific conditions and scenarios in the course of a long evolutionary history have shaped this basic and very stable capacity. It is more than a product of chance, or an "invention" as some pre-Darwinian fictions made believe. If the invisible hand of evolution has formed language, the question of language origin must be asked in the context of modern evolutionary biology and genetics. Actually the most adequate theoretical context is the (neo-Darwinian) *synthetic theory*. Controversies within the field of evolutionary biology today have to be considered in research on language origins. Although this discipline is now well founded on Darwinian principles and on genetics, it is still developing along with its sub-disciplines from paleontology to molecular genetics.

The first question is: In what period did language first evolve and how old is our language capacity? The second question is: Did it grow gradually, e.g., starting from communicative abilities common to mammals, or were there catastrophic transitions, i.e., rather quick (e.g., 50 ky) developments, which changed the genetic outfit of the species? A third possibility is that a series of such transitions could have occurred, such that smooth and catastrophic changes merged. The third question, which opens the way for an explanation, concerns the forces (both internal and external) which shaped the evolution of language. There is no reason to consider this evolutionary process as finished and it is conceivable that the evolution of our language capacity, or the capacity for its "reading out", is still going on. The processes of a cultural "reading-out" of the capacity for language are dealt with in the Chapter 4 to 7.

The three questions mentioned above are not independent from one another, because different forces or scenarios where these forces act imply different rates of change and, therefore, different timing of language evolution. If rather quick evolutionary processes are considered, a catastrophic scenario must be found in order to make this speed plausible. In Chapter 2 I shall discuss four basic scenarios that imply different evolutionary rates and different forces. The choice of these scenarios has consequences for the questions dealt with in later chapters.

The time scale for the origin of language is fixed by the evolution of the species' specific physical features: skeleton, head, teeth, hands, four-legged vs. upright locomotion, etc. Traces of these features were conserved or can be inferred from archeological records. The following dates help to establish the basic time scale:

–   The evolutionary lines which separate the primates, who are living today (chimpanzees, gorillas, orangutans) from the branch of hominids bifurcate at a period after 10 my BP. Chimpanzees have been shown to be genetically nearest to humans and their bifurcation line could be 7 my BP. (The archeological discovery of a skull called *Sahelanthropus tchadensis* was dated to 6 or 7 my BP; this would mean that the bifurcation line between chimpanzees and humans (*anthropus*) was earlier.)

- The Homo erectus already had many features of modern man (up-right locomotion, tool use) and reached many places in Africa and Eurasia (not in the Americas) that were later populated by humans. Two million years (2 my) ago is, therefore, a possible early date for a specifically human language. The earlier hominids had brains which were too small and it is plausible that no human-like protolanguage existed before that period (although semiotic capacities as those shown by chimpanzees and gorillas today probably existed before that period).[1]

- Calculations based on the genetic diversity of mitochondria (mtDNA) in living human populations and a genetic clock allow the dating of a point of bifurcation from which all living humans diverge (in biblical terms the birth-date of Eve). This date is 400 to 200 ky ago; this means that the language capacity common to all living populations was already present say half a million years ago. With dates beyond 200 ky ago, we would already reach the classical Neanderthals and the rise of Homo sapiens.

The most plausible period for the origin of language (comparable to human languages today and excluding primate languages) is therefore 2 my to 0,5 my BP. Preparatory stages in a continuous evolution may have evolved previous to the emergence of actual language. Insofar as cognitive abilities like sensory capacities, memory, action planning, and manual skill are concerned, much earlier evolutionary contexts have to be considered. Thus our 3-D-vision system probably is related to the 3-D-motion of monkeys, grasping at branches in the move from one tree to the other, etc. and many types of social communication were present before the 10 my bifurcation we started from.

CHAPTER 2

Basic scenarios and forces in the evolution of human language

In order to reach an adequate explanation of language origin we must distinguish the different physical (behavioral) and cognitive competences necessary for the evolution of human language and the evolution of language itself. In the first scenario, language is considered more or less an outcome of a diversity of other features, which developed and contributed a separate benefit for survival, fitness, and population growth. In this case the force fields of language evolution would have existed and persisted long before the bifurcation date of 7 to 8 my, which has separated our lineage from that of chimpanzees.

2.1 First scenario: Cognitive and physical predispositions for language

In evolutionary biology, the phenomenon of predisposition or preadaptation is known in various species. Thus certain insects are resistant against pesticides, some bacteria against antibiotics, although they never had an opportunity in their evolution to adapt to a situation where pesticides or antibiotics were part of their environment (and, therefore, no selection for this ability could have occurred). In these cases, other evolutionary processes (under the principles of variation and selection) have created a feature, which (by chance) was also relevant in the case of pesticides and antibiotics. In a similar way cognitive evolution (e.g., of the brain and the sensory organs) probably had fitness-advantage in the sensory and motor field linked to environmental fitness and reproduction. Thus an increase of memory and of imitative faculties could have improved environmental fitness and created a predisposition for language. Walking upright and the transformation of the forehead and the mouth could have produced the typical phonetic apparatus of man between the vocal cords and the lips. Thus, predispositions may be at least one factor in language origin. As language capacity involves motor, sensory and neural abilities, all three domains must be investigated in terms of preadaptation. The development of the larynx is possibly the most specific predisposition or preparation for language. Alternatively, it may be a consequence of a gradual increase of language use. As such, it would fall under the second or third scenario.

2.1.1 Motor rhythms and programs as predispositions for language

Few motor programs are inborn as are the newborn's reflex actions of gripping and stepping. The reflex-action of stepping is lost before the real programs for upright locomotion are learned. For linguistic capacities sequential patterns of muscular control of the hands (cf. gesture) and the rhythms of articulatory movements (cf. lips, mouth openings, the tongue) are the relevant motor rhythms; while for the semantics of languages the understanding of control and causation is basic, and could serve to lay the groundwork for the basic sentence schemata (deep cases, valences).

A scenario for the evolution of motor-control, which in turn creates a predisposition for language production, has to consider areas of cerebral motor control in the domain of the *fissura Rolandi*, which mainly consists of the subareas for tongue, lips, and other facial muscles. In the neural neighborhood, one finds the Broca center, the major area of linguistic motor control in humans. The general trend for an expansion of brain size created brain capacities without a specified purpose between areas of the brain with already specified motor and sensory functions so that a predisposition for a functional expansion was established. Thus motor patterns of chewing and breathing could have been sophisticated to develop motor patterns of vocalization. The capacity of sequential motor-activity and motor planning would have affected internal motor patterns, such that a higher control on the syntax of verbal productions was created. The development of mirror-neurons enabling a quick learning (copying) of motor-patterns from other individuals of the same species would have allowed the quick adaptation to traditions or rituals of vocalization (languages) in the social context of an individual. Possibly a gestured language which used predispositions involving motor skills in performing a series of controlled activities with the hands preceded the higher syntactic organization and fine-motor skills of vocalization and articulation patterns. As soon as the muscular control (a basic coordination of visual and tactile cues seems to be inborn) of hand-movements was achieved and learning capacities were increased (cf. the function of mirror neurons), partial and ritualized hand movements could support semiotic activities on a gestured basis. Condillac (1746) had already considered the hypothesis of a gestural origin of language in the 18th century. The plausibility of this hypothesis stems from the parallelism between the gestural communication of deaf mute persons and the vocal communication of humans without such disabilities. Actually, Allott (1989, 1991, 1994) advocates such a model. The cognitive parallelism of gestures and language is also prominent for McNeill (1992). Such hypotheses either assume a fully developed gestured language as a predisposition for the evolution of a sound-based language or a co-evolution of gestured and sound languages based on the evolution of complex motor capacities in the brain. Kien (1994) proposes that the evolution of man brought about a more efficient working memory enabling more complex planning procedures in general (e.g., in hunting, fire-making, tool-making, social behavior). This could have created a predisposition for syntactic planning and utterance complexity.

The flaws of such a scenario are that even if motor-programs achieved a preadaptation for language, the transfer of motor capacities to language would have created a conflict in the use of resources (muscular, respiratory, and cerebral). As cerebral resources are very costly (a big brain consumes a high amount of energy), such a transfer is only possible if it "pays". Therefore, one still needs a complementary Darwinian scenario, in which even initial linguistic achievements pay in terms of survival and reproduction.

2.1.2 Sensory preadaptations for language

One cognitive predisposition relevant for language concerns the evolution of upright walking and our sense of equilibrium. A set of footprints in volcanic ashes was discovered by Mary Leakey in Laetoli, Tanzania. They were dated to 3,5 my BP. Skeletal evidence from Ethiopia could be interpreted in favour of bipedalism existing even 4 my BP (cf. Foley 1997: 51).

One observes an evolutionary transformation of the inner ear, which changes the axis between the windows of the cochlea (the basic organ of sound analysis) and the rotation of the bones of the inner ear (cf. Daniel 1989: 260). This evolution created the conditions for a three-dimensional representation of the individual's body and its movement. The ear protected by the skull and with the double pathway of the self-produced sound through the air (outer path) or directly the bone (inner path) constitutes an efficient module of our language capacity (and is operative already in the womb). Such an efficient organ could have evolved (after 3 my) in the context of predator detection or avoidance (cf. Calvin & Bickerton 2000: 111), and hunting (possibly to facilitate hunting at night or otherwise without sufficient visibility). Thus a predisposition for acute hearing and recognition based on sounds in contexts not involving communication could have created a platform on which sound communication could evolve rather quickly. There are astonishing morphological differences between the inner ear of Neanderthals and that of modern man (this seems to also be true for the outer and middle ear; personal communication by J.-J. Hublin). The preferred frequency bands could have been different for Neanderthals and modern humans so that it would have been difficult for them to analyze the formants typical of human language, as we know it today. Consequently, vocal communication with Cro-Magnon man was probably difficult (beyond the problem of effective language acquisition).

The acoustic, visual, olfactory, and tactile senses together with motor schemata are necessary for the creation of stable object-concepts and the construction of relations between these (based on the concepts of them). K. Gibson (1983:46f.) says:

> Similarly the ability to construct an object image from varied properties is apparently absent among reptiles, but present among most mammals. All monkeys and apes construct visual object concepts. Only the most intelligent primates, however, (cebus monkeys, some baboons and macaques, and all great apes) construct and manipulate relationships between two or more objects. (…) Only humans, for instance, use tools to make tools or construct tools from multiple raw materials and then apply these tools in a second goal directed object–object manipulation. Humans also by far exceed other primates in their ability to construct objects hierarchically.

The capacity of relational thinking allows complex strategies in the search for food (memory for places, category of food, time of ripeness, value for different purposes, medical effects, etc.), in its preparation (cutting, grinding, cooking, etc.) and in the collective hunting of animals. The social relations may be better controlled, coalitions and power-positions independent from actual force can be managed, intrigues, strategies, politics can be devised. In the context of this increase in instrumental and social intelligence, language may have become a basic faculty. The behavioral and social consequences of such a cognitive evolution created the conditions under which linguistic competences "paid", i.e., they triggered a secondary Darwinian scenario, which selected individuals or groups based on linguistic skills. Nevertheless some behavioral and cognitive structures preparing the evolution of language must have evolved independently from selective effects linked to language. In such a scenario the (latent) language capacity could have evolved at the time of Homo erectus (ca. 2 my BP).

2.1.3 The evolution of the neo-cortex as predisposition for language

The growth of the brain is a general survival strategy and represents a trend in the evolution of mammals from basic insectivores upwards. The first massive pressure towards bigger brains occurred at the transition to active daylight hunting in the trees. Not only the increase of the volume of the brain but also a key development of its form consisting of a preference for rather spherical brains may be observed in this period before the hominids and apes separated. The second major transition occurred when early hominids adapted to life in the Savannah by behaviors such as walking upright and hunting as groups. Thus the general trend towards bigger brains can be understood as a kind of rescue mechanism in situations of ecological crisis or change and because of this and its much earlier occurrence should be understood as emerging independently from the origin of language.

The brain changed functionally while it became bigger, as the different parts of the brain had different rates of growth. The cortex and at a different rate the brain stem grew most quickly, while other parts like the olfactory bulbus lost size proportionally. In the neo-cortex, the temporal lobe and much later the frontal lobe increased specifically. The prefrontal cortex competed for synapses in midbrain and brainstem during fetal development, i.e., for limbic and diencephalic projections, which support stereotypic calls and displays of primates. For Deacon these changes constitute the major change in the hominid brain which caused the transition from primate alarm calls to human combinatorial language. It could have emerged with the Homo habilis; cf. Deacon (1991:61–69) and Deacon (1992). Linked to the temporal lobes and their growth the asymmetry between the hemispheres also increased. Even this very specific feature was not "new" for humans, but involved a quantitative change, which may have triggered qualitative and functional changes. Figure 2.1 shows the relation between body weight and brain weight (on a logarithmic scale, which transforms growth-curves into lines).[1]

The linear progression (on a logarithmic scale) is characteristic for all families of animals in Figure 2.1 but there is a kind of parallel progression in favor of brain weight which distinguishes basal insectivores, monkeys, apes, hominids, and humans. Insofar as brain growth and the shift to higher ratios is a general feature and not new in the case of hominids, brain size is probably not the effect but the precondition for language origin. If we compute the correlation only for the neo-cortex a similar progression is shown (cf. Dunbar 1997:78).

If one compares the absolute cranial capacities of five fossil hominid species and modern humans, a large amount of overlap between Homo erectus, Homo

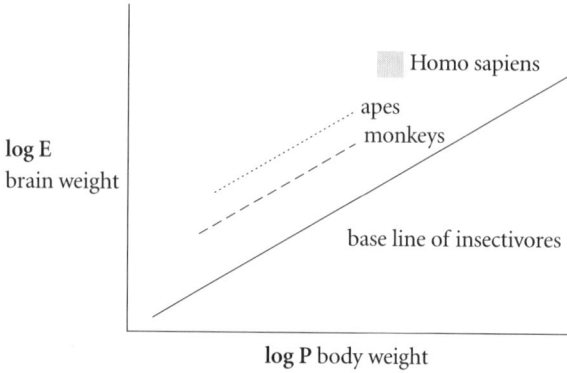

Figure 2.1 The relation between body weight and brain weight (adapted and translated from Changeux 1984:59)

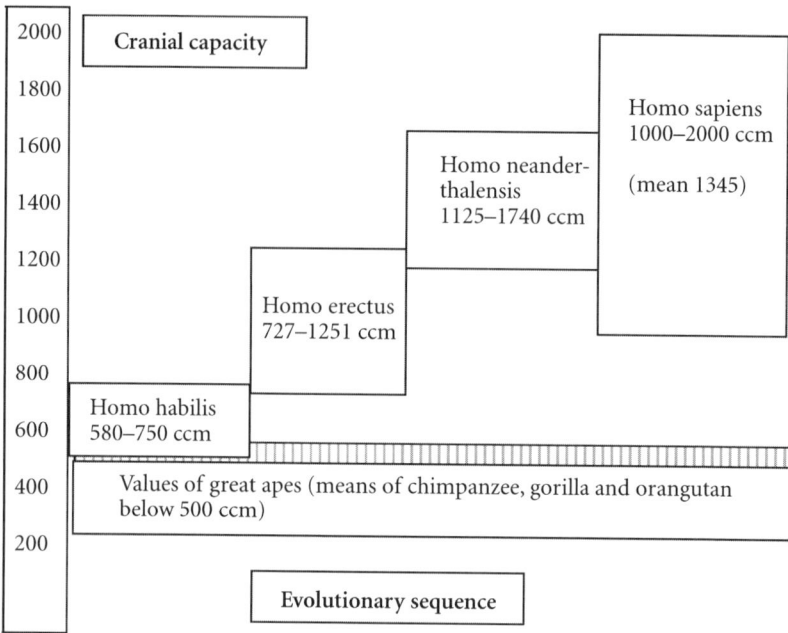

Figure 2.2 Cranial capacity and statistical variation (cf. Martin 1998:51)

neanderthalensis and Homo sapiens appears. The Homo habilis overlaps with the zone of modern great apes but only minimally with Homo erectus (the graphics are adapted from Martin 1998:51).

On the basis of these data the group of Homo erectus, Homo neanderthalensis and Homo sapiens form a sub-group; the Homo habilis seems to be a species in transition from more apelike creatures (the Paranthropus boisei has a range of values from 475 to 630 and the Australopithecus africanus a range from 425 to 485).

A larger brain involves a set of preconditions and consequences. First, brain size depends largely on in-utero growth in contrast to the growth of bones and thus of overall body size which depends on nutritional and environmental conditions after birth. In-utero growth is controlled by the energy supply available to the mother, e.g., the quality of her food. Therefore a change in hominid diet (and probably food sharing between males and females) was the major precondition for an increased brain. The first consequence of a bigger brain in the newborns is the difficulty of delivering the baby through the birth canal. The "solution" found was an almost boneless infant and an oblique position of the birth canal (which had been modified due to upright posture) and a correspondent rotation of the baby before it is born. Both features could only have evolved based on some favorable mutation being selected for. The basic causes of this evolutionary change were more likely the new nutritional conditions than the demands for higher intelligence in a new environment. The effect of a bigger brain could only stabilize the condition of nutrition at a higher level of energy, as it enabled a more efficient hunting and meat preparation; this effect could by itself guarantee that the genetic innovation survived (cf. also Ragir 2001).

The individual growth dynamics of brain and body are another key to language evolution. In Lenneberg (1967: 173), humans and chimpanzees are compared based on relative age from birth to adulthood (18 y. in humans, 11 y. in chimpanzees). The growth of the brain in chimpanzees nearly reaches its maximum at the age of two (corresponding to the age of $3\frac{1}{2}$ in children), it intersects the growth curve of the body before the chimpanzee is one year old. The growth curve of human babies is very quick until $3\frac{1}{2}$ years and crosses the curve of body growth only in adulthood (ca. 17 years). The human growth curve of the brain is linked to its maturation, its plasticity and the length of the intensive learning phase. Now if the birth of the human body in a rather early stage of brain maturation and the huge difference of brain plasticity and adaptive capacity had evolved before language appeared as a stable human feature it would constitute an important preadaptation for language use and language learning.[2]

Some authors argue that there is a threshold of brain volume for the possibility of language at ca. 750 ml (cf. Oubré 1997: 107). This critical value has been called the "Cerebral Rubicon". After the recognition of the Homo habilis as a separate fossil species (mean value 631 cc) the value was reduced by some specialists to 600 cc (cf. Martin 1998:51). The human child reaches this threshold after one year; the Homo erectus would have reached it after six years. As he had a rather short period of life, language acquisition (if possible) would have been correspondingly slower and its completion (even at the level of some protolanguage; cf. Chapter 8) would have overlapped with the critical period of sexual maturation and reproduction. Therefore it would not have paid for this species in the first stages of its evolution; cf. Chapter 8 for further discussion.

A final transition to bigger brains in human evolution may be linked to better control on hand movement and to the manufacturing and usage of stone tools, which reduced the muscles for biting and mastication and thus the forces applied to the cranial case. The earliest stone tools come from the Oldowan culture (ca. 2 my BP). If tool making and tool-usage had a selective impact on brain-size then it could have created indirectly (via brain-size and corresponding motor controls) a predisposition for language.

2.1.4 The evolution of the larynx as predisposition for language

The basic evolutionary constellation in the larynx concerns the spatial and functional relation between the pathway of air from the nose (to the lungs) and of food (from the mouth to the stomach). This constellation is already present in fish, where two separate pathways exist (cf. Wind 1989:181). As the trachea is ventral (below) and as the opening (later the nose) lies above the mouth, both pathways have to cross. In many mammals (e.g., the dog) the paths cross laterally, the epiglottis and the soft palate have to open and close in order to regulate the flow of air and food/drinking on the two paths. In humans, both organs are separated and thus cannot fulfill the original gate function in parallel. This is a danger or at least a disadvantage, which has to be compensated. The change in the geometry of the larynx is one of the preconditions for spoken language, it separates two major concavities; the tongue which moves between them can regulate the proportion between these "resonators". This proportion controls the formants, i.e., the major frequency bands of vowels. Thus the articulation of vowels and velar pharyngeal consonants is due to the deeper and vertically transformable larynx.[3] The vertical position of the teeth and the closed circle of teeth in humans make the articulation of frontal consonants (dental, alveolar) possible. This change of morphology was probably linked to the use of tools and fire in the preparation of food which made chewing less hard; the power of the jaws decreased and allowed for a new shape of the mouth (more

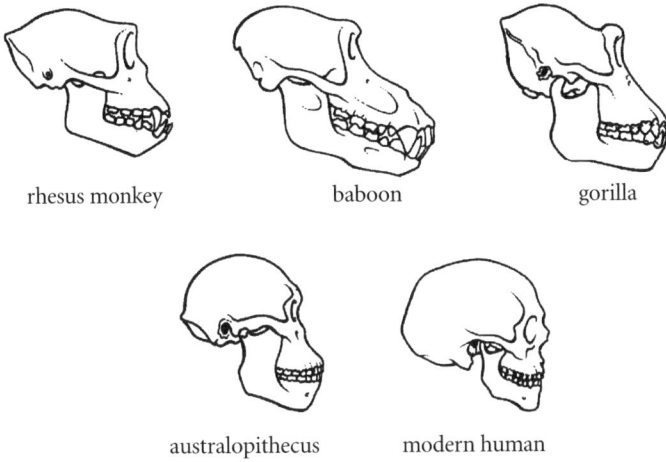

Figure 2.3 Transformation of the cranium in human evolution from rhesus monkeys to baboons, via gorillas and australopithecines to modern humans (cf. Weiner 1972: 32)

rounded) which made it perfectly fit for sound modification. Figure 2.3 shows the transformation of the cranium and the mouth in human evolution.

Laitman et al. (1979) have reconstructed the basic cranial line of Neanderthals which is a relevant measure of evolutionary change.[4] The index K computed by Budil (1994) shows a positive change of the index from primates to modern man and from (reconstructed) skulls of early hominids (2 my) → Neanderthals → archaic Homo sapiens (e.g., hominid from Petrolona, Sternheim, 0,2 my BP; other measures proposed are the Landzert angle or the Larynx-Height-Index, cf. Boë, Maeda, & Heim 1999: 53f.). These skulls have even values above those of average European skulls, whereas the factor K puts the Neanderthals in the neighborhood of living primates. In general it seems that the morphological dispositions for articulated language were already present 300 to 400 ky ago. There are *no* hints at a sudden (catastrophic) transition to a new morphology which allowed for articulated language. Possibly the protolanguage of Neanderthals was less rich in vowels, more nasal, less musical than ours and this could have been a sufficient basis for behavioral (negative) selection in reproduction across subspecies of humans.

The first scenario of language evolution described in this section is probably responsible for the evolution of language at an early stage (e.g., 2 my BP). As far as the vocal apparatus is concerned, it can be proved that a very specific adaptation for vocal language had reached the level of modern humans before 100 ky BP. Thus the skull base found at Qafzeh (Skhūl V) "had a completely modern supra-laryngeal vocal tract around 92 ± 5 ky BP" (Liebermann 1989:406). Even if we accept Liebermann's results and conclude that Neanderthals did not participate fully in this evolution, the bifurcation point of the two lineages from the erectus lineage (cf. ibidem:404) is at 700 ky BP. This means that even under this restriction the capability for a vocal language would have evolved between 700 and 100 ky BP. If the Neanderthals had a language capacity (oral language production) comparable to Cro-Magnon men then the evolution of our articulatory capacity should have evolved in the period before the bifurcation, i.e., after the Homo habilis, in the period when the Homo erectus began to expand into Europe and Asia (e.g., after 1.7–1.6 my BP).

In the domain of referential content and contextual use of language (semantics and pragmatics), cognitive preadaptations were probably the major force or cognitive capacities like motor-control, recognition, memory, and action planning co-evolved with language. It is hard to conceive of a specific selection on language performance in the semantic domain, whereas the scenario of sexual selection can better explain the evolution of the behavioral surface, e.g., the type of vocalization (cf. the third scenario below). This would underscore the claims of cognitive semantics that language is strongly integrated with other cognitive abilities and would restrict the Chomskyan claim of modularity. The claim that syntax is highly species-specific for modern humans could be further sustained if one can show that it follows from principles of speech production and that it has socio-semiotic qualities which may be selected.

The Darwinian principles operative in the case of long-range preadaptations for language are the same which are responsible for hominization in general, and the whole discipline of Evolutionary Anthropology has as one of its major aims to find these principles, i.e., to tell us what were the relevant genetic determiners (mutations) and their anatomical, physiological and behavioral consequences. Other disciplines (e.g., Physical Anthropology or General Biology and Geophysics) can tell us the possible ecological frames responsible for the selection of these characteristics.

It may be plausible that due to long-ranging causes and some ecological changes, like adaptation to daytime hunting in the forest and the transition to the Savannah, a selective effect on cognitive and communicative capacities of early hominid species occurred. For the more specific evolution of linguistic capacities in a shorter period, say in the range of 500 to 50 ky, it becomes much more difficult to imagine how genetic variation and environmental selection could control the evolution of language. The following scenarios present possible answers to the question: How was a specific evolution of language capacity in a rather short time possible? We assume at least that preadaptations (cf. the first scenario) are not sufficient in themselves to explain language origin.

2.2 Second scenario: Bottleneck situations and the rapid evolution of language

The bottleneck scenario is a general model of genetic speciation. If a large population accumulates genetic variations over a long period, these changes do not transform the average of the species because by gene exchange the differences are distributed homogeneously. Only if gene exchange is interrupted and subpopulations are (geographically) isolated does a selective effect occur. In an extreme case, one small group (e.g., one pair), which by chance has specific mutations in its gene pool, is isolated from the population and further gene exchange is interrupted. Now if the ecology is very specific for the isolated group and if the mutation they represent turns out to be highly competitive, then this population will expand successfully. In other cases of isolation, the subgroups will not survive and their specific genetic outfit will be lost. If both factors – genetic isolation and ecological pressure (dramatic selection) – work simultaneously, some genetic variants will survive under pressure and even be selected for an optimal representation of the beneficent genetic variation; all other variants are lost in the isolated groups though they may still be represented in the main population. The bottleneck scenario means that only a very small subset in the genetically variable population goes through the bottleneck (loosing the richness of genetic variations of the total population). After the bottleneck, the surviving individuals expand and form a large community sharing a specific altered genetic pool. If this process is repeated, i.e., if subpopulations are isolated, and a small minority survives under ecological pressure, a selection-tree is produced on which only those branches fitted to the ecological niches survive under separation. After a series of such bottleneck situations occur in a species, some remaining groups will be so far from the main population that they do not interbreed (for biological or behavioral reasons), i.e., the species has been separated into two or more subspecies. The separation may be enforced by ecological changes as when lakes or rivers separate former ecological units, or may be caused by migration.

In the context of human evolution the species Homo erectus had extended the territory they inhabited into Asia (cf. the Java man or the Peking man), while the Neanderthals had occupied the rims of the glaciers in Europe and Middle Asia. The adaptation to specific environments isolated these populations and created specialized subspecies. Probably populations of early modern man expanded along riverbanks and coastal areas whereas the remaining Homo erectus populations preferred ecological niches in the interior. The gracile modern types of man, adapted to the tropics, did not initially enter the European area south of the ice rims where Neanderthals lived, but only immigrated later as the climate became warmer.[5]

If a bottleneck scenario may suffice to explain the rather quick separation of species, specific contexts, which provoked a selective bottleneck and tipped the scales in favor of selection for language capacity, must still be established. One theory in this context is the aquatic ape theory. Some hominids in East Africa would have been isolated in ecologies where they wholly depended on fishing and food gathering at the shore or in the water. They would have readapted to swimming and diving (thus the direction of hairs on the human body and the partial loss of fur, traces of web between the fingers of the human hand could be indications for such a move). In this case sound communication could have replaced visual signs (gestures), because signing with the hands is more appropriate for creatures standing face to face and being free to move their hands in space. It is true that this theory has found no acceptance in the community, but some dramatic ecological shift in the criteria of fitness in favor of sound language must have occurred in a bottleneck situation such that very specific mutations should have survived (in a rather small population). These individuals with their narrow range of genetic variability at the abyss of extinction could have been the starting points of the subspecies leading to modern man. Nevertheless, the variants surviving in bottleneck situations can only select patterns already present in the original population. This means that language capacity must represent in some way continuity with capacities for communication and cognition found in earlier stages. For some language functions, this means that warning calls, sounds for social identification, and signals for the delimitation of areas of control were probably specialized and elaborated in the transition to protolanguage. Other language functions may develop based on rather small functional domains due to functional transfer or functional bifurcation.[6] This could have been the case for cognitive functions originally not accessible for social communication, e.g., spatial orientation, causal understanding, instrumental control, which then became included in the repertoire of social communication.

Just to fill the gap left by archeological research one could postulate a series of bottlenecks corresponding to the series of fossil human species discovered up to the present day: Homo habilis, Homo erectus (possibly distinct

Table 2.1 Correspondence between possible bottleneck situations, kinds of selective pressure and linguistic consequences (some details refer to the model of Lovejoy 1982; cf. Wenke 1999: 140f.)

Species	Bottleneck	Selection	Language
Homo habilis	Life in the Savannah enforced by climatic change in Africa.	Change of diet, hunting instead of gathering fruits.	Communication in food sharing, child rearing, communication.
Homo erectus / Homo ergaster	Geographic separation into isolated subgroups, sudden changes of the fauna.	Adaptation to colder climates during migration; ice age fluctuations of climate.	Learning and teaching of tool use, communication in families (parents-children).
Homo neanderthalensis	Subarctic climate separates the groups ecologically.	Industries for tools, clothing and housing determine a social selection of groups.	Accumulation of cultural knowledge, vocal communication in the dark (night or cave).
Homo sapiens	Explosion of the volcano Toba (70,000 BP)	Competition with Homo erectus and Homo neanderthalensis.	Larger communicative networks and symbolic organization of social life.

from Homo ergaster leading to modern humans), Homo neanderthalensis and finally Homo sapiens.

Only mutation, genetic drift, isolation, and ecological pressures on small populations in danger of extinction (and the genetic loss by extinguished sub-populations) are allowed in this scenario. Emergent language capacities could have gained definite advantages for survival during such bottlenecks and in the expansion stage after the bottleneck this trend would have been continued and further strengthened.

2.3 Third scenario: Sexual selection and a run-away evolution of language

Darwin's theory of evolution draws some of its plausibility from the analogy with the breeding of domestic animals like dogs. All the highly specific variants of dogs stem from one basic population of wild animals: wolves. The systematic selection of specific features by the breeder has created all the known varieties in a rather short time. If one could find natural processes acting like breeders, i.e., deciding to prefer a specific set of features (body size, color, character) one would have a good scenario for a rapid evolution of language. In 1871, Darwin directed the attention of biologists to the rather strange preference for features without manifest ecological profit in sexual selection. Thus deer have enormous anthers; they are mainly profitable in the period of rut when the deer has to conquer or defend a group of hinds. In many birds and fishes beautiful colors attract the attention of predators and are thus negative for environmental fitness, nevertheless the advantage in the situation of selection by females/males causes an overall benefit for reproduction. In general, Darwinian fitness has to consider different, possibly conflicting advantages. Survival against predators and exploitation of ecological resources are one type of selective controls, while attractiveness compared to rivals in the eyes of a female/male is another. Sexual selection is in some ways comparable to the preferences of the breeders. They *imagine* that a specific feature is an advantage and they select for it. If all females select the same feature in males (or vice-versa) this feature will become very prominent in the next generations. Moreover, these preferences may shift (and the shift will depend on the statistical increase of the selected feature). This creates a self-referential process, which is called run-away, because as soon as a certain preference gains some importance it may be reinforced repeatedly and go quickly to a maximum eliminating all features not obedient to the preference. As the overall ecological selection criteria continue to exist, the run-away scenario presupposes that the sexual selection does not intervene dramatically with overall fitness or that the level of fitness or the tolerance of the ecological niche is such that minor losses of overall fitness have no effect on selection.

Even if linguistic communication is not a basic precondition for sexual partnership, it is rather natural to assume that the sexes (one or both) developed a preference for communicatively proficient partners and selected in majority on this criterion. This preference could be rather superficial, e.g., the sounds produced by the partner should have some accepted range of frequency or other remarkable features. In this case foreign sounds or strange vocalizations would be rebutting. In a society with a stricter control of the adequacy of mating partners (eventually controlled by the parents or other relatives), more refined criteria of communicative competence may be applied. Finally the transition from sexual to emotional selection ("love") can modify the criteria of sexual selection. As we do not know the details of the social organization of Paleolithic and Neolithic societies, we cannot reconstruct their communicative codes (cf. Chapter 9). The criteria of sexual selection are therefore underdetermined and the scenario remains vague.

The evolution of human sexual behavior itself may be a factor, which brought linguistic behavior into the frontline of sexual selection. Thus sexual activity became more and more independent from the female menstrual cycles and therefore sexual selection became a permanent and socially dominant mechanism. As females had to care for more children (and for longer periods) food sharing of males with females and children became necessary for the reproductive success of the clan or family. On the one side, females needed more and richer information on the males to select in order to be able to predict their future behavior in the caring for females and children. On the other hand, the males, who did not want to invest in the children of other males, had to know enough about the females in order to trust them when they were on long hunting excursions. In general the new quality of social organization required a kind of "theory of mind", which allowed partners to trust one another (some authors say romantically that sex changed into love under the new conditions). Information about others' attitudes, beliefs, and dispositions to act can only be transferred if a language beyond the expression of actual feelings and reactions to present situations exists (cf. the role of "displaced reference" proposed by Hockett in 1960, then reanalyzed in: Morford & Goldin-Meadow 2001). This includes a capacity for deliberate and strategic deception. Although this scenario can only be described roughly based on what we may infer about the social organization of early stages of man (even actually existing societies of hunters and gatherers show a larger variety of role distributions and relations between the sexes), it remains plausible that sexuality is a key to the evolution of language. Other social relations like kinship relations, partnership between members of the same sex (friendship-networks) follow from the fundamental relation between the sexes and may influence the selection of preferred features via sexual selection. Another kind of selection may be determined by social exclusion, which diminishes the chances of survival and of reproduction (and may even have lethal consequences if protection against murder is lost). If males and females were selected in view of different linguistic competences this selection still contributed to the overall pattern of linguistic competence, but left some traces in gender differences. Several sub-scenarios, which result from cost and benefit evaluations in mating behavior, can be imagined.

Dunbar (1997) has found that chimpanzees employ 20% of their time in grooming. These practices are necessary to uphold social solidarity, social roles (hierarchies), to control conflicts, etc., i.e., grooming is a semiotic activity, a ritualized behavior abstracted from mutual hygiene. In bonobos, sexual activities are ritualized for social purposes. Dunbar argues that the percent of time spent on grooming-activities depends on the size of the group. If the social organization of the group tends to larger communities, these techniques of solidarity and social peace become energetically too expensive. Vocal communication, chatting, simply construing vocalized contexts of solidarity is an alternative. The most proficient actors in social communication get dominant roles in the tribe and reproduce at a higher rate. A run-away process makes this competence desirable *and* creates the necessary social power. Very soon a population may be organized by selection on communicative, i.e., linguistic competence.

Although the analogy with chimpanzees and bonobos is tempting, the positive social effects of chatting and making small talk cannot explain the emergence of highly sophisticated grammars. One could easily imagine a combination of scenario one (preadaptation) with this scenario. The social function would have selected the permanent use of vocal productions and the independent cognitive evolution with its preadaptation for language would have filled in the complexities of conceptual thinking. Sound language as a permanently ongoing social activity would have become the medium of cognitive processes and another runaway process would have started. As soon as the cognitive capacities of the species became an object of social attention and awareness, the expression of cognitive content became a routine, gathered behavioral and ecological significance and entered into the preference pattern of sexual selection. The expressed (practical and social) intelligence would be a much better candidate of sexual selection than the socially invisible cognitive fitness of individuals. The fact that women show less linguistic pathologies and that their abilities for social communication are higher than those of men (statistically), may be interpreted in the sense that it was rather communicative than instrumental competence which correlated with linguistic evolution. Men could have inherited their part of communicative competence by genetic redistribution of features to both sexes. In more recent research (Dunbar 2002) evolutionary criteria are applied to study the mating choices visible in personal advertisement and in history (marriage records in Eastern Frisonia, conflict in a Viking society, and others). Although cultural rules govern the transmission of choices over many generations, the choices themselves follow criteria of an evolutionary game with the number of offspring and their chances for survival as guiding criteria.

2.4 Fourth scenario: Language as a universal symbolic medium

In the last scenarios environmental factors like climate and the availability of food resources, and, depending indirectly on the former, social factors like group size, birth rate or division of labor and migration were considered the driving forces in the evolution of human cognitive and communicative capacity. It became clear, however, that pre-human and human societies moved gradually into self-made ecologies, and that consequently the dramatic dependence on ecological forces, which are independent and uncontrollable by humans diminished. Finally the replacement of the highly specialized subspecies Homo neanderthalensis by Cro-Magnon men, whose bodily constitution was not arctic but rather tropical, was the most dramatic signal, showing that modern humans were able to become (fairly) independent from natural forces and that they could cope with any variation of these forces. Therefore one must look for other than naturalistic forces as governing the evolution of the human species surely after 50 ky BP (possible much earlier). However, these forces cannot come from nothing; they must have evolved and gained relevance in the course of evolution. Instead of arguing in terms of biology or some other natural science, one could take the opposite view and say that the symbolic medium was there at the beginning and that all the biological adaptations were dependent on their relevance to the symbolic medium. This approach constitutes an alternative argument conceived in terms of semiotics and other social sciences, and has the advantage that the semiotic function does not suddenly pop up in the evolution of man; it was present from the beginning and just became more prominent or even dominant on the path of human evolution. The plausibility of an original symbolic medium can be established based on different explanatory endeavors.

Two such alternative explanations have already been proposed. In a philosophical (epistemological) context. Cassirer posits a symbolic capacity already implicit in perception, insofar as the flux of spontaneous impressions must be halted and a meaning (relevance) must be imputed to the chosen (frozen) segment. This is a basic capacity, which humans share with many animals. The meaning associated with a selected and stabilized perception (i.e., a memory) may trigger a spontaneous expressive behavior, which becomes a "natural" symbol, because it is causally linked to the process of perception and immediate memory. If the domain of expression itself is stabilized and gives birth to expressive gestalts, which are socially recognized, i.e., linked to stable reactions in others, a second level of the symbolic is reached (a "symbolic form" in Cassirer's terminology). Language and other highly ritualized and repetitive social behaviors (dance, rituals, and the production of artifacts) accumulate and organize the products of a symbolic culture at this level. Chimpanzees and other higher primates only reach this level if humans instruct them but it is the normal level for humans. A third level is attainable, if these symbolic objects (signs) become themselves the objects of perception and reflection, e.g., in language acquisition after the age of three, when a critical level of consciousness and an episodic memory are developed. Multilingual and multiethnic experience contributes critically to this level of language consciousness (for the discussion of "language consciousness" cf. Bateman & Wildgen 2002). In summary, (cf. Chapter 9 for symbolic forms and their genres) the cognitive system (perception, memory, expression) of higher primates contains the germ for the unfolding of a symbolic competence, which is the driving force in the evolution of language. Climatic and social contexts define proper contexts for the "growth and flourishing" of this capacity. This process of development probably requires higher brain capacity, which depends on a better quality of food (more energy, less time demand); it also creates new problems which have to be solved, e.g., a type of social organization or of social networks beyond the clan. As long as these conditions are not met, the development does not continue or, if it occurs locally, it is lost again. This line of argument may evoke the "vitalism" of the end of the 19th century, but it could fit into a generalized Darwinian framework, insofar as some natural evolutions (explained by mutation and selection) have long-range consequences; they create a potential, which only unfolds under proper conditions. This type of explanation does not exclude the other scenarios; it rather completes them. The symbolic function of behavior could have been relevant at different stages of human evolution:

The erected locomotion of early hominids (e.g., australopithecines) can be interpreted as a generalization of a current posture in conflict and competition (e.g., horses and bears adopt such upright postures in critical situations). It could have been selected for its symbolic content, which would have supported an evolutionary one: the need to survive by dominating the environment and coping with conflicts and crises.

The reshaping of the skull (cf. the cranial lines discussed in scenario 1) produced a face optimized as display for expression (mainly the eyes and the mouth) and concentrated the signals emitted during sexual selection, child-raising and fighting with rivals.

The increase in the size of the brain with social complexity (cf. Dunbar's results) could have its origin in the augmentation and differentiation of social signals in courtship behavior, alliances between physically inferior individuals, sharing of food and control of reciprocity (book keeping), and many other behaviors including deception as well as truthfulness.

In the competition between Neanderthals and Cro-Magnon man a higher level of symbol use, e.g., in art and ritual may have allowed Cro-Magnon man to establish and organize larger social networks, a more effective exchange of

genes (by exogamic reproduction) and of cultural innovation.[7] It is rather im-
plausible that they were superior in force or better adapted to the near arctic
climate in Europe than Neanderthals.

A second proposal is less philosophical and relies on a comparison of Paleolithic civilizations with existing cultures of hunter/gatherers in Africa and
Australia.[8] Livingstone (1983) argues that the normal communicative means
found in primates and other animals would have been sufficient for social
cohesion and conflict management. Referring to social tribe structures in Australia he shows that many different social groups share rather homogenous
territories and need symbolic means to distribute common resources, common
goods (e.g., water), and women (to prevent inbreeding). They use very complicated rules to achieve this and this level of rule-governed social organization
is only possible if language exists. Language, myth, religious beliefs, magical
techniques are different means to solve the central problem of a distributed
multi-tribe and multi-ethnical system. In this perspective language would have
coevolved with a whole set of social and cultural practices and would in its
origin been functionally nearer to rituals, magic and myths. This scenario is
plausible as it may be linked to existing cultures in Australia and other conservative social systems. The problem with this scenario is that modern man came
to Australia 50 to 40 ky ago (cf. Bower et al. 2003: 837) but we have seen that
the origin of full-fletched languages is rather in the period after 500 ky. In order
to maintain this scenario, one has to assume that the social structures found in
Australia in the 19th and 20th century were conserved (in principle) during the
intervening migrations. Moreover they should have remained stable in Africa
between 500 and 100 ky.

2.5 Initial conclusions

The biological character of a genetically coded language capacity does not allow for scenarios with time scales shorter than 100 to 50 ky. Even then only very
specific scenarios like those described by the bottleneck scenario and the run-
away scenario of sexual selection must be chosen (and very specific contexts of
their application). In general a multilayer model must be found with scenario
one as foundation; the bottle-neck scenario is plausible enough to explain the
evolution of modern man in general, the run-away scenario of sexual selection
may complete the picture for more recent evolutionary steps and the scenario
of a symbolic medium can account for the cultural dynamics since Paleolithic
art. The general hypothesis of an evolution of language (and possibly mod-

ern man) driven by his (latent) capacity for symbolic behavior which unfolded under proper circumstances is tempting. It puts language in a larger context (together with technique, art, ritual, religion and other cultural phenomena) and makes the transition to later development in the Neolithic period and the first large civilizations in Egypt, Mesopotamia and the Indus valley look more natural. It is difficult to imagine a theory of the historical developments that humankind witnessed on purely biological (genetic) principles.

The functional contexts, which could explain the selection of linguistic competence in a Darwinian framework, are the following:

– Communication in sexual partnership (choice of partners).
– Communication and identification in breeding; females may consider possible help by males in future breeding in the context of sexual selection (see above).
– Communication in conflict management; this allows lower costs in ritualized conflict scenarios and differentiates social roles.
– Collective action and signals relevant for others: warning, ganging up against predators, collective hunting or preparations for it (forerunner of common knowledge).
– Marking of symbolic frontiers by naming and the creation of myths (forerunner of literature).
– Establishing and stabilizing the rules of social behavior (forerunner of laws and social conventions).
– Power management by strategic symbolic behavior, alliances, techniques of cheating, duping (forerunner of political and economical management).

Human vocal communication monopolizes many of these functions although gestured and olfactory communication is still relevant. In human societies, a specific profile of communicative functions is elaborated. Shifts in these functions can bring about rather quick changes in the symbolic system (e.g., in language) without affecting the basic language capacity, i.e., the protolanguages of Homo erectus, Neanderthals and archaic Homo sapiens were probably different from modern languages in respect of their basic functions. Even later rather deep changes in the linguistic system are possible in the tolerance domain of our inherited language capacity. This makes it very difficult to infer features of our language capacity from the analysis of existing languages and their grammars (cf. Chapter 8 for recent positions in the discussion of this topic).

The analysis of the evolution of symbolic communication beyond language could help to uncover the deeper (biologically rooted) language capacity, which goes beyond currently described typological differences between languages.

CHAPTER 3

Expression and appeal in animal and human communication with special consideration of laughter

In his classic text "The Expression of the Emotions in Man and Animals" (published in 1872) Charles Darwin claims that the continuity between animal and human communication has its origin in the emotional function of language, in its "expressivity". For example, the emotional value of behavior and an other organism's reaction to it (its "appeal") can be a decisive factor in sexual selection, i.e., females/males prefer partners who show a specific behavior during courtship (inter-sexual selection) or females/males display specific behaviors in order to win out against rivals (intra-sexual selection). Darwin says: "A strong case can be made that the vocal organs were primarily used and perfected in relation to the propagation of the species" (Darwin 1888: 566). The evolutionary forces linked to sexual selection have been discussed in detail in Chapter 2.3. Darwin had a straightforward view of how this evolution could have happened based on Lamarckian principles: He saw a parallel between the evolution of the human hand adapted to specific purposes (liberated from others) and the vocal organs (which are also relieved of biting in attack or masticating a large amount of tough plants).

> The structure of the hand in this respect may be compared with that of the vocal organs, which in the apes are used for uttering various signal cries; ... but in man the closely similar vocal organs have become adapted through the inherited effects of use for the utterance of articulate language. (Ibidem: 50.)

The "inherited effects of use" are a Lamarckian trait in Darwin's argument, which cannot be accepted today, as only marginal effects of use or context are 'inherited'. Thus the higher level of nutrition may influence the height of a new generation, which has consequences for the height of later generations. These effects tend to have a short range and cannot explain a long-term evolution. It is possible that in the chain of gene-reading and in the production of proteins variations of morphology and behavior were brought about in shorter periods (cf. Enard et al. 2002). Nevertheless Darwin was on the right track, insofar as he pointed to the evolution of behavior (and not only of morphology) as the proper field for an evolutionary explanation of human language. He introduced three interesting principles based on "habits", i.e., stable behavioral "forms". The principles formulated right at the beginning of Darwin's book are:

> *The principle of serviceable associated Habits.* – Certain complex actions are of direct or indirect service under certain states of the mind, in order to relieve or gratify certain sensations, desires & c.; and whenever the same state of mind is induced, however feebly, there is a tendency through the force of habit and association for the same movement to be performed, though they may not then be of the least use.   (Darwin 1872/1969: 28f.)

> *The principle of Antithesis.* – … when a directly opposite state of mind is induced, there is a strong and involuntary tendency to the performance of movements of a directly opposite nature, though these are of no use; and such movements are in some cases highly expressive.   (Ibidem.)

> *The principles of actions* due to the constitution of the Nervous System, independently from the first of the Will, and independently to a certain extent of Habit.   (Ibidem.)

In today's terms, the first principle is related to the phenomenon of "ritualization" described in ethology, while the second points to a semantic space (completed by negation) still dependent in its major forces and its dimensions on behavioral effects (sensory inputs, motor outputs and their coordination). The third principle may stand for a self-referential cognitive organization of mental representations (which is largely autonomous in relation to input and output).

I shall take the first principle as a discovery procedure (in the spirit of Bühler's critique; cf. Bühler 1933/1968: 131) and ask how and why behavioral habits, abstracted to sign-behavior were the source-domain, in which semiotic behavior evolved. In Darwin's description, two steps in the process of selection are lacking. Namely, the role of the social profits of sign-behavior for its emergence and the dynamics of its stabilization must be elaborated; cf. the (reliable) appeal-character of signs mentioned by Bühler. Both refer to the pragmatics of sign-behavior. Insofar as they reflect environmental pressures, they may be responsible for the selection of sign-behavior in a strictly Darwinian sense.

Darwin's view of continuity between vocalization in animals and humans based on the expression of emotions and the social profits of this expressivity led to comparative work on behaviors in animals and men. Konrad Lorenz's ethology and modern comparative research on primates (including humans; cf. Boesch & Tomasello 1998) develop this line, which will be discussed in the

Table 3.1 Psychophysical basis, type of emotion and type of expression

Psychophysical system	Type of emotion/feeling (Gefühl)	Type of expression (Ausdruck)
Heart and breath	Excitation/calming down	Modes of motion as expression
Face	Desire/aversion (Lust/Unlust)	Mimical expression
Muscles of the trunk and the limbs	Tension/release	Pantomimic and gestural expression

next section. Earlier Wilhelm Wundt took up this topic in his "Lectures on the soul of men and animals" ("Vorlesungen über die Mensch- und Tierseele", first edition 1863, and seventh, augmented and revised edition 1922). He starts from Fechner's "Psychophysik" and develops a three-dimensional model for the expression of emotions in animal and human communication. The cultural dimension of expressivity is the basis for Wundt's "Völkerpsychologie" (psychology of populations). Table 3.1 shows the system proposed by Wundt in the volume "Language" of his "Völkerpsychologie" in 1911.

Vocalizations are linked to the psychophysical system of breath and facial muscles and they integrate the two first types of emotions. Paralinguistic features like loudness, stress, intonation refer to excitation/calming down and facial motion (lips, teeth, motions of the chin); those of the (visible) tongue may be related to desire/aversion. Parts of the vocal gesture, mainly the changes in the shape of the larynx and the motion of the tongue inside the mouth between the alveoli and the velum are neither part of the facial nor of the pulmonary psychophysical system. Therefore, the evolutionary change in the shape and mobility of the larynx is the key to a type of expressivity beyond excitation and desire. It can be neither read from the face nor from the level of activity of heart and breath and is therefore rather neutral in relation to global emotional states. It opens the field for a more "rational" type of expressivity, which points rather to the "body" of the social group than to the body of the individual who utters the sign. This "social body" creates a social expressivity, which transcends individual expressivity although it is energetically dependent on it (cf. Hobbes' Leviathan & Wildgen 2001a). In the tradition of Humboldt, one could say that a specific language "expresses" the "inner form" of a social group, the "Weltansicht" (worldview) and the subjectivity of a cultural entity (later a nation) (cf. Humboldt 1963:21, 19).

3.1 From animal motion to animal sign behavior

Konrad Lorenz wrote the foreword to the 1965 edition of Darwin's book "The Expression of the Emotions", in which he makes clear that his own animal ethology stands in Darwin's tradition although other, more philosophical, i.e., Kantian or Goethean traditions are respected. So-called "intentional movements" give the basic distinction between motion and sign-behavior in birds ("Intentionsbewegungen", coined by Heinroth 1930). Thus a gray goose while showing the behavioral pattern of soaring reduces the intensity of the movements and thus gives a signal of soaring to other geese. Eventually the whole group soars in a coordinated fashion. The intentional movement is a semiotic act because it announces the intended act. Insofar as it is a signal for other geese, it has a social and communicative value. In general, all inborn action patterns may give rise to semiotic patterns; Lorenz distinguishes instinctive behaviors and their "taxis" (specification for a context); e.g., a goose rolls back the egg with instinctive motions. If a real egg and a real nest are given, then the motion pattern is adapted to the egg and the nest. If one removes the egg or the nest, the motion pattern is realized in a reduced mechanistic way. Thus one could say that inborn motion patterns are either adapted to specific contexts or they form the basis for a simpler behavioral pattern which may attract semiotic functions; the semiotic pathway is a kind of generalized or socialized variation of basic developmental patterns. Figure 3.1 illustrates this bifurcation.

Lorenz compares instinctive motion patterns with language:

> "It is characteristic for them, that they can be described easily and completely in a language by words in spite of the linear sequence of words in language."
> (Lorenz 1978: 135; translated by the author.)

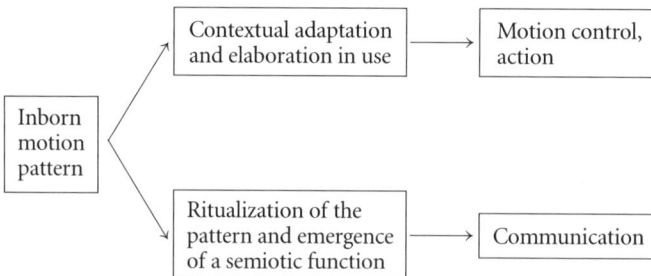

Figure 3.1 The bifurcation of motion patterns and the rise of communication

He adds an explanatory remark on this fact:

> For the evolution of the sensory-neural system of higher animals it is not possible to produce an inborn, i.e., a phylogenetically programmed stimulus-response mechanism, reacting selectively to complex qualities, whereas it is easy in the process of learning gestalts, to produce reactions, which respond to very complex configurations with a tremendous, almost incredible selectivity.
> (Ibidem: 136; translated by the author.)

Applying this concept to language, one would expect inborn capacities to be extremely simple and non-selective. Categorical perception patterns in newborns are candidates for patterns, which later shape complex articulatory processes by learning. In the domain of semantics, simple action patterns of grasping and object-constancy (as soon as the visual system is mature enough) are basic levels for the development of complex behavioral and semantic capacities. The Chomskyan view of a universal grammar (UG) containing virtually all possible linguistic structures is extremely counterintuitive in a biological context.

Now, if inborn motion patterns or patterns for their recognition are the starting line, one may assume that any animal behavior not yet specified for practical purposes is a possible starting point for semiotic behavior. Consequently, semiotic behavior may be understood as a latent capacity in the whole animal kingdom. Beyond the intentional movements already mentioned, a large field of movements (habits in Darwin's sense) may be ritualized, i.e., performed without practical use but with a socio-communicative function.

As the ritualized patterns have no specific context of use they appear rather bizarre, i.e., the "real" (practical) world is replaced by a fictive (only possible, not real) world. Lorenz (1978: 102f.) gives several examples in which instinctive behaviors of nest-building are performed in the absence of nest-building materials or branches, in another example the starling catches "flies" in a cage where no flies exist, etc. The semiotic patterns are referring to imagined, fictive, only socially relevant entities, whereas the active patterns are adapted to real-word conditions. The bifurcation shown in Figure 3.1 thus makes a basic distinction between acts and communication. In the following, I shall discuss recent results on referential sign-behaviors in non-human primates.

3.2 From animal communication to human language

If ritualization and the formation of cultures (i.e., the transmission of behavioral patterns by emulation, imitation and teaching) are compared in chimpanzees and humans (cf. Boesch & Tomasello 1998), the characteristic features of *human* communicative behavior become obvious. Contrary to instrumental behaviors, communicative behaviors are created "by two individuals shaping one another's behavior in repeated instances of a social interaction" (ibidem: 600). The authors call this process "ontogenetic ritualization" (ibidem). These results point to an important difference between instrumental and communicative learning. In the latter case, innovation does not originate with an individual but is based on play or interaction with a second agent whose feedback brings about ritualization. The results are not simply the product of individual invention constrained by the affordances of objects or materials or by identical needs and purposes. They are driven by chance and cannot be disseminated by parallel invention or emulation in practical contexts; imitation and in many cases instruction is necessary. They are neither pre-selected by the context nor do the results of such communicative learning follow stable and unique models. The major difference between young chimpanzees and children is that imitation (and teaching) is much more prominent in children. If humans create a rich environment for the training of chimpanzee gestures, these may come near to the semiotic capacity of young children, but this situation is artificial and does not belong to the natural environment of chimpanzees. The bias for imitation, which is more abstract than emulation as it is not controlled by an evaluative testing of the model, triggers another process called the "ratchet effect" by Boesch and Tomasello (1998: 602), i.e., the inventory of accumulated behavioral patterns does not decrease; change consists of further elaboration and sophistication of the accumulated "cultural goods". The acquisition of such a very complex system, e.g., language, a ritual tradition, a religious or political system, requires a long and intensive learning and teaching period, which only human societies can afford. The general picture is that of a gradual shift from emulation, to imitation (and teaching); the accumulation of results of ontogenetic ritualization creates a distance between animal and human behavioral and semiotic systems. The result looks like a dramatic qualitative difference. It is true that the increase of complexity is astonishing but this should not make us think that the basic principles are radically different.

A major difference between animal and human communication was thought to relate to the referential function unique to human language. I shall discuss, therefore, the results of research reporting referentiality in alarm calls and other vocalizations of apes.

Animal calls can be referential in relation to objects and events external to the caller. In these cases, they are easily identified by human observers and may be controlled experimentally by checking response to playbacks. Fischer and Hammerschmidt (2001: 30) label these vocalizations as "functionally referential". Examples are food-associated calls and alarm calls in vervet monkeys (Cercopithecus aethiops), Barbary macaques, and others. Categories distinguished in the alarm calls may be: eagle, snake, leopard (vervet monkeys) or dog, snake, human (Barbary macaques). The calls can be acoustically distinguished by means of frequency amplitudes and formant like structures (cf. ibidem: 33).

A second class of calls is given in social contexts; they "are commonly viewed as expressions of the internal state of the caller, and the observer may experience difficulties not only in describing this state, but also in pinning down the context eliciting a specific vocalization" (ibidem: 29). Thus the major semiotic functions of Bühler's instrumental (*organon*) model of the sign: expression – appeal – reference are fulfilled in these calls. The social meaning is difficult for human observers to assess, but one may guess a rather complex semantic space of caller external (referential) and social meanings (shared expressivity). The latter may be associated with the connotative meanings in natural languages analyzed in Osgood's "semantic differential" with the parameters: E (evaluation), P (potency), A (activity). Thus basically the semantics of animal calls may be not fundamentally different from the semantics of human languages. In order to assess the relation between more archaic forms of expressivity and language I shall analyze the case of laughter and the comical, which can be considered as a transitory genre between non-linguistic expressivity and linguistic codification.

3.3 Laughter and the origin of the comical genre

The comical is neither a universal genre, independent of historical and social developments, nor does it constitute a homogeneous and unambiguous category. Although comedy has been known as a dramatic genre since antiquity, the sense of the comical, of humor and wit changed dramatically in Renaissance and Victorian England, Voltaire's France, Jean Paul's Germany to name just a few of the cultural contexts through which comedy has moved. Even in the 20th century, humor may be rather serious as in upper-class England or raucous and slapstick as in some American comedy films, so that the category of the comical may refer to one of these many rather different behaviors.

Our concern here is however not some universal ideal of the comical, but the semiotic status of the comical. The fundamental character of the comical is demonstrated by the fact that comedy may be produced by reference to objects, situations, or behaviors themselves considered laughable, or by enacting them with a certain distortion of gesture and posture. It can also be manifested through a sort of verbal art, most commonly in the telling of jokes and humorous anecdotes or the performance of comic drama on stage. Thus comedy has an aspect related to referents (the world) and to behavior and one referring to verbal signs and texts and it asks for a proper interpreter who can perceive and react to the comical. The historical development of the comical (cf. Wickberg 1998) affects the interpreter and his social context and thus indirectly the comical objects and relevant sign structures. The cue for an attribution of the label "comical" to a behavior or a text is given by laughter, whereas the type of behaviors and texts eliciting laughter may be very different in different societies or periods. We could therefore reformulate our topic and say that our concern is any semiotic activity or type of activity, which systematically induces laughter (or smiling in a calmer context).

3.3.1 Classical analyses of laughter and the comical

Two pathways lead to modern theories of the comical: the literary genre called "comedy" based on theories of comedy, e.g., in Aristotle's poetics, and the rhetorical technique of making people laugh mostly at the expense of someone. A specific analysis of the comical (e.g., of humor) outside these main lines has only existed since the 17th century. In his "Leviathan" (1651), Hobbes says that "laughter":

> (…) is caused either by some sudden act of their own, that pleaseth them; or by the apprehension of some deformed thing in another, by comparison whereof they suddenly applaud themselves.   (Cf. Burtt 1967: 152.)

"Laughter" is treated in the chapter on passion and preceded by "vain-glory" from which it is distinguished as "sudden glory". It is followed by "sudden dejection (…) the passion that causeth *weeping*" (ibidem: 153). For Hobbes, the criterion of sudden effect applies to both "laughing and weeping". If Hobbes considers laughter as a natural passion linked to "vital motions" (ibidem: 148), he belongs to the classical tradition since Aristotle and points to the theory of humor in the medical context of Galen (i.e., humor as a typical mixture of the four liquids in the human body).

In Kant's "Kritik der Urteilskraft" (1790) the scope has changed; the comical object, situation, or person is no longer the center of the argument, it is rather the hearer and his mind, which specify the genre of the comical:

Laughter is an affect resulting from the sudden transformation of a tense expectation into nothing. This transformation, which is surely not pleasant to the mind, still pleases indirectly for one moment in a very vivid manner. Thus, the cause of it must be sought in the influence of imagination on the body and its reciprocal effect on the soul.

(Kant 1790/1974:273; translated by the author.)

Kant's definition refers to expectation, sudden transformation and nothing. After Kant the romantic philosophers Tieck and Novalis tried a "deeper" specification of Kant's "sudden transformation to nothing". The comical causes the ego to step out of itself and establishes "Being outside Being inside Being." (Novalis cited by Frank 1992:218.) This analysis contains an interesting point: The comical relates consciousness to sub-consciousness or simply to lower cognitive activities like perception, memory and imagination. In a sense, it transforms a conscious activity of the mind (a level only accessible to humans) into an activity at a lower level of the cognitive system (shared with evolutionary predecessors of man). Thus the intuitive analysis by philosophers (Hobbes, Kant, Novalis) indicates that the comical is grounded in pre-linguistic, preconscious and thus pre-human modes of communication. Laughter and the culturally derived forms of the comical genre activate pre-human communicative skills, which coexist with the linguistic type of communication.

As this analysis does only minimally consider the social nature of laughter (Hobbes pointed to the individual who laughs, Kant to the hearer affected by the comical) I will turn to the communicative aspect of laughter.

3.3.2 Laughing in communicative contexts

If one defines the comical by those factors in objects, persons and their behavior, which elicit laughter, one should start with an inventory of the contexts of laughter. Empirical studies show that laughter occurs permanently, that the triggering contexts are minimal or even inexistent and that laughing must be understood as one type of behavior in a larger field of communicative behaviors like silence, listening, responsive facial expressions, smiling, and language.

Laughter has a very simple phonetic structure and respects the boundaries of linguistic utterances like conversational turns, sentences, and phrases. The phonetic realization begins with a voiceless spirant (e.g., [h]) of 200ms duration followed by a vowel-like sound (in average around 278 (±95) Hz in the case of men, 502 (±127) Hz in women). The rhythm of spirant-vowel sequences is constant and neither of the two elements changes substantially. In writing laughter is noted as: ha–ha–ha, ho–ho–ho, hi–hi–hi, etc. The repetitive, rhythmic structure of laughter has parallels in animal calls, insofar as intermittent calls allow for a quicker identification of the sender (this can be shown to be relevant in the mobbing calls of birds and apes). The laughing person allows the listener an easy localization of the source and he may focus the listener's attention to his body and his communicative actions.

The sign-structure of laughter is drastically reduced and super-regular compared to language. In evolutionary terms, it comes nearer to animal calls than to language and may have similar functions, i.e., the coordination of attack or flight or other social activities. The subordination of laughter to speech indicates that it is a relict of older communicative behaviors marginalized by the development of language. Provine (1995: 296) says:

> The finding that laughter seldom interrupts speech indicates that there is a lawful and probably neurologically programmed process responsible for this temporal organization. The near absence of speech interruptions by laughter indicates further that speech has priority over laughter in gaining access to the single vocalization channel.

Contrary to the model of laughter proposed by Kant, most occurrences of laughter do not follow witty or humorous remarks of other persons, they just occur at a regular rate in normal communication (like pauses or breathing). Provine (ibidem) summarizes his empirical findings:

> The frequent laughter heard in crowded social gatherings is not due to a furious rate of joke telling by guests. Most pre-laugh dialogue is that of an interminable television situation comedy scripted by an extremely ungifted writer.

He found interesting gender effects. Men elicit more laughter in the audience than women do, but women contribute more to the laughter of the audience. This asymmetry could play a role in sexual selection.

Another social effect of laughter is its contagiousness. It can diffuse quickly in a group and young female adolescents are known to react strongly to the group effect of laughter. Empirical studies by Provine and Fischer (1989) using diary reports showed that the frequency of laughter varies in range after speech and smiling and it is more social (rather seldom found in situations of solitude). Laughing and smiling are less dependent on individual mood than on social context.

The "meaning" of laughter is strongly dependent on other behaviors, which run in parallel. In a study on communication between males and females Grammer, Filova and Fieder (1997) filmed behavioral sequences and analyzed the correlation between postures and laughter. They came to the following conclusions:

> It was possible to show that postures which are taken during laughter might well transport the meaning of laughter. The acoustic event 'laughter' does not alone distinguish interest from no interest. Highly interested males or females do not laugh more often than persons with no interest do. Moreover, people who are together with strangers of the same sex laugh more often. In sum, there is no contextual evidence that laughter alone is a sexual signal. When combined with postures, however, laughter may take different meanings on a continuum from rejection to appraisal of the partner.
>
> (Grammer Filova & Fieder 1997:93.)

Laughter is only one factor in a multidimensional behavioral space and it interacts with posture, body signals and speech. Determining the differential contributions of these individual factors and the manner in which they interact will be a task for the future. It can already be seen that verbal speech (let alone the content of the utterance) is not the principal factor in the determination of communicated meaning in a comical situation.

3.3.3 Neural mechanisms responsible for the comical

If one compares the vocalization of other primates with that of humans, very different neural pathways can be found to exist in the brain of a monkey and a human as Deacon (1992) reports. In primates, specific circuits in the forebrain and the midbrain control calls. They rely on structures in the limbic system and are linked to arousal, facial gestures and display postures. Human 'innate' calls, laughter and supra-segmental phenomena in speech such as intonation, tone and rhythm may correspond to similar pathways. In humans, language tends to activate different pathways. Parts of the left neo-cortex, prefrontal Broca's area, the motorcortex and Wernicke's area are centers for the control of linguistic activity and produce a much more complex motor-pattern than animal calls; they also control the tongue via the hypoglossal nucleus and not only the larynx. Deacon (1992:146) says:

> The fact that speech articulation is so resistant to disturbance by arousal state is evidence that the articulatory system is functionally dissociated and anatomically separated from the system for emotional experience and expression.

Deacon interprets speech as reducing the emotional types of phonation we find in apes, and Jürgens (1998) uses physiological results in order to prove the continuity between the vocalization of apes and human emotional expression. Comparative analyses make it plausible that laughter is a more archaic behavioral pattern, which may be put on the same process level as primate vocalizations before the evolution of articulated speech. It is highly integrated with facial expressions and postures and more dependent on arousal and emotion than the evolutionary more recent speech behavior. This explains some of the results of behavioral studies reported in the last section. In the transition to language, it is interesting to consider more specifically human evaluation of comical texts and cartoons. Such studies were done using the technique of brain imaging and comparing patients with a brain damage to normal persons.

Studies on patients with frontal brain-lesions (Shammi & Stuss 1999) were able to show that there are areas of the brain whose damage influences the capacity of humorous reaction to texts and cartoons. The authors compared 21 patients with cerebral lesions, partially in the frontal area partially in non-frontal areas and a control-group of 10 normal persons. A standard test: "Appreciation of Verbal Humorous Statements and Joke Completion Test" and behavioral observations of smiling and laughing showed a significant correlation with frontal lesions (identified by computer tomography or spin-resonance tomography). The reduced capacity of frontal lesion patients to recognize humor was explained by four factors.

- The frontal lobes (in these cases mainly the right frontal lobe) are important for cognitive integration. In cases of indirect interpretation as in jokes and humor, this capacity is necessary.
- In many cases, understanding humor requires an individual enacting of situations and presupposes access to the episodic memory of personal experience. The access to this type of memory belongs to the functions of the analyzed brain area.
- The perception of oneself and self-monitoring are important for humor interpretation and are also linked to the right frontal lobe as a relevant domain of organization.
- The linkage between cognitive processes in the neo-cortex and emotional processes in the limbic system involves the frontal lobes and is important if visual or textual inputs trigger laughter (the limbic system is responsible for emotional processes).

The study of Shammi and Stuss (1999) and other studies they refer to can only contribute to an understanding of the basic phenomenon. As the last section suggested the situations and processes, which trigger laughter, are multiple and many of them may be rather trivial. Nevertheless, certain phenomena of the comical open a deeper insight into the embodiment of communication and the roots (neural or evolutionary) of sign-behavior in general. As language is also embodied to a large extent (cf. Lakoff & Johnson 1980) the comical (laughter) is not so fundamentally different from language as it seems to be at first sight. I will try to reflect this perspective further.

3.4 The place of laughter in the evolution of semiotic behavior

Laughter is a sister behavior of language. It goes beyond comparable gestures of inoffensiveness or submission in animals. In the sense of Darwin's principle of antithesis, it is the complement of the sign for latent aggression, in which the teeth (for biting) are uncovered. As the aggression by biting has been reduced parallel to the reduction in the size of the incisors (e.g., in apes) the ritualized sign of non-aggression changed its meaning. It became the antithesis to the more important behavior of speaking. In a certain sense, laughter continues in its archaic phonetic shape the pre-linguistic behavior of alert- and alarm-calls and signs of presence and self-presentation. Hands now communicate the signs of non-aggression as in hand shaking. Laughter is in the network of bodily signs a mimic complement to linguistic expression and serves the communicational effect of social bonding which in higher primates is served by grooming and calls (cf. Dunbar 1998).

3.4.1 Critique of emotional expressivity (and appeal) as origin of language

Since the 18th century, two major fronts exist: the position of Condillac (following Locke's empiricism) starts from sensations, proceeding to memory and imagination, and credits language with the effect of stabilizing memory and imagination and thus enabling a much more complex system of ideas, which ultimately could even explain such abstract operations like mathematics. In a certain sense Piaget's theories of mental development continue the tradition of Condillac, which dominated French psychology in the 19th century. The other position was developed (but not published in his life-time) by Rousseau. For Rousseau the human passions, which find their expression in music and dance, are at the origin of our linguistic capacities. This line of explanation was probably not the basis of Darwin's ideas reported earlier, but in a Darwinian framework (where sexual selection plays a dominant role) it seems much easier to use the schema introduced by Rousseau. Both explanations fail, however, if the specific nature of human language, its high intellectual (rational) capacity and the very abstract character of its system of rules have to be accounted for. The historical lesson could be that:

Both emotional expression (and its social appeal) *and* the cognitive (rational) functions of language have to be considered in a proper model of language evolution, i.e., Rousseau *and* Condillac were right in pointing to the links between language and passion (language and music) and between language and cognition (language and visual art, language and science). However, language is different from both music and visual arts and science and only if we respect this uniqueness can we arrive at an evolutionary explanation of language.

In reviewing the history of biological thinking since Darwin Ernst Cassirer concluded that the evolution of language and other symbolic forms is the proving ground for any naturalistic theory, on which they consistently fail. In his opinion, the "categorical jump" from a language of expression and appeal to a "propositional language" remains the major hurdle for any biological explanation of language. In modern philosophy of language, the term "proposition" became the center of a controversy in which Fodor (and others) defended the propositional character of language and Paivio (and others) doubted it by putting forward mental images and imaginative thinking as alternatives (cf. Wildgen 1994: 4–8).

If we go back to the Aristotelian notion of proposition, then it becomes clear that the reason why the level of proposition is taken as a fundamental basis is that it has to do with Aristotle's syllogistic. In order to prove a sentence by the application of syllogistic schemata, i.e., in order to establish a scientific discourse beyond rhetorical persuasion, one needs a starting level with units which allow for affirmation and negation, i.e., which refer to truth and falseness. The syllogistic calculus then establishes chains which link true or false "unities" ("propositions") to true or false unities (proved by deduction or disproved by contradiction). Thus scientific argument, which became an ideal opposed to sophistic make-believe, was the motive for the introduction of the term "proposition". That level of cultural development was achieved in Greece in the 5th century B. C. In a very radical view, language does only seem to be propositional if translated into a logical calculus. Insofar as logic is an artificial code for specific purposes the fact that in (classical) logics the concept of "proposition" is central, does not necessarily mean that a model of the evolution of language must explain the propositional structure of this artificial language (thus it would be rather a topic in a history of logics). This reflection induces two consequences:

In the context of a theory of language evolution, which has at least a time depth of some hundred thousand years, the specific development of logics cannot be a crucial criterion of evaluation.

Instead of "proposition", argumentation is the critical level in the transition to language capacity. How was argument possible for humans, what role did it occupy in early civilizations (before Aristotle), i.e., in the oriental civilization, in the Mesolithic, Paleolithic societies or in the "civilizations" of Neanderthals and possibly Homo erectus? What are the pragmatic and political frameworks in which argumentation played a crucial role and had consequences for selection? Can the argumentative function, which is still present in contemporary discourse, be projected into the prehistory of man?

Answers to some aspects of the last question will be developed in the next section.

3.4.2 Argumentation in archaic societies

The question of truth/falseness of a proposition p is grounded in *propositional attitudes* like: know that p, believe that p, not know if p, and not believe that p; these in turn refer to subjects and their *awareness* of certain facts. In order to be aware of facts and to share such awareness, an advanced level of consciousness is necessary, which is only accessible to humans (Homo sapiens sapiens). It remains an open question, if Neanderthals were at the same level of consciousness and could use argumentative structures and the social coordination reached by means of argumentative discourse. Even in human communication, arguments are often hidden by insinuation, voluntary ambiguity, and indirect speech acts and some societies even consider plain arguments as aggressive, impolite and follow a taboo of explicit arguments. The metaphor: "Argument is war" discussed by Lakoff and Johnson (1980) is characteristic for the Western view of argumentation. Moreover, individual consciousness, individual knowledge, individual propositional attitudes are not sufficient. The speaker must be aware of or reasonably able to use shared knowledge, to infer the epistemic state of other people. To do this, she/he must use external criteria. Thus, a complicated pattern of interpersonal comprehension, shared knowledge, and negotiation in a variety of situations is required.

The first level, just being aware that a state of affairs holds, is already achieved by an animal, which reacts properly to a given situation. Even if there is no consciousness (or a low degree of consciousness) given in the animal, one may assume a mental state which represents a state of affairs or even its absence. In this sense, one could say that the "mind" of the animal "contains" a "true" proposition. The distinction between correct and false "proposition" was therefore not the problem that had to be solved in the evolution of language. It is the next level, i.e., the inferring of an epistemic state (of knowing, believing) in another person using *external* information, which is crucial. This transpersonal inference not only concerns epistemic attitudes, but also the desires, needs, and motives of another person.

In a social system, in which status and power are not only decided by brute force and in which they have to be defended and maintained continuously, communication becomes crucial insofar as it gives the information necessary for the inference of "knowledge" about the other; her/his beliefs, desires, etc. As intellectual capacities increase, this faculty develops further. Thus, a person may control the information given by his/her behavior in order to control the knowledge/belief of the other and this cycle may go on until limited by cognitive capacity. The emergence of symbolic forms is the proper solution for stability and chaos-control (cf. Wildgen 1998b); i.e., multi-person epistemic dynamics can only work profitably if the stability of shared knowledge and the input-connection of this knowledge (its "realism") are granted. If not, a system of knowledge, although cognitively possible, cannot be socially enacted and culturally elaborated. As in complex social networks Darwinian selection operates at the level of social entities (which survive or disappear), only species, which have solved this problem, can exploit the benefits of a higher level of cognition.

The question is therefore: How does language, or do other symbolic forms contribute to the evolution of social awareness, social consciousness, social cognition?

Firstly, there are symbolic forms (cf. Chapter 9 for a definition) like technique, which have a straightforward relation to human practice, are specifically referential, and there are other symbolic forms like art (painting, music) which are less referential, more removed from practical concerns. They define a neighborhood on a scale of "realism", in which language occupies an intermediate position. I shall come back to the plurality of symbolic forms in Chapter 9.

Secondly, the very existence of a shared lexicon and shared syntactic rules already provides a body of shared knowledge and thus establishes a core of coordination for a society (group, clan). Insofar as it is not itself the object of desire, is not consumed or the object of rival interests, it is the experiential form of society, social rules, social obligations and mechanisms of social control (beside "cultures" in technique and art).

The next chapters (Chapters 4, 5, 6) will consider the evolution of language in the context of the evolution of technique and art, whereas later chapters (mainly Chapter 6 [partially], 7, 8) will deal more specifically with languages, their grammars and lexicons.

CHAPTER 4

The evolution of cognitive control in tool-making and tool-use and the emergence of a theory of mind

The problem of how the human experience of force and its consequence and causality in the physical realm are related has been at the heart of the philosophy of science since Aristotle, who postulated different kinds of causality reaching from material and formal causality to the causality of effect (causa efficiens) and teleological causality. Whereas modern physics (since Galileo) reduced the scope to the basic causality of effect, modern psychological theories have continued to consider a broader spectrum of notions of causality. From a developmental perspective, Piaget took up this thread of ideas in his book "The representation of the world by the child" (Piaget 1926), in which he distinguishes two basic attitudes towards causality, which emerge in the child in different developmental stages. On the one side, every entity may be understood as the product of skilled human labor. Piaget calls this view "artificialism", we shall show that from an evolutionary perspective human tool-use, and tool manufacturing is the source domain of this schema of causation (Aristotle further abstracts the schema of artificial production, rooted in human skillfulness, to artificial production by Nature and God.). On the other side, every entity may be endowed with a force, an implicit form-giving energy, a germ for future evolutions, a soul. This position is called "animism". As Piaget shows, "animism" in children (until 12 years) contains a series of stages, although the development is not always linear, but follows an internal logic. In the first stage, everything has consciousness, in the second only moving objects have consciousness, and in a third, self-locomotion is the major criterion of consciousness and finally only living beings like humans and animals may have consciousness. In the last case, motion/change requires causation, which is found in an internal disposition to move, change or to experience motion and change passively. Self-locomotion requires control and control is associated with consciousness. Entities like wind, or the sun and the moon have a high degree of apparent self-control and, therefore, are good candidates for animation. The generalized "artificialism", inferred from the apparent omni-presence of parents and their total control of the child-milieu, has an antagonistic relation to the distributed forces of an animistic explanation of the world (in Laurendeau and Pinard (1961) Piaget's empirical investigations were replicated and the phases postulated by Piaget were slightly modified). I will consider simple and higher order consciousness as one pillar for the interpretation of causality by humans and its categorization in language in Section 4.4. The developmental perspectives, which Piaget focused on, can be related to evolutionary stages, where the animistic stage, still present in religions of nature, corresponds to one dimension of hominid evolution involving the symbolic and religious reinterpretation of man's ecology and his society. It shows up in basic rituals, demonstrated by the worship of ancestors and natural powers.[1]

The other dimension, which could be called technical, has to do with tool-usage and tool manufacturing. The second cognitive principle of causation in Section 4.2 takes up this stage of evolution (2 my–50 ky). The symbolic behavior elaborated in art (which presupposes instrumentality), its evolution is the topic of the next chapter, and I will concentrate on the evolution of tool-use and tool making and its relevance for the evolution of human intelligence and language in this chapter.

Tool-use has been found in the whole animal kingdom from mollusks to insects to vertebrates. The latter mostly have well developed brains, which facilitate the learning necessary for tool-use (cf. Becker 1993, for an overview). Tool-use therefore is correlated with the cognitive capacity of the brain, mainly with visual and motor control, coordination and learning (emulation, imitation, and teaching). Throughout the discussion on animal and human tool-use, the importance of inherited cognitive skills versus learned behavior is a basic topic. Other fundamental problems include the materials used for tools (their affordances for manipulation and shaping) and the contexts of use (functions in ecology). Tools are not communicative per se, although the indexical function of signs can be related to exact pointing towards a goal with the help of a stick or another tool. They unfold their communicative function only in social cooperation, e.g., the use of weapons in chase or the use of handy tools in the opening and dissecting of an animal, in the cleaning of its hide, in the preparation of food, the manufacturing of cloth and huts (or parts of cave-openings), etc. Thus, one cannot infer directly the level of linguistic or communicative sophistication from the level of tool use or making, but the schemata of complex causation and instrumental control are a semantic-cognitive preadaptation for complex linguistic structures. The level of tool-industries points to a level of social organization, which makes the existence of language plausible.

In order to start from a very basic level, I will go back to insects and to the problem of describing a path and distance in space. This problem must also be solved in any use of a tool, although in the case of bees tools do not directly intervene (indirectly the shape and acoustic qualities of the honeycombs are a kind of instrument for the transmission of acoustic information and the bees manufacture them). Any causal action must occur in a space and the direction and path of the action must be properly controlled. In the context of social cooperation, which is prominent in bees, this causal structure must be communicated properly in order to enable other bees to use the spatial information to find the food and to exploit it collectively. Therefore, visuo-spatial control and its collective enacting is one of the pillars of causality, which must reappear in communication about external events and action in space and time. Individual experience with causal connections has to be transmitted in order to allow a collective control of causality (and of forces active in space and time).

4.1 The vector-space of goal directed motion

Already for basic mammals (and even insects), the control and pursuit of a path in space can be considered a goal directed activity, which must be mentally controlled. If we consider bees and their social communication about sources of food (the so-called "language of bees"), we recognize that they have an orientation in space due to a kind of biological clock and to the perception of direction (relative to the sun enabled by the perception of polarized light). With their rhythmic motion-pattern demonstrated to other bees upon the arrival in the hive, bees may "designate" the direction and distance of food in relation to the beehive and the sun. Figure 4.1 shows the basic pattern (cf. Frisch 1974: 203; Hauser 1996: 496–504, where the experimental work after von Frisch is described).

The length of the path is designated by the rhythm of the "dance" and the duration of it and by parallel sound-patterns (which are perfectly transmitted by the hexagonal surface of the honeycombs). Now, insects and mammals are in different zoological orders. However, similar cognitive and semiotic capacities may be found in different orders (the social system and semiotic devices of bees are at a very high level in the order of insects, perhaps correspond-

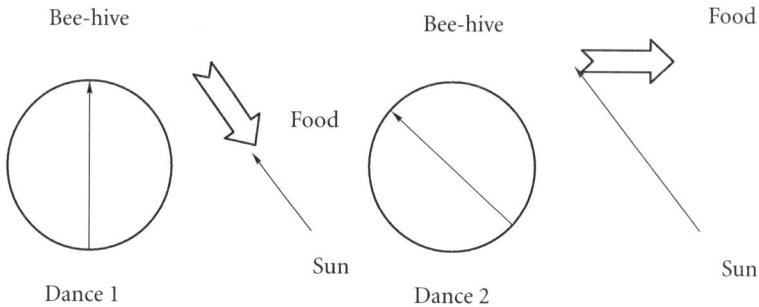

Figure 4.1 Basic patterns of signaling of path and direction.

ing to the extreme position of human language in the mammal order). Hauser (1996: 504) remarks:

> The honey-bee dance language is unquestionably precise and provides detailed information about the external environment. This claim would appear to fly in the face of historically ancient discussions of animal communication [...] favoring the view that animal signals merely reflect the signaler's affective state.

In fact, we assume in the following that there is a continuity between communicative functions in animals and man and that the reference to the ecology, in which the animal/human lives, is basic for all types of communication. It is rather the high level of sophistication which makes honey-bees and humans comparable; the basic referential function is in one way or another realized by all means of communication of socially organized animals.

A cat or a dog which finds its way back home, a predator seeking and catching prey, prey hiding or fleeing, all need basic techniques of spatial orientation and devices for correct and quick control of a path in space. Therefore, the basic scenario of goal-oriented behavior may be characterized by a vector space, with direction, distance (possibly speed and energy functions) integrated into the communicative behavior. If such a cognitive capacity exists, it must necessarily show up in communication, if the animals act in groups and the major motive for communication is the integration of individual cognition into a kind of collective "mind". This motivates the first principle for causation scenarios in cognition.

First cognitive principle of causation: Specification of a vector space

The cognitive system has to represent space and motion in relation to the body (actual position) and some stable environment.[2] It must specify a vector which points to the goal and indicates its distance. This cognitive capacity shows up in communication behavior where socially coordinated motion occurs.

That this principle is also valid for human languages is shown in spatial and directional prepositions and in the syntax and semantics of the phrases they govern. The imagistic space (cf. Wildgen 1994, 1999a) underlying their use contains distances, metrical spaces, and open/closed environments, i.e., those basic "naive" concepts, reanalyzed later in topology.

Zwarts (1997) has exemplified the vectorial content of linguistic structures in prepositional phrases (in Dutch) and similar devices, which may be found in all languages:

(1) Near the church (bij de kerk).

(2) Above the church (boven de kerk).

(3) On the church (on de kerk).

(4) Between the church and the pub (tussen de kerk en de kroeg).

(5) Deep in the tree (diep in de boom).

(6) Far outside the city (ver buiten de stad).

(7) Two centimeters above it (twee centimeter er boven).

(8) More than two meters outside (meer dan twee meter buiten).

Basically we have a three-dimensional space, which may be flattened to two or one dimensions, a center (departure, origin) and a peripheral position (goal), with a vector (line segment with a direction) and a distance (in examples 5, 6, 7, 8). In most cases, we further need an equivalence relation, e.g., all points below a distance from the center (in 1). Thus the prepositional phrase with locational and directional information realizes the first basic principle in a human language. Different strategies or techniques may appear in different languages, thus creating a typological profile at this basic level of causation. One can say that human language contains structures parallel to the socio-cognitive abilities of animals, which have no direct evolutionary continuity with man. The parallelism is not biologically caused but has to do with basic conditions valid for both the ecology of bees and that of men. These can be inferred from the physics of light and motion, which are a common background for any kind of social communication.

4.2 Instrumentality in higher mammals and man

The use of instruments and the goal-oriented adaptation (manufacturing) of tools can be observed in many orders of animals: ants (insects), birds, and mammals all use simple instruments. In some cases, this allows them to access difficult areas of their body (elephants) or to reach under surfaces. Chimpanzees shape twigs to facilitate "fishing" for termites in termite-hills (cf. Immelmann 1979: 128). The use of instruments may be inborn and even the evolution of limbs may be connected to instrumental functions, i.e., limbs are "shaped" evolutionarily to adapt for specific instrumental functions. Thus, primate and human hands take over functions originally located in the head (mouth) for attack, defense, preparation of food, for mastication, etc. Our gestural language, facial expressions, and vocal language presuppose a kind of "instrumental" evolution of the human (and hominid) hand and face (cf. Wildgen 1999b, for the synergetics of hands and eyes).

The development of tool-use and tool making implies learning, social imitation or even teaching. Tembrok (1977: 186f.; following Napier 1962) distinguishes six levels:

- ad-hoc tool-using (but cf. Davidson & Noble 1993).
- purposeful tool-using
- tool-modifying for immediate purpose
- tool-modifying for future eventuality
- ad-hoc-tool-making
- cultural tool-making

The last stage, "cultural tool-making", can only be observed in primates and in man.

In a certain sense, human cultures are represented by the production of permanent tools, the techniques of their usage and the social organization enabling and supporting their use. The precise use of tools becomes apparent in the throwing of shafted hand-axes, and later in the use of arrows.

In the evolutionary line of primates, tool-use is reported both for new world apes and old world apes. The first show only the behavior of throwing objects (from above down to the bottom of trees) in attack and defense,[3] whereas the second show a higher diversity of tool uses (cf. Becker 1993: 79–110). Rather sophisticated tool-use with beginning tool modifying is reported by Boesch (1993), who describes the nut-cracking behavior of wild chimpanzees of the Taï National Park (Côte d'Ivoire). The animals transport both nuts and hammers to roots, which are used as anvil. As stone hammers are rare and necessary to crack very hard nuts (Panda oleosa), they are transported and preserved. Wooden hammers may be shortened using fallen branches until they fit (Boesch 1993: 173f.). Infants must learn the use of tools and different ways of passing on the proper method of use have been observed: *stimulation* (e.g., leaving the hammer near a nut), *facilitation* (providing good hammers and intact nuts), and *active teaching* (ibidem).

Another type of tool use by chimpanzees is called "leaf sponging", i.e., drinking rain water from the hollow of the trees using leaves. Although not all chimpanzees in all ecological environments show these types of tool use, one can say that they are able under proper circumstances to develop a system of stable tool use and even tool modifying. A moderate amount of teaching of tool-use is possible without the use of language but complicated actions or their perfect enacting require special linguistic tools; this is clear in the case of normal musical education or high level athletic training. A simple level of tool-use and tool-making does not require language and the immediate question is, was language a necessary condition for the further evolution of tool-use, be-ginning with stage four in the list above, or did the general (social) evolution, which demanded an enabled level of "cultural tool-making", have as (social) precondition the existence of a language? A third possibility would be that tool-making at stage four demands planning beyond the present and at further stages the control of a series of goal-oriented activities, i.e., in a sense a *syntax* of manual activities. The production of tools becomes a part of a larger set of social practices, i.e., tools found by archeologists are only indicators for a very complex social and cognitive interaction. Thus stone tools of a certain material and size presuppose knowledge about places where one finds the material, a mental geography of proper resources. The stone tool in use can help to shape other tools of wood, horn or bone; these again are helpful in manufacturing clothes, parts of the furniture and dwelling.

On this view a stone tool is only the single remnant of a whole system of cultural traditions, which were learned by children, taught by adults and as-sembled in the memories of the older members of the clan together with the stories of the family and the clan (of the world and the spirits possibly). One can easily imagine such a social complex if one considers the embedding of ba-sic manufacturing techniques into the community life of Australian aborigines (cf. Reynolds 1983).

Another key to the evolution of tool-use and language is possibly cerebral lateralization, which is a long-range tendency in primate evolution:

For example, hemispheric specializations similar to those that characterize *Homo sapiens* appear to be present in macaque monkeys (Macaca) who are left-hemisphere dominant for processing species-specific vocalizations (...) and right-hemisphere dominant for discriminating faces.

(Reynolds 1983:224.)

In the course of the evolution towards man the left hemisphere subsequently became specialized for right-hand manipulation and bimanual coordination. Thus the evolution of manual skills was responsible for the cognitive ability of planning and coordinating the motion pattern of hands. In parallel the anatomy of the hand changed and as archeologists have discovered enough bones of hands one can deduce from the characteristics of these bones, that:

- The Australopithecus afarensis already had a higher mobility of the hand in comparison to chimpanzees living in that period, but that there remains a clear qualitative difference compared to modern humans (cf. M. Brandt 1992:76).
- The Homo neanderthalensis of Ferrassie 1 and 2 has specific features, which do not coincide with those, found in humans, but the mobility of their hands was presumably at the same level (cf. Piveteau 1991:62ff.).

The parallel question for an archeologist is: Did Australopithecus afarensis or Homo erectus make tools (beyond level 3 mastered by chimpanzees, see above) and was Homo neanderthalensis as fit for tool making as the Cro-Magnon man was?

The earliest tools are dated to about 2 million y BP. They were found in the Olduvai Gorge (East Africa) and show a variety of forms of flaking using pebbles, which had been brought from other places to the sedimentary context in which they were discovered. The basic technique of stone flaking had been discovered and elaborated to a "culture". For these cultures, the correspondent findings of human bones got the name "Homo habilis".

The next stage is called the "Acheulean industry" and related to the Homo erectus. The shape of the bifacial hand axes is (at least locally) standardized (cf. Davidson & Noble 1993:370f.). The archeologists are still debating whether the hand axes or the flakes (or both) were the tools "intentionally" produced. The stone-industries of late Homo neanderthalensis (Mousterian industry) improved and reached a similar level to that of Cro-Magnon men/women (perhaps out of rivalry with him/her).

In the context of lateralization gender differences may be relevant. Tool-use and tool making require specific visuospatial skills, in which modern human males score higher than females (cf. Falk 1993). This sexual dimorphism may be either linked to "a recessive X-linked gene of intermediate frequency" (ibidem: 211) or to brain-lateralization. If selection (sexual or other) primed spatial orientation in a larger territory and the use and making of large tools (weapons) in males and small scale orientation and vocal communication in females, this (benign) sexual dimorphism could have pushed the evolution of both capacities in parallel, because "of the way genes are transmitted from one generation to the next, characteristics that are selected for in one sex are extremely likely to affect the other" (Falk 1993: 227, Fn. 1). Even a small sexual dimorphism in brain lateralization due to differences in the rate of growth or the effect of hormonal frequencies may thus create, if the selective tendency is stable for large periods (millions of years) a specific intellectual profile in which both female and male specificities are increased and redistributed between the sexes.

Continuing in the line of such a hypothesis of a cognitive co-evolution of visuospatial scenarios and cognitive-semantic competence, I shall compare tool-making scenarios and schemata for simple sentences. The underlying hypothesis is that the semantic (deep) structure of sentences is prefigured in visuospatial scenarios as those mastered by early toolmakers (Homo habilis, Homo erectus).

The basic script of tool manufacturing contains the following schemata:

- Seeking for materials (this may include the cultural transmission of knowledge, where the materials may be found and even trading of materials).
- Using both hands, such that one hand fixes the material, which has to be shaped, and the other controls a tool used for shaping. This means the holding of both objects and the control of a stroke of the bone-tool on the stone. Figure 4.2 shows a simulated picture of the process (cf. Jelinek 1975: 171).
- The products of tool making in the late period (about 30 to 10 ky BP) were highly differentiated and served many purposes. Figure 4.3 shows six objects (cf. Weiner 1972: 124).
- The tool is adapted to specific contexts; it becomes the blade of a knife, the point of an arrow, the body of an ax, etc., or it is used to perform one phase of a process, e.g., cleaning the fur of an animal; the fur is already the result of a longer goal-oriented process beginning with the hunting of the animal. If a social distribution of functions exists, the tool-producer may exchange his product for food or other tools. It becomes an object of value. The mastering of tool-production allows the production of cultural

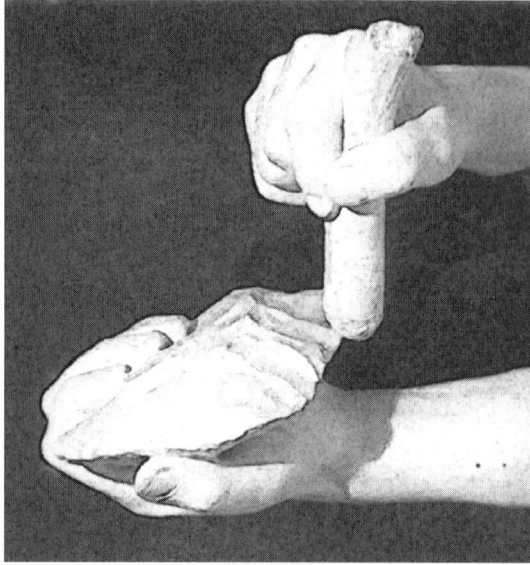

Figure 4.2 A simulated tool-making scenario (cf. Jelinek 1972: 171)

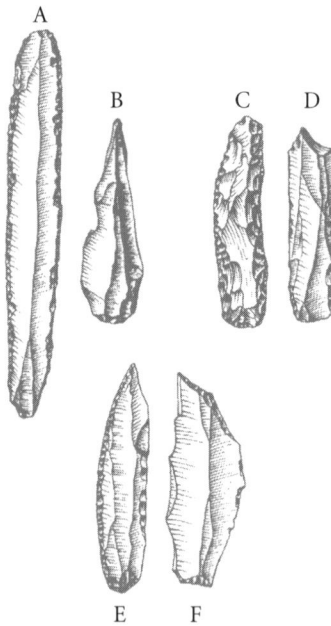

Figure 4.3 Six tools: A: a blade found in Laugerie-Haute; B: graver found in Corbiac; C, D blades found in Siberia; E: Capsian-blade; Capsian-graver

objects and art; these may again become objects of value. Elaborated tools and objects of art show geometrical abstraction (triangles, symmetrical or asymmetrical shapes) and iconicity (with abstraction).

– A further stage produces pictures (signs) of the hand, the "instrument" which shapes tools. Cf. Table 5.8 in Chapter 5.4.

The last stage points to a first cycle of self-reference. The painter refers (iconically) to the (his) hand, which he uses in painting. The causal scenario, which underlies tool-use and tool making, may be schematized in the following fashion:

1 Seeking of the material for the tool   Finding of the proper material

The path may be the result of a chance trip or the image of a path is stored in memory.

2   Object fixing   Tool fixing

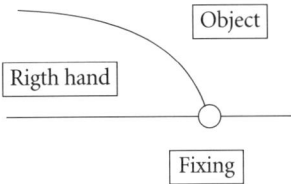

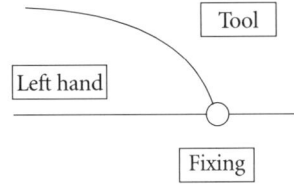

3 Shaping of the object with the tool
Result: two objects controlled by the (L) left and (R) right hand choke together

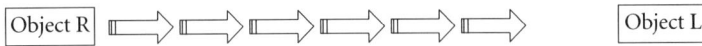

Repetitive action of object (R) on object (L)

4 The shape of the object is changed by subtraction
Object (L) changes its shape by withdrawing pieces

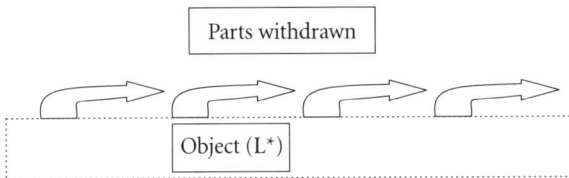

Result: object (L*)

Figure 4.4 Sub-schemata of tool manufacturing

The interesting and new process is No. 3; it applies principle 1 in the first section, i.e., a vector-field prescribes the path of the shaping energy from (R) right hand to (L) left hand. If we magnify the zone of contact, we see the bouncing of the tool on the zone. It has two effects:

- It creates a hole at the point of contact.
- It triggers a shock wave, which may split the zone.

Archeologists can recognize the goal-directed activity of hominids (humans) by the small hole; the intended effect is the splitting and a specific result in certain materials is the sharp edge of the tool. We may formulate a second principle (further consequences are discussed in Chapter 7).

Second cognitive principle of causation: Instrumentality

The cognitive/functional map of human hands with its force and its fine grip specifies a type of causality of form giving by an intentionally controlled shock wave and splitting of a body (i.e., stone, bone, etc.).

From the second principle, we can derive an "idealized cognitive model" of events (cf. Lakoff 1987:68–76), which applies the body schema of human hands and their instrumental use and includes non-linear effects. One can distinguish *simple* and *complex* (interactive) sub-models. The first four sub-models may be called simple:

1. Simple events are linked to one (left or right) hand.
2. Simple events involve a body acting on an individual object (bone, stone, etc.).
3. Simple events are modular insofar as they may be repeated, inserted into other contexts and combined with other events (self-containment is provided by the body).
4. The transmission of force is prototypically asymmetric. One hand moves (and a tool in this hand), the other hand fixes the object which has to be shaped. As the shaping instrument is deformed to a lesser degree, an asymmetric effect is produced.

The simple causal model is insufficient at the level of the basic instrumental action: shaping a stone to obtain a hand-axe (or the flints, which are cut off; cf. Davidson & Noble 1993). One has to consider an interaction between different types of causation:

5. An agent perceives/experiences affordances centered in the objects (cf. Gibson 1966); they have to be respected or exploited.
6. The cooperation of hand and eye (acting and perceiving) is strengthened in an adaptive cycle.
7. The cooperation of right and left hand, of thumb and fingers is further elaborated.

The simple billiard-ball schema of linear transmission of momentum fails as a causal model. One has to define a concept of causation, which includes:

– Cooperation of body and environment, body-center (e.g., brain) and periphery (limbs, e.g., hands)
– Nonlinear-causation, as catastrophic effect after the accumulation of minor causes
– The branching (or diffusion) of effects

The complexity of the relation between cause and effect requires the cognitive stabilization of an intermediate resource called controller or controlling system.

4.3 Controllers and their semantic consequences

Brennenstuhl (1982) introduced the concept of "tunnel", i.e., a controller (controlling system) allows a range of actions and excludes another range; e.g., if a missile deviates from its ideal path, then the controlling mechanism corrects the trajectory such that it returns toward the invisible line inside the "tunnel". In English the verb "let" marks a domain of allowed (uncontrolled) action and presupposes that the action does not enter the excluded area; if it does, the "permission" will stop: e.g., *Let the children play in the garden*.

Locutions like the German proverb *Der Krug geht solange zum Brunnen bis er bricht* (literally 'The pitcher goes to the fountain until it is broken'- the nearest English equivalent would be 'It's all fun and games until somebody gets his eye poked out.') may guide us in the analysis of another type of a causal schema. The agent of the breaking remains invisible, and different persons may use the pitcher with varying degrees of carefulness until it breaks. The cause is accumulative, i.e., in the pitcher minimal cracks accumulate and the responsible agents are distributed by chance, i.e., different users or circumstances may cause the breaking (even in the first instance of usage). Moreover, the independent probabilities are additive, i.e., if the container is used very frequently its breaking becomes almost necessary. Other causal schemata combine local effects and their interaction, which produces a global effect.

The types of causation humans may distinguish in the world are also relevant for our understanding of the internal organization of language itself. Thus single lexical items *control* the constructions to which they contribute and this parallelism is more than an easy metaphor, because even the most abstract forms of human behavior use the basic cognitive resources of man. Grammatical laws are not elements of some spiritual third world. This becomes evident as soon as they are understood as a natural product of evolution (and not as some God-given law or ready-made convention). This has been shown in the grammar of sentences (under the heading of control, valence, rection, etc.); i.e., the semantics of causation reappear as formal restrictions in the syntax of sentences. The question arises: How did the cognizing of forces enable/create the syntactic dynamics in language. I shall come back to this question in the final chapters of this book.

Controller and controlling systems define a bottle-neck in cognitive (and social) evolution and I assume that a rule system like the one exemplified in human grammars was either a precondition for an achievement like tool-industries or coevolved with it.

4.4 Mentally or communicatively caused events and theories of mind

In the following, I will concentrate on the specificity of mentally or communicatively caused events.

Mental causation may be rooted in the basic animistic attitudes of children discussed in the introduction to this chapter. Beyond manual control of objects, a child has to give sense to the action of his parents or other persons, i.e., he or she must build-up a cognitive representation of other persons. In order to do this, the child must build up a theory of mind. The following stages have been found in psycholinguistic research (cf. Thommen 1991: 199).

- By the age of two, children learn to situate themselves in the triangle of their caregiver and objects.
- When children are three or four years old, they become able to consider the existence of a foreign perspective without guessing its content.
- Being between three and six years old the child learns to attribute first order knowledge to others (e.g., the other knows that **p**).

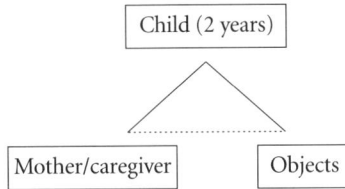

Figure 4.5 Basic triangle of relations

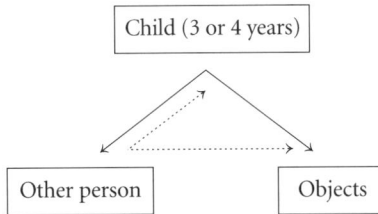

Figure 4.6 Elaborated triangle of relations

- Between the ages of seven and ten children learn to describe second order knowledge of others (e.g., the other knows that person **x** knows **p**) and to guess dispositions for action of others in relation to their knowledge.
- Until the age of twelve, a child becomes able to calculate based on knowledge of others and their specific dispositions to act.

This cognitive development is crucial for the understanding of causation in social and communicative interaction. If a person (P) knows that a state of knowledge K will motivate Person Q to do A; he becomes able either to foresee A or to make Q know K in order to have him do A. But if Q guesses that P wants him to do A and that he controls K, he will either check K or do B in spite of K in order not to be controlled by P. Thus knowledge of first and higher order becomes a cause, which may or may not be controlled by a person.

The acquisition of knowledge of others may be gained by the observation of others, their actions and expressions. On this level, P may guess how Q interprets his movements, his behavior, his expressive gestures and may make him believe that he has certain dispositions by manipulating his own behavior in the perspective of its perception by Q.

In a more complicated scenario, knowledge is transferred by language. In this case, it is even easier to manipulate the knowledge of others, and every society must develop techniques in order to guarantee a certain degree of honesty. This can be done by moral rules: Thou shalt not lie, or by a penalization on lies and deceiving. A rather natural penalization is the general unreliability of communication and its breakdown as a useful tool, if a critical threshold of deceiving is crossed, or the group may ostracize or refuse to cooperate with individuals with a reputation for being deceitful before communication breaks down further. This leads to a new principle of causation:

Third cognitive principle of causation: Theory of mind and mental causation

Mental (communicative) causation may take one or several of three channels:

- visible behavior (e.g., motion in space)
- gestures, facial expressions, and other expressive behavior
- language

In any case deceiving is possible and higher order knowledge (and deceiving) is accessible (for adults). This requires specific norms and a value system centered on truthfulness and sincerity.

Speech acts themselves are members of a larger field of "controllers", some of which are non-linguistic (they may even be more forceful than linguistic ones):

- coercion: its direct force is higher than the stimulation or frustration force of speech acts. The force may be due to threat (your money or your life) or simply by showing power (pointing with a gun at a person);
- punishment or reward,
- giving an example which stimulates imitation,
- emotional manipulation like seduction, demoralizing, frightening, arousing disgust, etc.

Other controlling speech-acts types are:

- commitments
- obligations
- duties (cf. ibidem: 69)

The felicity conditions of speech acts frame the background condition for control, i.e., the environment and social rules are themselves controllers and speech acts only specify the parameters or concentrate symbolically a given constellation of control features.

Table 4.1 Speech acts of stimulation or frustration in order of force (cf. Brennenstuhl 1982:68)

	Stimulating speech acts	Frustrating speech acts
High force	order	prohibit
	command	
	demand	frighten away
	tell	
	persuade	dissuade
	ask	talk out of
	beg	
	wish that A does x (in A's presence)	warn
	advise	advise against
	suggest	
	encourage	discourage
	recommend	
	advocate	mar (show disapproval)
Low force	praise	

If a theory of mind is present in higher primates and specifically in man, a system of causation scenarios by signs in proper contexts and under the rule of social conventions shows up, which is reflected in speech act verbs, and corresponding syntactic devices: to promise that, to persuade / dissuade someone to do something, etc.

The structural properties of complex causation reappear in these contexts, e.g., distributed control inside larger organizations, accumulation of controlling causes of different kinds such as power, positive/negative values associated with persons and situations, desires and their diffusion by imitation, arguments in persuasion, procedures of evaluation or devaluation, etc. In any case mono-causal chain effects seem to be rare exceptions and the controller/controlled has to consider a complex ecology of affordances, proper situations, shifts in evaluation/desire, etc. In large sociological contexts, rational control is only possible if very strong (or subconscious) flows control the dynamics and guarantee the stability necessary for collective activities. In general these social systems have higher degrees of freedom than animal communities have and therefore are less stable over time.

Evolution has not only enriched the potential of humans to exploit their ecological niche and to manage more complex social organizations, it has also brought into being a hyper-complex dynamics of causation. It enlarged the field of (social) control and thus made necessary a kind of "hyper-controls".

This is the basis of human freedom and responsibility. Two extreme types of consequences may be foreseen:

1. The loss of control (even on the local level) by a chaotic socio-political evolution, which causes a breakdown of communication.
2. The enslavement of local controls by global ones. This means loss of freedom and thus of intelligent, self-responsible choice; such a phenomenon could be called the "Big Brother syndrome" or the "Orwell problem" (cf. Chomsky 1986).

These consequences force human societies to develop rituals, i.e., fix sequences of actions which have been chosen and/or further developed in cultural evolution and which are learned and enacted by persons. Ritual or automatic action patterns, whose parts do not give sense to the user restrict the degree of freedom in social behavior and allow for easier control.[4] In a compact way grammars are the product of such a long-term control over rules of behavior; i.e., the restrictive character of grammars is at the same time the precondition for a complex intellectual life; freedom and limitation are inscribed as complementary principles in the structure of human languages.

CHAPTER 5

The evolution of pre-historic art and the transition to writing systems

5.1 The evolution of art from the Paleolithic to the Mesolithic

The development of symbolic forms in the period from ca 40 ky BP[1] to the first oriental civilization in Mesopotamia and Egypt may be called "evolution", but this term does not have the same meaning as in the case of the "evolution" of animals, hominids and modern man. The time-scale of thousands and hundreds of years is too small for a purely biological interpretation of semiotic evolution, although the human brain witnessed an acceleration of change via gene expression rather than via genetic information per se. The rather quick evolution of symbolic capacities may therefore be linked to the new mode of gene expression in the brain rather than to overall genetic changes (cf. Enard et al. 2001). Thus, "evolution" properly concerns the exploitation of biological potential, adaptation to new ecological niches, development of special skills and mainly cultural evolution under the condition of population growth and intensified contact between human groups and societies. The basic question is: Why did new symbolic activities like the engraving of tools and the painting of caves emerge in a certain period, in some cases in areas, which were not in contact with each other? Was there a transition (catastrophe) line, which triggered the appearance of a new kind of semiotic activity? This question is important because if we are able to describe and explain the emergence of new symbolic activities, we may reach new insights into the underlying cognitive capacity of man, its potential for communication and the factors, which played a role in uncovering the biologically latent possibilities of sign-usage.

The beginning of graphical arts can be dated by the first appearance of concentrated color pigments in the context of hominid dwellings. Barham (2002) reports that in south central Africa pieces of iron hematite (often called ochre) and specularite were recovered from an archeological site near Twin Rivers, in Zambia. They had been brought to the site, processed and rubbed against surfaces. One can infer that these materials were used to color objects, bodies or surfaces. The use of such pigments establishes a continuity, which reaches from the archeological sites mentioned (i.e. from 270 ky BP) to contemporary hunter-gathers in the Kalahari. The first engravings on stone were also found in Africa and can be dated to 70 ky BP. One can conclude that archaic Homo sapiens used colors to paint (e.g. their bodies, objects, and/or large surfaces). The period I will try to interpret from a semiotic perspective concerns the first engravings on stones, bones and ivory dating from about 30 ky BP, the first sculptures from 27–20 ky BP and the paintings in caves from 30–15 ky BP. I will consider four stages of figural symbolization ("art"), which preceded the development of writing. Roughly speaking, this evolution/development covers the period between 40 ky to 12 ky BP:

– The engravings on tools
– The first "sculptures"
– The painting of caves

In the last section of this chapter the evolution of writing systems in the late Neolithic and in the bronze age will be sketched. The periods of Paleolithic symbolic activities may be related to different "industries" of stone shaping described in Table 5.1.

Table 5.1 The periods of Paleo- and Neolithic stone-industries in Europe and of cave art in France (cf. Gamble 1986:82, 84, 136 and Prideaux 1973:63)

Stages of glaciations (measured by isotopes of oxygen)	ky BP	Lithic technologies (Neanderthals, recent man)	Stylistic periods of cave art in France (recent man)
Interglacial (5e)	128–118	Core/chopping tool	
Early glacial/temperate (5d–a)	118–75	Flake, core/chopping tool	
Early glacial, glacial (4,3)	75–32	Handaxes, scrapers	
Full glacial (2)	32–13	Blades	Perigordian (ca. 34 ky–19 ky) Aurignacian (33 ky–18 ky)
Late glacial (1)	13–10	Microlithic elements	Solutrean (18 ky–16 ky) Magdalenian (16 ky–10 ky)
Current interglacial	10–0		

5.1.1 The engravings on tools

Engravings on tools and other small objects belong to the category of trans-portable pieces of art ("art mobilier") and thus rather to profane life than to ritual or sacred contexts. The artistic forms found are mainly either decorative, or representational, i.e., the shape of an existing object may be inferred. In many cases they are both. One can clearly distinguish between a kind of self-contained form giving, i.e. in the ornament, and iconic art, which uses realistic contours and colors perceived in external objects, animals, etc. A trend towards abstraction on the one side and towards mimesis on the other is present from the beginning and points to two basic dimensions of pictorial/sculptural activity: abstract signs (symbols) and natural (iconic) signs.

A sign (a picture, a sculpture) can be observed and imitated without temporal restrictions whereas the phonetic form of an utterance is only remembered for a short time; in most cases the structure of the sign itself is forgotten as soon as the message is understood. Moreover, the engraved bone in the possession of a person and the engraving on it may be used as a prototype (or a model of imitation) which orients further perception of similar objects. It is also an object of value (it can be given, stolen, inherited or buried with the owner). Becoming an object of value marks the point of transition to ritual and magical objects. The stability of the sign-form attracts other meanings and helps to organize a whole field of mythical or religious knowledge, which existed as belief or behavioral schema before the time-permanent sign was endowed with its meaning. Hence, the system of beliefs and practices becomes psychologically sizable with the help of permanent signs.

5.1.2 Paleolithic sculptures

These sculptures may be small as the famous "Venus-statuettes" found in France, Italy, Austria, Siberia, and many other places. They typically over-emphasize sexual attributes. In other cases, the sculptures are very realistic, as are the bison made out of clay in the cave Tuc d'Audoubet (cf. Leaky 1981: 174). The sculpture may even be a decoration on a weapon or a ritual instrument. A typical type of sculptures appears in Western and Eastern Europe. They show naked women and are concentrated in areas of actual Austria, Czechia, Moravia, Ukraine. Another more slender style (probably not naked) is found in the East of Moscow (mainly in Siberia). Figure 5.1 shows a number of "Venus"-statuettes from: A) Willendorf, B) Lespuge, C) Grimaldi, D) Dolné-Vêstonice,

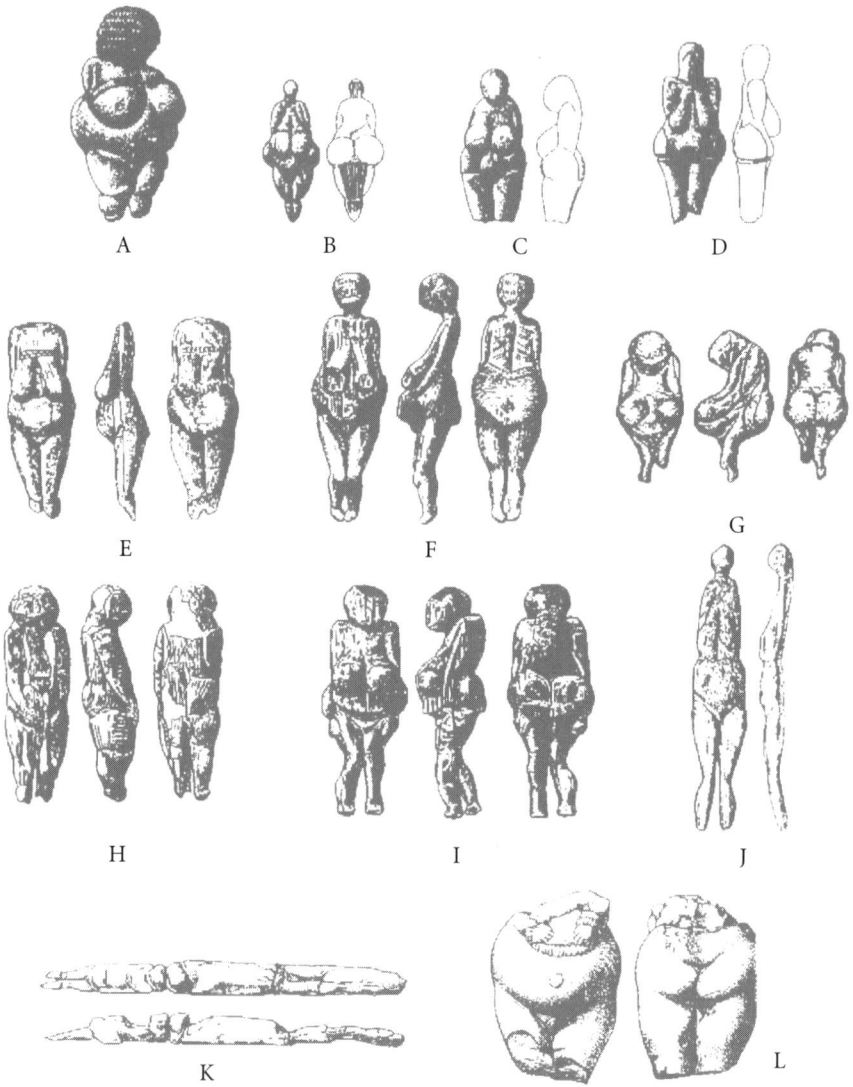

Figure 5.1 "Venus"-statuettes from Middle and Eastern Europe

E, F and L) Kostienki, G) Khotylevo, H and J) Avdeevo, I und K Gargarino (cf. Sanchidrián 2001:126).

Female attributes are overemphasized; cf. the breast, the abdomen and the backside. The hair is fashioned in a very specific way. Although these figures are not universal, they define a certain style of art. Simultaneously they create models for human bodies, ideals of the human body. The dominance of female statuettes and female symbols ("vulvas") was interpreted as the consequence of a more "gendered" society in the Upper Paleolithic. Eventually a more egalitarian society was replaced by a society with social differentiation and a divergence between female and male roles (cf. Foley 1991).

The three-dimensional sculptures of human bodies and animals may point to norms valid for sexual selection in certain societies and later for animal selection in breeding (cf. Chapter 2.3). In this case, the sculpture (or the painting) does not primarily represent existing entities, it rather symbolizes a rule for how to shape and transform existing entities. The sign becomes a medium of invention and innovation; it transports a "logica inventionis" in the sense of Leibniz, a design for how to shape things. The transition between a semiotic system, which represents the world and thus helps to achieve a level of collective perception and a system, in which the future of the world is designed *in abstracto*, is decisive. It allows for a new pace of cultural evolution guided by innovative and goal-directed imagination.[2]

5.1.3 Paleolithic cave paintings

Cave paintings occur mainly in an area north and west of the Pyrenees: mainly in Périgord, Toulouse (France) and Cantabrica (Spain). Probably the area was a very early economic "Kulturbund" (network of civilizations) in Europe. The herds of reindeer (as in northern Finland today) defined the relevant ecological dynamics. They probably came to the plains in winter and returned to higher grounds in the Pyrenees, the Cantabrica Mountains or the Massif Central in France in summer. The populations of Cro-Magnon men followed the herds and thus met other populations in southern France and northern Spain. This contact and common basis of survival would explain a common (or similar) system of beliefs, myths, and rituals, the expression of which are the cave paintings in this area. Consequently, these paintings are the result of a rather specific, although geographically large "civilization" and it is even possible that some painters/medicine-men were able to circulate in this culturally homogeneous area. Reindeer typically do not figure in the paintings. This could mirror a fundamental difference between Paleo- vs. Mesolithic societies. The animals in the cave-paintings would, on this account, stand for the world outside the context of human society and the world controlled by humans, i.e., the separation of an autonomous human ecology from a wild, dangerous, uncontrolled outside world. Shamanism, magic and finally religion are symbolic tools to "control" the domain outside real, practical life, to control chaos in a modern

Figure 5.2 Three representations of a deer (cf. Rhotert 1956: 23)

sense. Animals like the bison, the wild goat and the wild horse were in a certain sense "candidates" for domestication but were still wild. The symbolic control of these animals thus precedes their control in domestication (and prepared it unconsciously).

The fascination of the Franco-Cantabric cave-paintings comes from their vividness and the amount of movement "frozen" in the work of the painter. This points to a basic dynamism of figural art and could be linked to dance and to rituals in the context of which these paintings had their place, e.g., in initiation rituals.

The high points of cave painting occurred from the late Aurignacian to the middle-Magdalenian (cf. Table 5.1) and declined rather quickly towards the end of this period. In the period of decline, the paintings became smaller, were reduced to contours, sketches and finally to schematic signs. Although this decline probably had economic or religious causes, it exemplifies a basic gradient of semiotic systems called "grammaticalization" in linguistics. A sign has a rich referential meaning (a realistic imaginistic content) at the beginning. Then it looses this content and is reduced to a functional schema in the context of a larger complex of meanings. In the context of a ritual, the painting may fill a slot in a complex of ritual activities, in the context of a sentence a prior lexeme may become a grammatical item linking other lexemes or integrating them into the sentential frame. Figure 5.2 gives a series from a detailed (3) to a sketched (2) and a schematic (1) picture of a deer.

Stage (1) may be further reduced to a symbol without iconic support. For the users of the cave the meaning was known (and even the hidden iconic cues could be read), but for those who did not participate in the ritual, they looked like ciphers of some unknown alphabet. As we know that alphabets are a much more recent phenomenon, we have to interpret these signs as mnemonic struc-

Figure 5.3 A bison with symbol-like drawings from the cave Font-de-Gaume (cf. Jelinek 1972:434)

tures. There was a corpus of common knowledge in these societies and the painter was aware of this knowledge. The awareness was probably established by formalized teaching in initiation periods and by rituals, or restricted to functional roles in the tribe (e.g., the role of the shaman). The "reading" of the paintings presupposed this knowledge, which had acquired social value. Even before a system of writing was introduced, a corpus of knowledge, of which persons in specific social positions were aware, could exist as a semiotic system. As this knowledge was not acquired in "natural" practices by emulation or imitation (as tool making) it had to be "objectivated" into signs, which could be rituals, paintings, sculptures, music, dance, prayers, etc. Because of this objectivation, cultural knowledge became a socially codified system of signs, which prefigured the later graphical mode of codifying it, i.e. writing. After this step, cultural evolution had reached a level of organization, which made writing possible and profitable. It had only to be invented and elaborated by use. In Figure 5.3 a painting, which mixes the figural representation of an animal and schematic drawing, is shown. In principle, one part of it could be the topic (e.g., the animal), the other the comment, or in grammatical terms, the subject and the predicate (to chase, to kill, to bring home, to eat, etc.). The figural language would be similar in its basic organization to the transition between one-word-utterances (either subject or predicate) to two-word-utterances (one part is more referential, the other more grammatical as in pivot-words).

5.1.4 The representation of humans in a social context

In the cave painting of the Franco-Cantabric tradition human beings are rarely represented (sometimes they appear in hidden places, are mixed with animal forms like ghosts or masks or look like caricatures). In the period between 12 and 7 ky BP, i.e., just before or after the rise of agriculture, a wealth of engravings is found in which humans occupy the central place. The arrow had been invented and chasing (probably also warfare) had been sophisticated. The individual huntsman or the group of hunters and the animal (sometimes the enemy) are the major topics. The scenes are very dynamic as they show people and animals running, attacking, fleeing. In many cases, there is a basic relation, e.g., a huntsman shoots at an attacking ibex, four huntsmen with a leader, or a battle between two groups, etc. We could say a relation or a valence schema is realized in the painting. Figure 5.4 shows an engraving from Cova Remigia in eastern Spain.

The engravings show a multitude of situations in every day life. If hunting scenes are dominant, a number of other social settings are also represented: groups with women, women with children, dances that involve men and women. Probably the social roles were separated between hunters exploiting the larger ecology and women controlling the family, the dwelling and

Figure 5.4 The chase at the ibex, Cova Remigia, Spain (cf. Weigert 1956:31; Sanchidriàn 2001:400)

the nearby ecology. The change in social structure (if we infer this from the catalogue of pictures) could have two sources:

- The warmer post-glacial period changed the ecology. Instead of hunting large animals and moving with the big herds of reindeers, the hunters exploited the diversity of smaller animals in their neighborhood, the settlements became more stable, the techniques of hunting and exploitation developed further.
- The Levante population was apparently in contact with populations in northern Africa and possibly had a different ethnic substratum. Thus the human bodies shown in the pictures portray ideal persons with slender builds (even women).

The Mesolithic art of the Levante culture is so different from the Franco-Cantabric one that these cultures seem to be both historically and ethnically independent. Possibly both cultures had parallels in northern Africa: the Franco-Cantabric style resembles the rock engravings in the Sahara Atlas and the oasis Fezzan (south of Tripoli). Between 7 and 6 ky BP cultures based on cattle breeding reached this area from Sudan. They continued the same realistic style (mainly with contours engraved in the rock) but with different contents. In a similar way, the Levante style is imitated by Mesolithic rock-drawings in the mountains further south: Hoggar, Gilf Kebir and others. Here the paintings on the rock show pictures of social life in a very vivid although formalized style. Figure 5.5 shows a family scene found in Kargur Talh.

If we imagine the religious or shamanistic contexts of Paleolithic and Mesolithic art, we may see how the dramatic change of climate may have trig-

Figure 5.5 Family scene in the Levante style from Kargur Talh (northern Sahara); cf. Rhotert 1956:41

gered a basic change of image-schemata. If in the deep and hidden caverns animals (or their souls, the clans they represented, basic natural forces) were the object of worship and magical rituals, the art on the rocks in Mesolithic (i.e., warmer) Spain and in northern Africa concerned rather the sun, the rain and other geo-cosmic phenomena. This could have reoriented completely the metaphorical and metonymical network, which grounds the semantic categorizations found in languages (cf. the basic ideas of Lakoff & Johnson 1980). Thus the change would have affected the make-up of the meaning-system (which probably triggered a change of linguistic categorization and of grammar at a deeper level than sound change). The structures often considered as universal, such as image schemata, cognitive models, mental maps, and blending (cf. Fauconnier & Turner 2002), may have undergone dramatic changes in the Paleo- and Mesolithic periods (and still today although the slow rhythm of such changes makes it difficult to observe them in a human life span).

As both cultures in the northern Sahara extended to Sudan, we have a link to one of the first large and historically important cultural systems, the art of Egypt and the invention of hieroglyphs in Egypt. This does not exclude the possibility that other Mesolithic cultures in Pakistan and India (cf. Brooks & Wakankar 1976), in the Indus Valley and in the "Golden Horn", i.e., Mesopotamia and the areas west (Palestine), existed. However, it is clear that the Paleo- and Mesolithic cultures did not disappear without leaving deep traces in subsequent human civilizations (rock art is also found in Australia and Tasmania; cf. Bahn & Rosenfeld 1991).

5.2 The topology of Cro-Magnon life space and the semiotic space of decorated caves

The term "life-space" as denoting the basis of human cognition was introduced by Kurt Lewin, who observed the quickly changing perception and interpretation of space as a soldier in World War I (cf. Wildgen 2001b). "Life-space" or "cognitive ecology" refers to the relevance pattern, the "meaning" given to aspects of the surrounding space insofar as it is cognitively marked as a memory-system for what we have lived through, experienced, enacted, imagined, hoped, and feared. These contents are attributed to spatial characteristics in a natural way. If in the first step of this process, real places receive memory traces, in a second step the memory-space becomes purely internal and an artificial (cognitive) space is constructed to receive and elaborate the mnemonic structure (cf. for the "art of memory" Yates 1966; Wildgen 1998a). I will first consider the evolution of objective spaces used for memory traces and then consider more abstract construed spaces. If we consider the life-space of Cro-Magnon hunters, two regions are most relevant:

1. The *space of hunting*; it consists of the habitat, the migration routes of bison, aurochs, reindeer, etc., the caves of bears and lions, the rivers rich in fish, etc. Together with this hunting space, the sky with the motion of sun, moon and stars was probably semiotically organized as a memory-system of spatial orientation (B1).
2. The *space of shelters*, abris, cave opening, where the clans stayed for certain periods of the year (B2).

These two base-spaces, B1 and B2, which subdivide the social life in an external (open) and an internal (closed) one, may be blended or transformed in ritual, religious contexts. Thus, the space of the sacred, magical, and ritual is one derivation, the space of burial and life after death another one. This allows us to state three major trends:

1. The space for *rituals* and magic is derived from B1 and B2. Thus, the painted caves are a derivation of decorated abris, cave entrances, by their transfer into dark and hidden (normally not accessible) caves. We call this transferred space, the *ritual space (R)*.
2. The space for *burials* was in most cases not in closed caves, but rather in open space. Nevertheless, these places could be *blended* with space R, e.g., in Neolithic dolmens an artificial closed space covered with soil is placed in open space but construed as a closed space. The Egyptian mastabas and pyramids correspond topologically to this type (are open, visible architecture with a hidden cave inside); the burial caves in the Valley of Kings in Egypt are also of the same type as the mountain above was considered as a natural pyramid.
3. The internal structure of the natural and the construed caves has topologically (ignoring all the topographical details) the shape of a closed tunnel, which may be broken up by sub-tunnels.

One could consider further *blends*. A cave is like the inner space of the body: mouth (nose) – stomach – intestines or it is a negative of the body itself with head (entry) – neck (narrow entry) – trunk (main room) – limbs (side-rooms).

   One could venture the hypothesis that the topology of life-space and body is the stable background of semiosis. The (catastrophic) transitions to reinterpretations in other (homologous) spaces constitute the proper semiosis beyond perceptual categorization. This corresponds to Peirce's concept of a symbol cre-

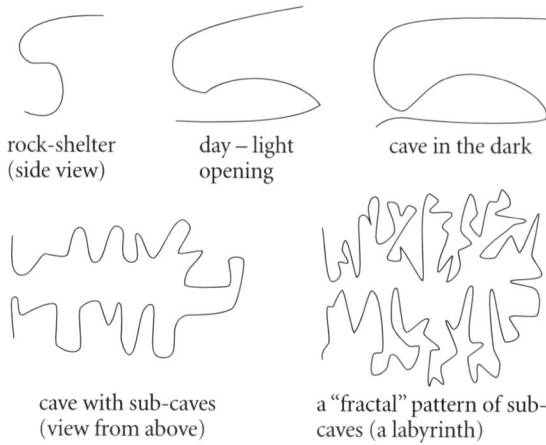

rock-shelter   day – light   cave in the dark
(side view)   opening

cave with sub-caves   a "fractal" pattern of sub-
(view from above)   caves (a labyrinth)

Figure 5.6 Topological structures of possible caves

ated by transfer from one sign-system to another (cf. Peirce 1865/1986: 105f.). The regress of further and further transitions may be controlled by topological invariants or by rather concrete, iconic signs like the representation of animals, which probably have meanings in a sign system beyond a description of contemporary fauna, but are anchored in visual experience (contrary to abstract signs which accompany them). Figure 5.6 shows the transformation from the concept of rock-shelter to that of a labyrinth tunnel.

The internal appearance of closed caves was further fragmented as primitive lamps gave only local views (possibly the irregular light produced the effect of a pseudo-animation of painted animals on the wall). In a certain sense, a painted cave is the simulation of a mentally realized space of imagination, memory and fantasy comparable to modern media like film, video or computer games. The local structure of the surfaces, the protrusions, holes, etc., added relief to the construed space and were systematically used by the painters. There were probably preferred paths for the visitors of the cave, i.e., a "hodological path" of scenes, views, and aspects. Rappenglück (1999) tries to prove that a rather hidden group of cave-paintings in Lascaux (Le Puits) gives an astronomical topography in which animals stand for astronomical pictures. The (rare) representation of a bird stands for the sun, the bison stands for the spring and early summer, the wool rhinoceros for late autumn and winter, the horse for (high) summer. The four animals horse, bison, rhinoceros, and mammoth also represent geographical directions (north, east, south, west). Leroi-Gourhan (1981) tries to show that the distribution of animals on the ceiling of the main cavern in Altamira has a formal structure with the 16 bison in the central field and other animals in the periphery. He interprets the animals as symbols for the sexes, whereas Freeman (1987:72) prefers a realistic interpretation. The central herd of bison has a distribution of sexes and "corresponds precisely to what one would expect had the artist intended to depict a herd in breeding condition" (ibidem:77).

Leroi-Gourhan (1992:Chapter III) presents a statistical analysis of the specific place for different animals (1.386 mammals depicted in 62 caves of the Franco-Cantabric area) and of their collocation (in pairs). A syntactic (sequential) organization is the result of this analysis. The author shows that the animals chosen for depiction are different at the entry, the central painted surfaces and the deep end of the cavern. In the mid-cave different animals occupy the center and the periphery (often they are smaller). The central panels show: 310 bison, 464 horses, 102 mammoth and 101 aurochs.

These four classes are the constituents of the central area and dominate it (with 83% to 93% of their total distribution). The back of the caves shows: bears, lions and rhinoceros, whereas deer dominate the entry, the ibex occurs more often in the periphery of the central panels, in the back and the entry. Other animals are rather evenly distributed over the four zones: wild goat and reindeer (the cave Chauvet discovered in 1994 shows a rather deviant distribution of animals, namely, the lions occupy a major place in the back of the cave, reindeer are more frequent than usual and the panther and the hyena are exceptional; cf. Roudil, 1995: 59).

The painted cave is not just a mental construal; the pictures have a syntactic and a rhetorical organization, which distinguishes the beginning, the center and the end (the result). As a summary, one can formulate two semiotic principles:

Principle of blended space
The cave is a blended space referring to an external and an internal base space (B1 and B2), with a specific orientation (preferred paths) and an exploitation of local relieves and the illusion of animation produced by flickering light.

Principle of functional and syntactic organization
The choice of themes (animals) and their arrangement shows a quasi-narrative structure (beginning, climax, and end) and a separation of center and periphery (comparable to head-satellite structures in syntax).

The symbolic interpretation of the single figures is still controversial, i.e., the lexicon, which specifies the definition (meaning), the function, and possibly multiple readings of an item cannot be reconstructed (different theories can only be structured guesses).

The space of the cave has received different interpretations based on supposed mythical or religious contexts. The cavern corresponds to the:

- Eating food or death by being devoured, as in the case of a human eaten up by a big carnivore, e.g., tiger.
- Giving birth, as the birth channel of a woman or alternatively receiving the sperms of a man.
- Openings of sense channels, which receive inputs from the outside and produce memories or imagination in the mind.

In all these cases, the dynamic schema is that of *capture* versus *emission*. In the case of sex and birth, both schemata stand in a causal relationship.

- The cavern is the place of origin and regeneration of animals (and men).

If one compares the Paleolithic rituals with frequent myths in societies of hunters and gatherers, then the representation of animals in the cave could mean that animals have an origin under the earth. Their renewal, their reappearance in big number in spite of heavy losses during the season of chase would ask for an equilibrating symbolism, which helps them to reproduce under the earth. The herd of big animals in the cave of Altamira would correspond to a belief that before the herds reappear again the next year, they reassemble to former magnitude in some hidden, sacred place. This place of regeneration would be symbolically recreated in the painted cave.

Two facts must be explained by any interpretation of the Franco-Cantabric caves:

- Why did this art disappear with the arctic climate after the climax of the last ice age (13 ky BP)?
- Why are hidden painted caves not found in other areas populated by Cro-Magnon men/women, although rock engravings were produced all around the world and up to modern times?

The myth of annual renewal of large herds can answer the first question. These herds disappeared in the Franco-Cantabric area and the large-scale organization of migrating hunters with them. Parallel to the ecological and economical shift the cave paintings disappeared (were not continued or forgotten). The second question could be answered if one considers the (almost) closed network of Franco-Cantabric civilization between 40–13 ky BP as an experimental "box" of cultural evolution comparable to the Nil valley (surrounded by deserts not ice) or Mesopotamia in later millennia. If for thousands (ten thousands) of years specific and benign conditions were valid in a closed area, then the sequence of cultural tradition could lead to a very complex and stable plateau of cultural evolution. It was defined by a system of symbolic forms (art, myth, economic exchange rules, rituals, etc.), which made them different from all civilizations under less benign, less stable conditions. The high level of the Franco-Cantabric civilization is therefore the result of different factors:

- A potential for cultural innovation common to the human species.
- A proper time span for the evolution and progress of cultural traditions in an area big enough for their accumulation and stabilization. Above all, the density and mobility of the population was a critical factor for this evolution.
- An amount of welfare, which was rather evenly distributed, and a social equilibrium between groups belonging to the cultural network (absence of permanent conflicts).

The last factor could make a decisive difference to later (Neolithic) societies of farmers. As many examples of hunter and gatherer societies in rich ecologies show the load of labor and warfare is rather low for these populations, i.e., they have an easy life. Nevertheless, a Rousseau-like romanticism or even an admiration for Palaeolithic populations must be avoided. Although they were genetically almost identical with ourselves, the conditions of social life have changed so radically that we cannot imagine what it would mean to live in Palaeolithic France or Spain.

5.3 Living and moving forms in the classical cave-paintings (Chauvet, Lascaux and Altamira)

In the following only the effect of apparent motion, animation, i.e., the dynamic aspect is considered. I assume that the categories of motion and causation are fundamental for the understanding of all semiotic processes (cf. Chapter 4 and Wildgen 1994). The following passages consider their role in Cro-Magnon semiotics.

The oldest cave with high-level painting yet known is the cave Chauvet in the valley of the Ardèche (confluent of the Rhône north of Orange). Different periods of visitation are dated between 31 and 23 ky and thus belong to the Aurignacian (cf. Table 5.1).

Motion and dynamics are expressed and represented in different ways:

The choice of the angle of view: plain profile or half-profile. Moreover, one part of the body (e.g., the head) may turn in a different direction. A rather extreme example is found in the cave Chauvet: a bison turns his head almost 90°, thus directly facing the spectator. Usually the whole animal is shown in semi-profile, so that four legs are visible and the moment of locomotion may be represented (by the relative position of legs).

Motion can be attributed to the legs as primary instruments of locomotion. The particular position of the head can also indicate forward locomotion. The group of lions in Figure 5.7 represents the head positions and legs in a group of attacking lions. In another painting more than four legs are visible in a bison (7 or 8), which could represent very quick movement (it is facing a lion, cf. Chauvet et al. 1995: 76f.).

Many animals form groups or herds in motion. The juxtaposition of animals of prey and predators, e.g., horses and lions may evoke a chase and if the animals stand for humans (as prey and predators), a chase or battle scene may be inferred. The periods, in which the paintings were made, span an extremely

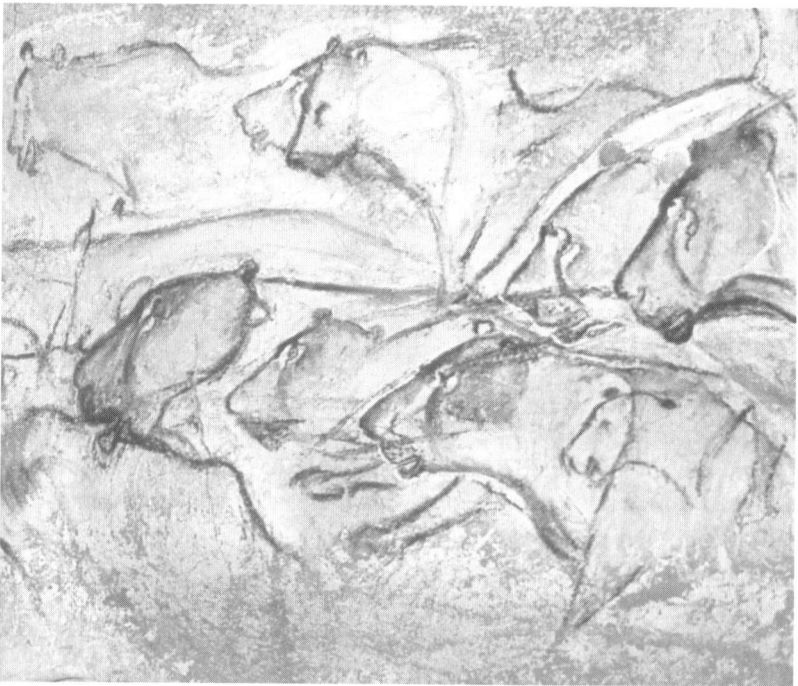

Figure 5.7 A group of lions (cf. ibid: 101)

long range of time. One cannot be sure, if the painters intended this effect on the viewer, or if they just filled the empty space left by prior generations. In some clear cases, two animals show a typical battle scene as the two rhinoceros in a painting of the cave Chauvet (Ibidem: 64f.).

From a semiotic perspective, which links pictorial and linguistic sign usage, two types of generalization may be considered (stated as principles but still hypothetical).

Principle of motion first
Although pictures and lexical items are basically static entities, the semiotic message conserves traces of the dynamics by selecting characteristic phases, which allow the rough reconstruction of processes.

Principle of dynamic metaphor
The locomotion, action and interaction represented by pictures (and verbs, sentences) create a basis for dynamic metaphors.

The central features may be attributed to humans or clans (this announces the art of "Physiognomy" developed in Greek antiquity and reassessed in Renaissance; cf. Wildgen 2001a). The following list is just a guess, which illustrates the last principle:

Table 5.2 Examples of metaphors; cf. the role of animals in a narrative

Animal which is strong, dangerous (e.g., lion, bear, rhinoceros).	→	Strong human, who is respected, protagonist.
Animal (herbivore) which can resist predators but is not a predator (bison, horse, mammoth, aurochs).	→	Resistant, defensive, human agonist.
Commonly hunted animal.	→	Food for humans, helper, object.

As Cro-Magnon men/women were mainly hunters (80% of their food was meat from hunted animals), the lexicon of animals is a natural classification of human qualities, of prototypical characteristics. These features may have been (and probably were) attributed to extant individuals, to groups, and possibly to clans and sub-societies. As a lexicon of collective values they were the natural basis for magic, rituals and later for religions.

Patterns of locomotion are not only relevant for the content of pictures but also for their production. Beltran et al. (1998: 72) have shown that painters in the cave of Altamira stood with their left arm on the cave wall and traced along it to get a long curved line; i.e. they used their (left) arm and hand as a mold for lines. In a similar way the natural motion of the arm with fixed body was the basis for larger curved lines, e.g., the shoulder and back of a bison, i.e. the human limbs were used as instruments in a ritualized act of painting. The drawing of a bison can thus be decomposed into a series of natural motion patterns, which begin at the head and end at the hind legs (variants of this technique are common). As in writing systems the natural motion patterns of the hand, the arms are the dynamic constituents of the lines in the painting. The surface can be further structured by lines which separate light and dark parts, or by areas with different color or texture and further details can be added. In this context it is worthwhile to note that certain body parts of animals receive special attention: the hair of a bison or its eye and nose (in Altamira), the heads of horses (e.g., a sequence of four heads with necks in cave Chauvet) and of lions (e.g., the sketched or elaborated heads and necks in cave Chauvet; cf. Chauvet et al. 1995:60f. and 101f.). The prominence and importance of body parts may be linked to the prominence of corresponding human body-parts like head, eye, ear, and mouth or to a physiognomic concept of the analogy between animals and humans (cf. Wildgen 2001a, 2003a). Smith (1992:Chapter 4) compares the possible ritual background of Cro-Magnon art with a shaman ideology, which considers life-powers in common to animals and humans (e.g., breath). He also gives a reason for the frequent superimposition of figures (mainly of scratched or engraved ones on a wall, ibidem:102f.). This would indicate that the enacting of the drawing was more important than the viewing. The avoidance of superimposition in the elaborate paintings of cave Chauvet, Lascaux and Altamira serves to distinguish between two techniques:

– An easy technique of scratching where the primary scope was the enacting
– A more formal, specialized technique of illusionist painting (or sculpture) for repetitive/permanent use in rituals or magic (or for other functions; our knowledge is still very spare).

A cognitive (and communicative) schema apparent in Palaeolithic art and related to the general form of this loosely organized, mobile and large-scale network of cultural unities is that of symmetric exchange. The exchange has two levels:

– Exchange between humans and nature. The equilibrium is established symbolically. Humans take from nature by chasing, gathering and in order to guarantee overall stability, e.g., the continuity of seasons, the reappear-

ance of big game, they have to contribute to its regeneration by acts of representation which in a literal sense help animals to be present again.
– At this basic level, which could be the fundament of the myth of equilibrium between man and nature, the equilibrium of giving/taking had to be guaranteed inside the human group, e.g., between hunters and those who stayed near the fire place (independent of gender roles which were perhaps rather variable).

In the season of collective hunting goods had to be distributed among groups of hunters. For rare and valuable goods a mode of exchange and value construction had to be invented and controlled. Mauss (1973: 145–279) points to the fact that the exchange of gifts is a fundamental practice in all archaic societies. If we use once more the basic archetype of action-control *capture* and *emission*, we see that a level of stable equilibrium is reached in the double transfer, i.e., if one gift is equilibrated by another. If formally a gift and a retro-gift are basic for the equilibrium, one still needs a measure of equivalence for them. This is simple, if the same type and quantity of gifts is exchanged, a stone for a stone, an apple for an apple. Such an exchange is trivial and without (cognitive and economic interest). If different types are exchanged or rare objects of very different nature and without practical use, e.g., colorful feathers for rare stones, amber or shells, the question of a common measure, a frame-work for comparing different entities, of measuring these at first sight incommensurable entities like food for care (love) becomes necessary. This asks for a semantic system, which is able to map every kind of entity onto a general frame of relevance and meaning.

The cultural achievement of Paleolithic art relevant for large areas beyond the normal action range of individuals presupposes a rather general grid of meanings on the level of values in a probably multilingual society of hunters. It would be exceptional if the existence of a large-scale system of values for exchange with equilibrium had not produced a linguistic unification on the content-level, in the form of a collective system of meanings. The phonological expression of these meanings probably remained by and large different. Thus, the diversity of conventional signs (cf. Leroi-Gourhan 1992: 137–140) shows a range of distribution corresponding in size to actual dialect-areas and suggests that the populations living in the Franco-Cantabric area had as many different dialects (or even languages) as were used in the same area before the rapid unification after the French revolution. Nevertheless these dialects formed an assembly on the level of basic semantics and pragmatics used in cultural contacts, rituals, in the oral tradition of myths and the practice of rituals. They formed probably one of the largest symbolic civilizations before the introduction of writing. All civilizations after the Neolithic revolution are for economical and ecological reasons incommensurable with Paleolithic ones and this limits our attempt towards an explanation (to members of contemporary societies).

5.4 From iconic schemata to abstract signs and to writing

Paleolithic paintings contain many signs, which cannot be interpreted as pictures or figures. The transition between iconic signs and abstract signs (symbols) occurs first with very frequent contents. Two human body-parts appear regularly in the paintings and engravings:

- The human hand
- The female vulva.

In the case of the hand the most concrete picture is created either by pressing the (left) hand on the wall and painting the contours (or by spraying chewed color with the mouth) or by painting the hand with color and pressing it against the wall. The picture is really the *trace* of the hand (it indicates the act of touching the wall with the hand). Other tokens abstract the shape of the human hand to a line (a band) with three, four, five branches (cf. Figure 5.8).

Figure 5.8 Pictures of "hands" in the cavern of Santian, Spain (cf. Jelinek 1975:465)

The relation of hands to their body is metonymical (pars pro toto), i.e., one can guess the whole if one has the necessary knowledge, which is easy in the case of the hand. In some cases, the hands are deformed (e.g. have only four fingers); they could therefore be the personal signature of a painter; some authors even guessed an underlying gesture language. Many other pictures cannot be linked with specific contents, from which they are derived. Leroi-Gourhan (1992: Chapter IX) made an inventory of the Franco-Cantabric signs and distinguished three major classes:

– small signs (e.g., sticks and ramified forms),
– full signs; e.g., triangles, squares, rectangles (tecti-forms), key shapes (clavi-forms), and
– punctuated signs.

He comes to the conclusion that all these signs have only a very indirect association with the animals represented in the paintings. They are a supplementary code. This is very clear in Lascaux, where signs and pictures are systematically combined into one gestalt and have corresponding sizes (cf. ibidem: 337).

The small signs could be derived by "disjunction", i.e., certain figural features from pictures are isolated, cut off. The general tendency is one of geometrical abstraction. Small pictures as in portable art could have triggered the abstraction. The conventionalized miniature signs were later added to full-scale pictures in the cave paintings. This is the same process as the one observed in the evolution of early writing systems, e.g., in Egypt. Some of the small signs assimilate the form of spearheads, i.e., they copy traits of their support. Figure 5.9 shows a selection of small signs (cf. Leroi-Gourhan 1992: 336 for a more complete list).

Leroi-Gourhan associates these signs with the male sex (as phallic symbols). Full signs are associated with the female sex. Either they are derived from the form of the vulva, or from a female profile (without head and feet). Beyond

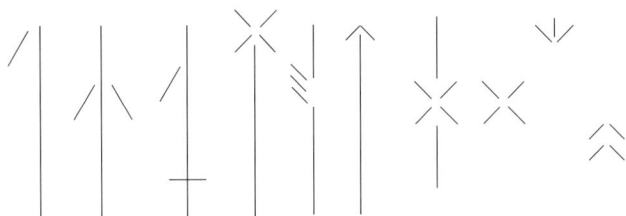

Figure 5.9 Examples of small signs

a normal form, which stands in an iconic relation to a relevant entity in life-space, e.g. a female contour or a sexual organ (vulva) and a simplified form, one can distinguish derived forms, which recombine simplified forms to form new, more complex entities or invert, rotate, or deform them (cf. Wenke 1999: 208). The signs called "tecti-forms" or rectangular (cf. Wenke 1999: 208f.) look like huts or shelters and could refer secondarily to the domain of females (in a matrilineal society, daughters inherit the house and objects in the house and these are associated with the female sex). Figure 5.10 shows some examples from Leroi-Gourhan (1992: 319).

The punctuated signs can be related to a basic technique of painting and engraving, i.e., to aligned points, which produce a curve or two rows of them, which fill a surface. It is thus a discrete variant in the representation of lines and

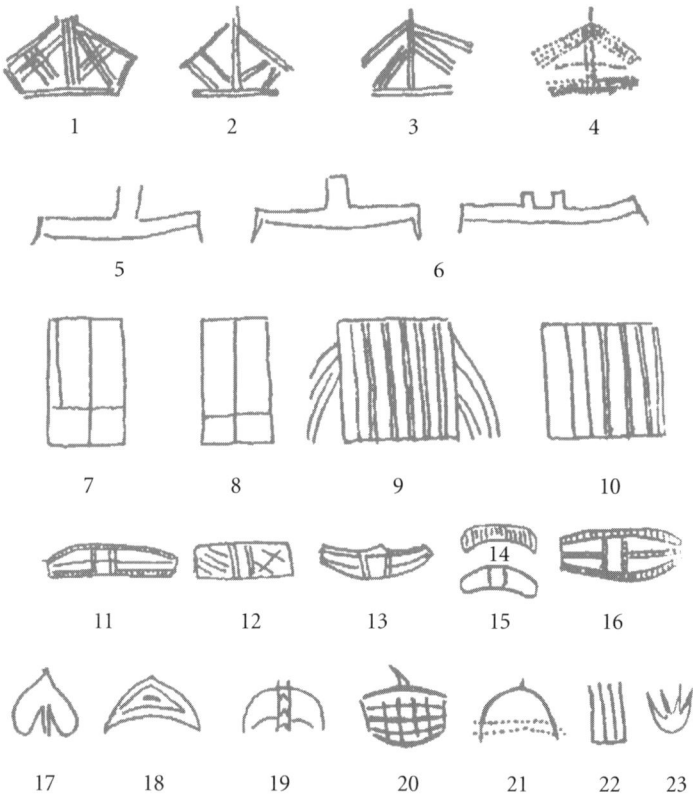

Figure 5.10 Examples of rectangular (tecti-form) signs

surfaces. There is some evidence that counting or representing mathematical structures may underlie these signs (cf. Marshack 1972).

A general feature of sign-usage is the fact that, on the one hand, the usage of specific signs is regional, i.e., we observe a diversity of "languages", while on the other hand certain techniques such as the abstraction from female characteristics are common to large areas (Central Europe). Thus the signs already show a typical pattern in Europe: large leagues of cultures (cf. Whorf's Average European) and fragmented languages and dialects (some signs appear in areas with a diameter of only 40 km which corresponds roughly to the space of dialects).

We may summarize these results in two further principles:

Principle of sign abstraction
Forms with a high level of emotional load are selected as the basis of abstraction; the process itself tends to geometrical and mathematical symbols (and prefigures the evolution of writing and mathematics).

Principle of regional separation
With the conventionality introduced via abstraction (which has many possible outcomes), semiotic subsystems appear and thus a fragmentation of the sign space. As some general motivations and trends are conserved, a duality between common (European) signs and local signs appears.

On the basis of this evolution all further developments are present, even if many traditions were lost and basic techniques, like writing, had to be introduced from the Orient.

Beyond the "sanctuaries" of Paleolithic art in the Franco-Cantabric area and their (possible) continuity in Meso- and Neolithic art (cf. 5.1.4), two large pathways link the Paleolithic period to our time: rock engravings and writing. I shall follow these two routes and try to uncover basic principles of form giving or semiosis apparent in these developments.

5.4.1 Rock engravings from the Paleolithic to modern time

Engravings on open rock surfaces or in caves are a universal code, which appears in every place where humans lived (and with a tremendous frequency) and at any time. Actually, so called "primitive" societies in Australia still practice rock-art, and in industrial societies the spraying of homogenous surfaces of buildings, or trains, busses, the scratching of window-planes demonstrates the unbroken vitality of this form. Some authors believe that the imitation of cave-bears who scratched the walls of the cave where they spend the winter-months were at the origin. (Bears could not perceive these "signs" in the dark, which were only "read" by humans who penetrated into these caves using light.) The universality of rock engravings contradicts such a hypothesis. One can say that any smooth surface (as a kind of black board) in places frequented by humans could be used for a graphical communication between creative individuals and anybody living in the area or frequenting these places. The rock engravings therefore highlight two basic tendencies:

1. Humans (Homo sapiens sapiens) are able and eager to use graphical expression (linked to hand and eye). This mode of expression is parallel to the acoustic-auditory channel used in language. This means that the duality of figural and acoustic communication is a basic characteristic of our species.
2. The smoothness of specific surfaces and eventually significant forms of the rock afford an interpretation as natural signs and the elaboration of a system of conventional signs which are added to the primary signs. This fits with the view of Leibniz (in his: "Nouveaux Essais") that our mind is partially like a tabula rasa, a table without signs like the Roman wax tablets, but that minimal deformations may easily be read as significant predispositions and then be used as germs for a quasi-natural semiosis (the final products are rather constructs of the mind than "natural" signs).

In both cases the sign is primarily an objectivation of structures and contents in the human mind. In this sense rock engravings give us an insight into the universal semiotic capacity of humans independent form space and time.

Anati (1991: 14ff.) enumerates 144 regions on (all) five continents where rock engravings were found. The concentration of engravings in some places with thousands of figures (graphemes)[3] shows that many generations have contributed in a long chain (of millennia) to accumulate, modify and interpret (by means of further additions) this "book" of engravings. Typically the populations engaged were rather small, lived in less rich environments and conserved their cultural and economical level for long periods. In Europe the Alps are a typical ecology for rock engravings, as the population density remained low (and more or less constant), migration was slow and only affected the larger valleys. Nevertheless these populations participated in overall European processes, as many political, military and economic flows had to use networks of routes through the Alps to communicate from north to south and vice-versa. In this context the function of these rock-lexica becomes clear; they show the common cultural knowledge of a large network of human groups linked by a similar ecology (and similar needs and techniques of life) and a long history which had only small windows for the change enforced by global processes (north and south of the Alps). They remained self-identical for millennia (the ethnical and linguistic substratum was probably influenced by Slavic migrants since 1,000 B.C. and later by Celtic, Romance and Germanic "immigrants").

Some of the more abstract engravings deserve special attention:

– Concentric circles and spirals.
– Concentric rectangles, sometimes linked by bridges" as in the game called "nine-men-Morris" in English, "mill" in German.
– Stars, trees, crosses, i.e., basically configurations based on straight lines.

These geometrical abstractions may still have a diagrammatic value, e.g., one may understand them as the plan of a house, a city, or a labyrinth, as stars in the sky, real trees as source-pictures. They are, however, on the way towards geometrical, i.e., mathematical abstraction, and can be understood as an objectivation of mental schematizations. Thus, regular geometrical figures like a square (a set of concentric squares), a circle, a cross, a star are insofar archetypical as they have a high level of symmetry. In the perspective of Leyton (2001) every natural and also every design object has a history (memory) inscribed which may be uncovered if the shape is transformed step by step into some symmetric and optimal source shape. In this sense the symmetric figures are archetypes found behind the diversity of memory signs in rock engraving, i.e., they represent the result of a self-referential process, of a reflection on signs. The topics of the "mill" and the "labyrinth" stand at the origins of more general schemata for strategic games, city maps and mythical stones (e.g., the labyrinth of Knossos with the Minotaur in its centre). As a consequence of the loss of memory, i.e., of cultural knowledge in the reduction of signs to geometrical archetypes, these graphs contribute to a lexicon of ornaments. One can sum up, saying that one path goes from vivid, reality-like pictures or pictograms (cf. Anati 1991: 162) to ideograms. These form the sign vocabulary which can be considered as the starting level for the development of writing. They were in some cases composed in order to describe a complex scene or even a story (if a linear reading sequence was marked or presupposed). The other path goes to ornaments. The neighborhood between writing and ornament is evident in Chinese calligraphy and Islamic art (based on words from the Koran).

Small pebbles found in Mas d'Azil in southern France (cf. Földes-Papp 1984: 36f.) are painted with abstract signs, and belong to the Mesolithic period. They were first interpreted as arithmetic stones or even as elements of an alphabet. The similarity to the object-signs which in Mesopotamia prepared the invention of writing is however superficial. The function of these stones is better described as soul-pebbles, i.e., they represent abstractly the invisible soul of ancestors. Nevertheless, if such a technique of shape and form abstraction could be developed for religious purposes, it could as well be used or reinvented in the context of trade in Neolithic societies with a reference to animals, goods which were transferred, sold and bought and thus preform the origins of writing.

5.4.2 The evolution of writing

As the Nilotic cultures melted into the civilization of early Egypt, there was possibly a continuity (in the Mesolithic period) between Paleolithic art in Northern Africa and early writing systems (e.g. in Egypt). The hieroglyphic characters are pictorial (although schematized) and sequential, i.e., they are at the level of semi-symbolic signs in the hierarchy. It remains controversial if Paleolithic sign systems really contributed to the evolution of writing. Coulmas (1992:17) enumerates three characteristics of writing:

> 1. it consists of artificial graphical marks on a durable surface; 2. its purpose is to communicate something; 3. this purpose is achieved by virtue of the marks' conventional relation to language.

The two first characteristics are also valid for abstract signs in cave paintings. The third presupposes knowledge of the underlying language, which can only be fulfilled if either these languages can be reconstructed from living languages or if a phonetic writing of them existed historically. Both conditions cannot be fulfilled in the case of prehistoric abstract signs. The question if they represent writing must therefore remain open.

The basic operations needed to achieve a consonantal alphabet follow a simple strategy:

– Reduce the correlation of the graphic sign to a part of the phonetic shape of the corresponding word. If the corresponding language marks variations in the morphological paradigm by changing vowels, the consonants are the invariants of the word family. If the word has only one consonant, there is a clear map from the picture to the phonetic segment (the consonant).

– Recombine the signs as "pictures" of the sequence of consonants. In the further stages of development, the common meaning of a family of words for which the consonant stands is given up and the pictorial shape becomes irrelevant (i.e. it looses its iconic grounding).

Both operations presupposed an awareness of spoken language. In the context of multilingual communities meeting in the valley of the Nile (forced to move by climatic change in the areas north and east of the Sahara), the conditions for a meta-linguistic awareness, or linguistic consciousness, were met. The deeper source for the evolution of writing was therefore the transition from spoken language as an unconscious routine of communication (learned only in early childhood which leaves no traces in individual biographic memory) to meta-linguistic awareness, linguistic consciousness. In the same period the confrontation of different religious and ritual (mythological) traditions created a meta-religious awareness and an effort to reorganize the system of religious traditions. Myth and language, the basic symbolic forms in Cassirer's philosophy, underwent a dramatic change (probably in Mesolithic Egypt). As a consequence writing became a deeply religious technique: This religious, ceremonial character stopped the inherent trend towards an alphabetic writing which was only fully realized by the Semitic populations at the rims of the Egyptian civilization. The western Semitic and the Phoenician alphabets were late consequences of the contact between oriental civilizations in the "golden crescent": Egypt–Mesopotamia–Indus.

The abstraction process from pictures to writing symbols corresponds to a general mnemonic principle. This is also valid for messages in an object language employed by Yoruba tribes and in Australian messenger-sticks. The message is coded for the messenger, who "reads" it when he arrives after a long journey. This guarantees that he does not forget important contents, but it presupposes that he knows the message. This means that the written message can only be "read" accurately if the reader has a knowledge of its contents independently from the "written" document (cf. Friedrich 1966: 17).

Full-fledged writing-systems presuppose a writing industry, i.e., the frequent production and usage of writing in proper contexts. The Paleolithic stone industries established the context for the manufacturing of functionally optimal artifacts (weapons, tools), the Mesolithic and Neolithic picture and symbol industries established the necessary context for writing systems and optimal communication across larger distances (times) and in larger societies (with distributed roles and functions).

The communicative/functional usage of writing was systematically developed in Mesopotamia, which became a melting pot of many cultures and concentrated large populations into one organized political system. The paths for the exchange of goods, values, and ideas became complex and difficult to control. The civilizations of Mesopotamia (and the "golden crescent") took their new shape between 11 and 8 ky BP. The first "token" systems, called "object languages" by Schmandt-Besserat (1978), appeared ca. during this area and were not dramatically changed for almost five millennia. Only in the Bronze Age, between 7,5 ky BP and 5,1 ky BP, did the number of tokens increase and their shape differentiate and finally give rise to Sumerian writing (ca. 5 ky BP; cf. also Friedrich 1966:42f.). The context was not religious but economic. The storage, transport and control of goods motivated a system of bookkeeping. A closed jar contained a number of symbolic objects, which stood for the goods sent to a destination. On the jar, a list of the symbolic objects in the jar was marked.

This system had two levels:

1. objects (e.g., sheep) are represented by object-symbols in the jar,
2. the content of the jar is listed in planar symbols on the jar.

Thus, step-by-step, symbolic objects come to represent the objects sent, received, sold, etc., and signs on the containers represent these symbolic objects. The recipient could assemble these messages in order to keep track of what he had received and he was able to transfer the symbolic objects across different categories: from received to sold, dead, lost, etc. In this manner the symbolic objects and the manipulation of them became a kind of holistic mimesis of economic transactions. The representational function is achieved by the symbolic system in its organization and its processing; the single signs may loose their pictorial content, but the representation of the writing system and its processing as a whole is still enriched.[4]

If we look closer at the symbolic objects in the table given by Schmandt-Besserat (1978:87f.) we notice the geometrical and abstract character of the signs: spheres, discs, pyramids, cones, tetrahedrons, biconoids, and ovoids are the basic shapes. On these bases, other abstract geometrical shapes are marked (in a lower dimension): holes, lines in/on the sphere, disk, etc. The Sumerian pictograms later flatten the symbolic objects to two-dimensional shapes.

The direction of writing was first rather accidental, later an organization into vertical columns came up with the order of columns from left to right and inside the columns from top to bottom. Finally the whole arrangement was rotated by 90°; the first column on the left became the first line on the top. In the same move the symbols were rotated by 90°.

The mapping of one word → one symbol was replaced by a syllabic mapping and sequences of (syllabic) symbols mapped into polysyllabic words. As a word (and its sign or sign-sequence) stood for a whole family of words with the same root, determinatives were used to distinguish different word-forms. As only consonantal patterns were mapped into written symbols, the written forms were still ambiguous. There were two major methods of disambiguation:

1. By a kind of "punctuation" the vowels could be marked. The method of punctuation was adopted by many civilizations and languages in the Near East (still observable today in Arabic and Hebrew).
2. Special symbols for vowels were inserted into the sequence of consonantal symbols. This method was first adopted by the Phoenician (Persian) and later by the Greek, Latin and Cyrillic alphabets.

The evolution of writing systems was linked to cultural and economic evolutions, which produced larger, more complex societies, and shaped a synthesis of different religious traditions and different languages. Thus the conditions for effective communication were changed by the growth of the communicative network. Ethnic, religious and linguistic diversity triggered an awareness of religion, myth, ethnicity, and language; these became objects of consciousness and reflection at least for a group of specialists (priests, politicians in the sense of people occupying professional roles in a state).

In the case of the civilizations in the "golden crescent" economy, traffic and administration first created a (poor) system of object symbols and later a very rich inventory of cuneiform characters which soon filled libraries with reports and commercial texts.

Different solutions for the design of writing systems were in conflict and in Europe and western Asia the ideographic systems disappeared and the alphabetic principle expanded in all directions. Only in China did the ideographic writing system survive. It had found its very abstract shape already in the old bone-engravings (1 400–1 200 B.C.).[5] The basic economy of these systems has, in spite of its ideographic character, structural similarities with the alphabetic systems:

1. The complex ideograms can be decomposed into ca. 20 elementary line-configurations. This corresponds roughly to the number of characters in an alphabet (23–30).
2. These elementary characters can be combined to form ca. 214 different radicals. This corresponds roughly to the number of syllables in an alphabet system.
3. The complete signs are fitted to an imaginary square. Similar tendencies can be observed in Hebraic quadratic letters, Roman capital letters and the "Antiqua" introduced in the Renaissance.

There are, as it seems, basic design principles which govern the evolution of a writing system and which are rather independent from the historical, social, cultural, and political forces which shaped the evolution of writing in its initial stages.

This evolution of writing transformed both the content- *and* the form sides of language. The basic principles may be linked to principles of mental economy, optimality, mnemonic adequacy, cultural universality, invariance in relation to sound change and meaning-shift. The emergence of pictorial art and writing systems altered language dramatically and this is also valid for modern spoken language for which written standards gradually became a norm or at least a control which smoothens natural sound change and meaning shift.

5.5 Is the esthetical function basic for art and language?

It is an astonishing fact that Cro-Magnon men developed a rich tradition of painting, sculpture, engraving and portable art only in Western Europe. They probably came from the Near East and had previously populated East or Central Asia, but left only poor traces of comparable art in these areas. Some authors link the "creative explosion" in Western Europe to a general scenario of human evolution, although the restriction to specific areas would forbid such a conclusion. Others even infer a dramatic mutation, which created art and language at the same time (i.e. after 50 ky BP). Another theory assumes a sudden evolution or qualitative increase in the cognitive capacity called "theory of mind", i.e. guessing at and mapping the mind of other people. The human mind would have changed from the state of "autism" to that of "social intelligence"; cf. Mithen (1998b: 171–175). It is more plausible that this regional evolution has to do with cultural evolution and more precisely with a large scale organization of Cro-Magnon societies in Europe related to population density in specific areas and larger networks of cultural exchange. Thus what changed was not the basic esthetic, semiotic or linguistic capacity but the context of its use.

Heeschen (2001) shows that the capacity for speech includes a predisposition for play, and art. In small societies the direct use of information procedures via speech may be a taboo, as it is considered too dangerous: Loosing face or accepting blame may be mortally wounding and a violent battle may be triggered by plain words. Indirect, veiled speech, wordplay, songs, and narratives were much more apt to transport socially relevant information and cues than statements, directives, or arguments. As a consequence language use became (and probably always was to some degree) an artful technique of allusion, narration, and playing with possible meanings, allowing for interpretations which cannot be fixed.

Now, a language capacity functionally linked to play and art, to the performance of rituals, the telling of myths and stories or jokes, may be sufficient if accompanied by music, dance, and gestured action in small communities. If the community or the networks of regularly communicating groups grows, new forms with more specific norms and standards have to be invented and Paleolithic art is probably an invention of this kind. It does not only presuppose the existence of language itself but the playful, artistic use of this capacity in the context of rituals, religious and communal life in general. The poetic function is, as Roman Jakobson assumed, a basic dimension of human language, insofar it goes beyond the aims of communicating some desire, interest and rather triggers a free play of imagination, creativity and humor. In order to fully understand Paleolithic art we must assume a highly developed verbal art and probably a high level of music and dance performance. Creativity in language, art, and science as a hint to basic principles in the evolution of the symbolic capacity will be the topic of the next chapter.

CHAPTER 6

Symbolic creativity in language, art, and science and the cultural dynamics of symbolic forms

6.1 Symbolic creativity and human evolution

Human creativity is, in Western countries, often understood as a personal faculty or a natural intellectual gift while society is seen as repressive in its relation to highly creative individuals, and as a force which seems to hate the genius and restrict his/her possibilities of expression. If one subscribed to this view, it would seem difficult, if not impossible, to conceive of an evolutionary process which is based on the positive effects of human creativity, in which these were welcomed and exploited by the group rather than repressed. A further objection to the idea of creativity as an evolutionary resource could be the assumption that the dynamics of creativity are based on individual competence and individual achievement, so that there is no way how, in a scenario of mutation and selection (a strictly Darwinian frame-work), the result of such personal achievements could influence the human genome and thus the competence and deeds of much later generations. Innovations due to individual creativity would, on this view, come and go. As a further consequence of this critical view, which I shall not adopt in this chapter, creative individuals would teach some of their new "tricks" to their children, thus having some influence on the next generation, but these effects would not be passed down as long as no technical means for the conservation of innovations, like writing, libraries, computer data bases, were in use. Our hypothesis is on the contrary that the language used by Cro-Magnon men was already a very efficient store for adaptations and innovations. It thus became a major alternative to biological adaptation in which ecological and sexual selection eliminate that part of the genetic heritage which does not fit and statistically strengthen those parts which happen to fit. This strictly Darwinian type of evolution is neither goal-directed nor consciously channeled; i.e., individual experiences and learning effects are lost forever. With the rise of symbolic forms, specifically with the rise of language, a new type of memory adaptation appears which is able to accumulate individual experiences and innovations. In its long range results it shows similar effects as Darwinian evolution, but it contains a goal-directed content resultant from innumerous *intelligent* adaptations and innovations. Only at this stage does individual consciousness, experience, learning, memory and creativity play a decisive role. The symbolic forms may be called the cultural "genome" or meme-structure which enables quick adaptations to ecological changes and pushes a societal development with an accelerating rate: first of 10 ky, then millennia, then centuries and currently decennia.

If we focus on the social conditions for the flux of innovations, their stabilization, and further development, a natural link between creativity and evolution becomes visible. A population which is able to *exploit* innovations (presupposing a general stochastic production of new ideas or practices) may reach a level at which it can overthrow rival societies in a period of conflict over natural resources. The evolutionary gain of innovation is most evident when military equipment or organization is the domain of innovation. The technological invention provides an advantage which may bring a group of warriors into a dominating position from which they may more effectively distribute their genes and finally outnumber the original population or force them to live under very harsh conditions which again diminish their chance of population growth. This view of innovation which makes "war the father of everything" depends heavily either on techniques of metallurgy (bronze, iron) or on the mass-mobility allowed by the use of horses (or ships). For the Paleolithic populations, i.e., in the period of hominization and the evolution of language, this view of innovation, related to a kind of "arms-race" is not helpful, because population density and the state of technology were still too low. There must be a deeper link between creativity/innovation and the evolution of man, the evolution of his/her symbolic behavior.

A general precondition for the selective value of creativity and innovation obtains when human ecology is changing at such a quick rate that populations optimally adapted and structurally restricted to a given ecology are endangered. Under such circumstances populations with a very high degree of ecological specialization and optimal adaptation to a very specific ecology risk extinction, so that survival requires behavioral adaptation beyond selection effects. A second precondition which encourages creativity and innovation is the presence of a plurality of rival sub-species all existing under difficult conditions and all competing for possession of land resources in an area which can only support the survival of one of those species. Both of these preconditions seem to have been fulfilled in the critical period after 500 ky BP (perhaps after 200 ky

BP). The quickly changing ecology was driven by the rhythm of glacial and interglacial stages. Possibly the most critical period is the one after the Riss-glacial which happened between 347 and 251 ky (deep sea isotope stages 8 and 9). The following interglacial (Riss-Würm; stage 5e: 128 ky) witnessed a sea-level above today's level with a "large mammal community that contains hippopotamus" in England (Gamble 1986: 83). The ice-ages interacted with the dynamics of the gulf-stream and the resulting climatic changes necessitated rapid changes in the flora and fauna. Thus the analysis of pollen at the "Grande Pile" (Vosges mountain, Eastern France) showed peaks of vegetation related to warmer climate in four stages, five smaller peaks in two stages and then again in the era leading to the current interglacial stage. In total 15 to 20 peaks are separated by bad periods, the longest bad period is just the one between 40 to 20 ky BP, which witnessed the arrival of the Cro-Magnon man in Europe and the disappearance of the Neanderthal man. This rapid sequence of ecological changes would have meant extinction (or remigration to Africa) for a species which could only adapt biologically (based on chance mutations and the selection from the range of variants produced). Culturally transmitted environmental adaptation based on creativity and its symbolic stabilization and transmission was the only solution which allowed the human species to survive in a quickly changing ecology. The history of mankind is therefore based on a "Copernican" paradigm change from biological to cultural evolution. In the long range the culturally induced adaptation (driven by creativity in behavior) defined an epigenetic field which could even govern small-scale biological adaptations, e.g., in the area of brain architecture and functionality insofar as the self-organization of the network-structure in human brains is not strictly determined by the genetic code and thus is readily adaptable to specific conditions in the long period of maturation and growth.

The original reaction of Homo erectus populations to climatic changes was probably to move towards the South, although this is likely to have triggered a conflict with populations established there. Thissen assumes that at least six waves of immigration (of flora, fauna and hominids) occurred from Africa and Eurasia to Europe and back again. After 200 ky BP archaic Homo sapiens, instead of going back to Africa, stayed in Europe and developed the subspecies of Neanderthals (cf. Weser-Kurier of 16.08.2003: 40). In the interglacial with its climatic peak at 118 ky BP another subspecies came to Eurasia and met Neanderthal populations in the Near East. The new invaders first spread to the South East. They were not adapted to the northern climate, but finally penetrated Europe at the end of the early glacial period (called Würm-glacial: 75–32 ky BP) and they were even able to replace the highly specialized Neanderthals despite the Neanderthal's ability to compete technically with the newcomers.

In terms of a non-biological, behavioral, adaptation, one can say that first the Neanderthals preferred to find a way to cope with the changing ecology rather than migrating with the climate. The way they achieved this was partially by behavioral (technical) adaptation, although they also had a survival advantage because they had enough time to adapt biologically (beginning 200 ky BP). The new sub-species arriving from a warmer climate (from Northern Africa or returning from South Asia) encountered a climate which had already become very severe but it was able to survive during the full glacial (32–13 ky BP), a period that witnessed the extinction of Neanderthal man. Unlike the Neanderthals, the new sub-species had no chance to adapt biologically in this short period; their only chance was behavioral adaptation. Their survival proves that they had the intellectual and cultural capacity to cope with the lethal danger of this climate and exploit their inherent (biological) capacity of behavioral adaptation. One must therefore assume that both Neanderthals and Cro-Magnon man had the capacity to innovate and to exploit innovation in everyday practice; they were able to exploit changing resources, to master fire, to use shelter efficiently, to redistribute resources in the tribe. They achieved high mobility in the search for food, had a good knowledge of the ecology, its affordances and dangers, and were able to transmit such knowledge.

We may call the biological or cognitive capacity for a successful adaptation (including the interpretation of the ecology in terms of affordances) and its social/cultural organization/transmission *social creativity*. As it is present (to a greater or lesser degree) in all individuals of the species, it constitutes a social force that can be systematically exploited, conserved and transmitted. The innovations brought about by social creativity need symbolic behavior, need language beyond alarm calls and phonetic grooming to spread quickly and be conserved for later generations.

In the following I shall analyze cases of innovation in language, art and science which give us insight into this capacity which we share with Cro-Magnon man. As empirical observations of social creativity in the Paleolithic era is not possible, I have chosen very clear cases of socially mediated creativity on a historical scale of millennia or centuries. I will endeavor to employ these in a search for the basic principles of *social creativity* enabled by innovation in the area of symbolic behavior. The methodological presupposition of this analysis is a biological one. As the social creativity shown by the cave painters in the Magdalenian period are only at a distance of 13 ky from us and as we are the descendents of Cro-Magnon man, our biological/cognitive equipment cannot differ dramatically from theirs and thus even contemporary innovative processes must use the same creative capacity as Paleolithic or Neolithic human agents and societies did.

The unfolding of the three major "symbolic forms" (cf. Chapter 9 for a more detailed analysis of this concept): language, art, and science follows a sequential order in the evolution of man. Although they all belong to the basic heritage of the human species, the systematic and highly complex expression of this capacity was probably first substantiated in language (say between 400–200 ky BP) than in art (say between 40 and 13 ky BP) and beginning with the civilizations in Egypt and Mesopotamia science began to flourish (between 7 and 4 ky BP approximately). This is also the time when writing, the second, more stable linguistic system, began to evolve (cf. Chapter 5).

The principles of human creativity, its unfolding since the appearance of Homo sapiens should therefore be assessed for the three major symbolic forms. Creativity in language can demonstrate the basic and long-range principles, creativity in art can highlight the dependence of further evolution on individual personalities which are able to accumulate and synthesize the innovative streams present in the surrounding culture. Finally creativity in science can point to conceptual crises and revolutions and to processes of mental modeling typical for expert communities. The following sections present case-studies of innovation in language, art and science.

6.2 Creativity and lexical innovation

Lexical innovation is perhaps the best example of innovation in language for understanding the dynamics of linguistic evolution on a historical scale. Phonological change, on the one hand, is rather determined by long ranging forces which are in many cases independent from human consciousness and human will. Syntactic change, on the other hand, may be rather quick in situations of language contact or in the formation of pidgin languages. In its underlying principles it is however stable over millennia and it is difficult, if not impossible, to detect the effect of individual creativity on the fashioning of syntactic patterns. The middle range evolution of language depends primarily on the augmentation of the lexicon, the store of linguistic items contained in a collective (long term) memory. (As Chapter 8 will show, the second major precondition for the emergence of grammar in human languages is the complexity of valence patterns.) The growth of the lexicon can be triggered by the spontaneous creation of new sound-meaning connections and this phenomenon seems to show up in some Australian languages, but it is marginal in most languages (cf. Dixon 1980). Most new items either follow some already established schema (or even rule) or are analogous to existing items. In the large range of possible subfields of innovation (e.g., blends or transfers from other languages), the field of nominal composition allows us to analyze the major principles. I shall therefore take nominal composition as the prototype of lexical innovation.

Simply putting a multitude of associations, thoughts, and immediate creative responses into words may easily result in incoherence when the content of the ideas is innovative and therefore unfamiliar to the hearers. In general, spontaneous creativity, ongoing parallel processing, imagining, and memorizing are all controlled by restrictions on semantic coherence. The underlying and fundamental problem is therefore first how to organize and synthesize a flux of perceptions and ideas which originate in ongoing thought and conversation and stem from a diversity of linguistic and non-linguistic sources and second how to make the organized and linguistically coded contents understandable to the audience. This task may be achieved in two distinct ways:

- Building up a spontaneous "image", a "composition" for the ideas the speaker wants to communicate. This can be called the *"imagistic"* composition of the message for the speaker.
- Planning the utterance with a fixed time budget, e.g., in a conversational slot, given a fund of lexical choices and syntactic (textual) techniques of linguistic production. This concerns mainly the *verbal composition* of the text.

These two processes run in parallel although the first may have priority in the starting phase, the latter in the final stage. In a sentence or a text, chunks in imagistic composition may be organized for coherent production (online composition) while new imagistic chunks are being prepared, i.e., we assume a phase-shift in favor of imagistic composition. Nominal compounds constitute a phenomenon within this framework which is important in several respects:

- It contributes to lexical variety and differentiation.
- It can provide structures which are shorter than existing ones, thereby contributing to language economy.

The creation and interpretation of novel compounds makes use of contextual and encyclopedic knowledge, and thus integrates memory content into ongoing planning procedures. I shall first enumerate the basic principles in the formation of novel compounds and then consider the effect of context.

6.2.1 Dynamic principles of nominal composition

In traditional treatments of nominal compounding, one point of departure has been the syntactic and morphological category of the constituents. For the semantics of nominal compounds we must, however, choose more fundamental categories. We consider this to be achievable by separating nominal-static entities from verbal-dynamic entities. This distinction has already been shown to occur in the phase of one-word sentences during language acquisition as a first functional differentiation (cf. Bloom & Lahey 1978: 110–113; McCune-Nicholich 1980). We hypothesize that a nominal compound must normally contain at least one nominal-static constituent and one verbal-dynamic constituent. In those compounds where this basic functional pattern is not realized, dynamic information may be extracted from one (or both) of the constituents.

Nominal compounds belong to the level of words near the boundary between word structures and phrasal structures. From a dynamic perspective, the boundaries of structural levels can be compared to semi-permeable membranes, which control structure maintenance and diffusion. Inside the "word-membrane", there exist certain criteria of completeness versus deficiency. If a noun contains two stems (if it is a nominal compound) it must have a relational kernel and nominal filler. Contrary to the completeness criteria at the syntactic level, the arguments of the relational predicate can be selected using a measure of prominence. If this normal structure is not present in a nominal compound, we can predict a flow of structural information through the membrane; i.e., a flow of structure diffusion:

– From the level of word semantics to the level of word structure, i.e., the internal semantics of the constituents is exploited.
– From the level of context to the level of word structure, i.e., thematically similar structures in the context are "absorbed" to repair the structural deficit at the level of word structure.

The internal structure of the constituents of the compound has several grades of accessibility:

Derivational accessibility. The verbal stem of a nominal constituent can be uncovered with its case frame. We assume that the access to this structural center is not easily or automatically realizable, but involves 'costs' to the cognitive system and requires specific contexts or motivations.

Lexical accessibility. The internal semantic structure of a simplex can be re-trieved. This process may be represented in linguistic theory using semantic features, semantic fields, networks, frames or stereotypes. The minimal condi-tion for such a type of representation is that it must allow for inference, i.e., it must describe how the speaker and hearer can infer more than just that which has been said, thus expanding and specifying their interpretation.

Metaphorical expansion. If the solutions (a) and (b) do not work or if the context calls for a different interpretation, metaphorical processes can change the interpretation of the constituents, thus yielding another interpretation. One must distinguish *actual* and *frozen* metaphors; for the latter there is an eas-ily recovered (conventional) reading, whereas in the case of actual metaphors the speaker tries to activate either a non-preferred reading or to create a new meaning by metaphorical transfer.

Finally, every constituent of the compound (and possibly the compound as a whole) gives rise to associations (syntagmatic and paradigmatic field re-lations, or owing to similarity of form or sound). These may constitute the material used by *analogical* processes (cf. Wildgen 1987:146–156 for the analy-sis of a corpus of such compounds). The first three processes can be influenced by contextual factors in such a way as to produce a coupled process out of the two types of dissipative processes, i.e., the constituents of the compound can be structurally enriched if derivational, lexical and metaphorical structures are uncovered. On the basis of these enriched structures, that reading is selected which fits best.

The complicated interaction between context, word semantics and the economy of language use can only be described within the framework of a specific language. I shall, therefore, turn to more specific features of nom-inal compounds in German and in related languages. The most prominent structural feature of German and English compounds is their asymmetry. It is always the right-hand constituent (on the first level of segmentation), which determines the number, gender and (usually) the syntactic category of the com-pound. We can say that the right-hand constituent governs the grammatical features of the whole. This grammatical asymmetry has consequences for the semantics of compounds.

The apparent symmetry of copulative compounds is unstable. Even with novel compounds the hearer tends to assign different meanings if the order of the constituents is inverted; Table 6.1 shows some examples from a corpus of 6,000 German nonce-compound collected at the University of Regensburg (1979–1980).

Table 6.1 Symmetric compounds from a German corpus of nonce compounds

German	translation	German	translation
Mann-Frau	man-woman	Frau-Mann	woman-man
Dichterkomponist	poet-composer	Komponistendichter	composer-poet
Kardinal-Ökonom	cardinal-economist	Ökonom-Kardinal	economist-cardinal

In many compounds one can observe one of the following two tendencies or both:

– Classificatory constituents are placed on the right. These compounds approach derivations if the right-hand elements are reduced to a small list and are subject to morphological decay.
– Evaluative constituents are placed on the left and thus approach prefixes.

These synchronic fields of attracting forces can explain the diachronic fashioning of prefixes and suffixes out of constituents in nominal compounds. The poles of the compound exert a selective force which is dependent on the grammatical asymmetry of this construction; this field leads synchronically to a typical distribution of constituents in the compound and diachronically to the creation of prefixes and suffixes out of constituents of the compound.

We have thus far dealt with cases in which no relational element is realized in the compound and the analysis of how the complementarity of static and dynamic constituents is preserved under these circumstances. We may now consider cases in which two constituents of the compound are relational. Our analyses showed that three solutions to this problem are possible, and they depend on the internal structure of the constituents. The dynamic facts expressed in the relational terms (mostly verbs) are interpreted as parallel and simultaneous. As already mentioned, the more general term is placed on the right.

1. Arbeits-Begräbnis ("working burial"; in the context of a meeting of political leaders) SP/80/20/23/3 (SP = Spiegel / the year of publication 19__ / the no. of the issue / the page and/or column where the compound can be found).
2. Horch-Angriff ("listening-attack"; in the context of tapping phone lines) SP/80/50/35/2.

Compounds of this type are very rare.

The second constituent (or its verbal center) governs a subordinate clause; the verb of the clause is selected and appears as the left-hand constituent.

This presupposes that the verb at the right can take subordinate clauses as complements.

3. Anzapf-Versuch ("attempt to tap"; in the context of a beer-festival) SZ/80/63/13/3 (SZ = Süddeutsche Zeitung).

In many cases the relational character of the left-hand element is not exploited and it is simply considered to be a nominal argument of the relation at the right. Thus the relational character of the right-hand element is exploited before that of the left-hand one.

To summarize, we can say that the local dynamics of compounds are very simple and can in fact be described in terms of structural diffusion and structural asymmetry. The fact that rather simple principles are at work could explain why nominal composition is learned before complex phrasal or sentential structures are acquired. In general, one can say that every constituent of the compound creates a single meaning-space, which has an "imagistic" content, i.e., some kind of possible spatial image with a restricted number of dimensions (≤ 3) and a syntagmatic value (field) which tends to prefer certain types of linearly combined entities (left, right or both). If two constituents are chunked in one compound, a coherent space must be construed such that:

– It leads to new "imagistic" content. The asymmetry (the right constituent dominates) makes this task easier because the imagistic space of the dominant constituent is (in most cases) preserved, whereas the imagistic content of the sub-dominant constituent may be deformed such that it fits the dominant space.
– It saturates basic syntagmatic relations. These dynamics can be partially predicted if the word class of the constituents is known, but as word-classes are semantically not very homogeneous and show a large variety of imagistic content types, this structural access is only a first approximation.

On the basis of our argumentation thus far, we can state that processes of compounding are either determined by the relational potential of their constituents or they are governed by textual and contextual, regularities and/or by analogical inferences. There remains, however, a small class of nominal compounds which can be interpreted out of context and contain no traces of covert relational structures. In these cases the relational part has been eliminated and we must find a means of recovering it. Two possible ways of doing this can be proposed:

1. The missing relational term can be inferred from our knowledge of the world. The constituents which are realized select a certain domain of knowledge, which suggests a connection between these nominal constituents.

2. We possess an inventory of basic relational terms, i.e., relational atoms. The constituents make a selection from among this set of alternatives using certain affinities between nominal constituents and types of relations. In Wildgen (1987) such a list has been established on the base of catastrophe schemata.

These solutions are not mutually exclusive. We assume that the first is broader as it uses a richer representation of culturally relevant knowledge. In the second case, a smaller set of invariant frames is sought. Without going into the details of archetypal semantics, we can say that the following relations with two or three arguments (i.e., dynamic types with two or three stable attractors) can be founded in catastrophe theoretical semantics:

a. Affecting   (A affects/influences/touches ... / B)
b. Effecting   (A ejects/emits/creates ... / B)
c. Transfer   (A gives C to B / B receives C from A)
d. Instrumentality   (A affects B with the instrument C)
e. Causation   (A causes C to affect B)
f. Localistic relations (entering, leaving, being in, changing from A to B, changing from A to B via C).

In Figure 6.1 two topologico-dynamic frames for the relations (c) and (d) are shown (for details cf. Wildgen 1982a, 1994).

Thus we can define a basic set of dynamic (= relational) primitives, whose features: structural stability, and irreducibility, can be mathematically proved.

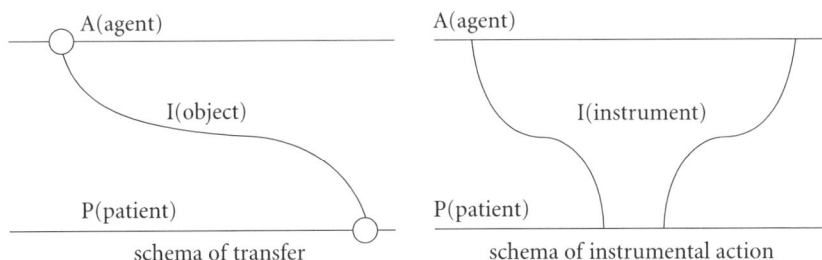

A(agent)

I(object)

P(patient)

schema of transfer

A(agent)

I(instrument)

P(patient)

schema of instrumental action

Figure 6.1 The major three-valent process-scenarios derived in catastrophe theory (from the elementary catastrophe called "butterfly")

We can assume that a similar list contains the most probable candidates for the completion of the relational slot in the nominal compound. It may be enriched gradually, so that an open list is created which structures major parts of our worldly knowledge (cf. alternative 1 above).

The synchronic (partially diachronic) analysis of nonce compounds in German shows that linguistic creativity is governed by elementary dynamic principles: asymmetry of structural and semantic scales, freezing (masking) vs. uncovering of information, principles of economy (least effort) and in the extreme case of nonce N+N-compounds the activation of relational constants.

We presume that in a protolanguage (used in Homo erectus populations) the spontaneous formation of new sound labels for old or new intentions dominated and was only restricted by phonological laws. The creativity framed by the functional dynamics of sequences (cf. the principle of asymmetry in compounds) and by an efficient information control (cf. the packaging, freezing and uncovering of word-meaning) as shown in this section is a phenomenon that was only accessible after the evolution of full-fledged lexicons and grammars. The principles shown to be relevant in current lexical innovation are therefore good candidates for a first set of evolutionary principles which became relevant in the period after the first protolanguages described in Chapter 8. It should have preceded the rise of a more specific rule-governed syntax, because it enabled the emergence of new and more complex linguistic gestalts based on existing lexical material.

6.2.2 The dependence of creative compounds on the context

If nonce-compounds are comparable in their situational spontaneity to the biological processes of mutation, the filtering of lexical innovations which leads to neologisms and to a permanent change of the lexical inventory corresponds to biological selection. The production and interpretation of nominal compounds in specific contexts condenses rather loose textual and sentential structures into a semantically rich and very short form. These interpretations are often not stable and tend to disintegrate immediately, if the context is lost (forgotten). This loss of information can annihilate the whole process so that the compound neither enters into the long-term memory of an individual nor into the collective lexicon. Under special circumstances however, it can lead to a state of stability. In these cases it tends to select a basic but stable interpretation and to fit the result of contextual creation into the lexicon. These processes exhibit two types of transitions, which are qualitatively different Table 6.2 gives a schematic view of this idea.

Table 6.2   Three strata of global processes in nominal composition

Stratum 1	Discursive organization of content Thematic structuring of texts and sentences In general: *short term* composition
	▼ Transition 1: condensation of information and stabilization relative to context
Stratum 2	Condensation of content Operation of economic principles Stabilization of contextual meaning In general: *middle term* composition
	▼ Transition 2: selection and stabilization independent from context
Stratum 3	Selection of structures Loss of unstable contextual keys Operation of economic principles in the knowledge system In general: *long term* composition; acceptance of *neologisms*

Two basic principles seem to govern the first transition:

The principle of variation. In the verbalization of a communicative intent the speaker makes a choice from among a set of alternatives, weighing them according to different scales. This range of alternatives can be further exploited when the speaker takes up the same theme in the sequence of his utterances.

The principle of framing. The speaker presupposes frames of interaction and of text-organization. The global processes of nominal composition exploit such frames.

We shall now illustrate the different types of processes:

The simplest case of *anaphoric composition* consists in the shortening of a nominal compound, by the elimination of a constituent (mostly in the center of the compound). More often the basic structure is not itself a compound but a phrase, a sentence or a text.

The material analyzed in Wildgen (1982b) shows that the transformations from text, to sentence, to phrase and finally to the compound are manifold. The basic principles are the resumption of a thematic complex and the reduction of the form by the elimination of non-central elements in the utterance. The above example 'Atombunker' shows how a set of novel compounds is created, all of which are candidates for a later lexicalization.

The cataphoric processes are variants of anaphoric processes, the difference being a pragmatic one. The speaker makes a jump to stratum 2 without

Table 6.3 Anaphoric motivation of new compounds in the progression of a text

Examples from the corpus	Translation (narrow)
Die Leute von Greenpeace ▼ Die Greenpeace-Leute SZ/80/54/1/1	"The people from Greenpeace" ▼ "The Greenpeace people"
Bonns Innenministerium möchte Kernkraftwerke künftig unter die Erde verlagern ▼ Ein Atommeiler unter der Erde ▼ ein verbunkerter Reaktor ▼ die Atombunker ▼ ein Untertage-Reaktor ▼ Nuklearbunker	"The Ministry of the Interior in Bonn would like in future to put atomic energy plants under the earth" ▼ "An atomic pile under the earth" ▼ "reactor in a bunker" ▼ "atomic bunker" ▼ "underground reactor" ▼ "nuclear bunker"

verbalizing the previous stratum 1 (cf. Table 6.2). The hearer will either imagine adequate contexts using the situation and the local processes as inputs, or he will give up. In many cases the speaker feels obliged to help the hearer in his task. These processes are basically variation processes governed by pragmatic principles.

The second main class of processes may be called *contrastive differentiation* (cf. Wildgen 1987) and is qualitatively different. Here an existing theme is divided into two (or, less often, three) sub-domains which thus constitute a scale with opposed poles. In dynamic terms we can call this phenomenon a bifurcation. The process of contrastive differentiation is a consequence of this structure-creating process following from bifurcation. I shall give only three examples from the corpus, which show that virtually any nominal concept may be split into sub-concepts adding a constituent in the front-position. The technique allows for analogical compounds defining a set and implicitly a production rule which may formalize the series established by stepwise analogy.

The process of contrastive differentiation exhibits a very basic dynamic principle which can be encountered in many domains of language use. It says: Every unitary entity of form and meaning can bifurcate such that a scale with two poles (and eventually a metastable middle attractor) is created. The anaphoric processes, which exhibit a process of contextual/semantic diffusion, do not normally lead to a stabilized compound on stratum 3. Secondary processes, specific for registers, styles, print media or situational talk can introduce further information and thus create semantically rich and more stable structures. If the contexts are stable or very suggestive, these compounds can achieve stability on stratum 3 (neologism). The process of contrastive differentiation as

Table 6.4 Examples for the process of contrastive differentiation

Examples from the corpus (narrow translation)

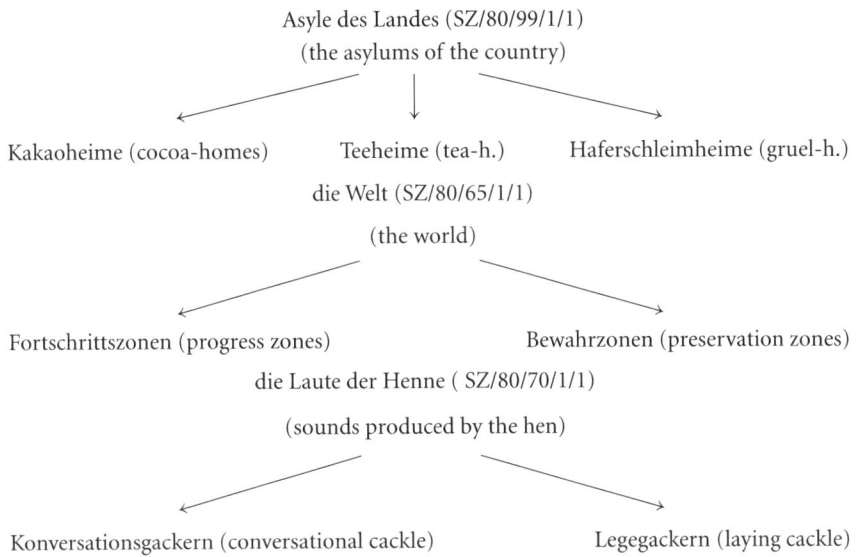

Asyle des Landes (SZ/80/99/1/1)
(the asylums of the country)

Kakaoheime (cocoa-homes)   Teeheime (tea-h.)   Haferschleimheime (gruel-h.)

die Welt (SZ/80/65/1/1)

(the world)

Fortschrittszonen (progress zones)   Bewahrzonen (preservation zones)

die Laute der Henne (SZ/80/70/1/1)

(sounds produced by the hen)

Konversationsgackern (conversational cackle)   Legegackern (laying cackle)

an innovative procedure is a possible source of changes in the lexicon of an individual or of a community. The result depends on the weight of the contextual
need for differentiation and on the position the new compound is able to take
on in the system of lexical items.

The stabilization of creative linguistic behavior beyond the situation of use
is relevant if we want to understand the historical evolution of language. But is
it relevant for our understanding of the evolution of language?

The process of grammaticalization, which has only been mentioned in the
context of prefixes and suffixes originating in lexical constituents of nominal
compounds, is in principle able to explain how grammars emerge on the basis
of lexical material. The lexical meanings are based on imagistic content associated in situations of deixis and contextual language use. Thus we may conceive
a path leading from contextual communication embedded in social action to
the emergence of a grammar. The case of pidgin language creation was rightly
used by Bickerton to observe how from an extreme situation of language loss, a
"bio-program" for language creation was triggered and could lead to a linguistically complete language, a Creole in the generation where the pidgin became
a mother tongue. Whereas Bickerton was still arguing in terms of some inborn "universal grammar" (in Chomsky's sense), I prefer to understand the

emergence of grammar as the result of more basic dynamic principles which also underlie our current grammars but lack the mechanical shape of rules in generative grammar. They are much more fundamental, and catastrophe theoretic semantics has shown that the underlying formal laws are shared not only with other cognitive domains as in perception but even apply to natural systems in chemistry and physics. Thus it is not a "universal grammar" but a "universal morphology" in the sense of Goethe, d'Arcy Thompson and Thom, which underlies the evolutionary and actual emergence of grammars in human societies.

However, linguistic creativity is not restricted to verbal codes. There is an inherent imagistic space of contents (cf. Wildgen 1994) which controls the coherence and simplicity of a meaning-construction. In the next section I shall therefore consider some cases of picture-word creativity, in which the imagistic background finds it own (specific) realization in a photo-compound or a fantastic picture.

6.2.3 The blending of image and compound in comical texts

One example of a traditional image-text composition is the emblem, which usually has three constituents:

- a short motto (word or sentence),
- a picture,
- a set of verses (a text), elaborating the relation between motto and picture.

I shall analyze some comical combinations between a nominal compound as motto and a picture. The comical genre prefers new and often deviant combinations and allows us to observe the interpretative devices used. The first example uses a photo as picture; the second uses cartoons.

The object shown combines image features from a cup and a saucer with those of a sponge adapted in its shape to a side-view of the cup. The coherence is achieved by replacing a part of the cup by the sponge. The shape of the cup dominates the image (and the object represented), although the major function of the cup as a solid container of liquid is given up. As the text further explains, the sponge is also a kind of loose container and has the advantage of being spill-proof ("auslaufsicher").

In the case of photos, the object must be first mounted in order to fit the nonce-compound and then the picture is taken. The cartoon allows even more freedom in the pictorial combination and a stronger deformation of

Figure 6.2 Schwammtasse ("sponge-cup"; cf. Stein 1994: Zwanzigster Tip)

the constituent pictures. The following examples are taken from "Halbritters Waffenarsenal" (Halbritter 1977: 90f.).

Five out of seven noun phrases or nouns use nominal compounds; three of them share the head constituent "Helm":

1. *Brauhelm*   (brew-helmet)
2. *Trompetenhelm*   (trumpet-helmet)
3. *Altfränkischer Daumenhelm*   (thumb-helmet from old Franconia)

In all cases the first (left) constituent of the compound is represented by major parts of the helmet or by objects referring to a verbal constituent as in: *Brauhelm*: Brau – brau-en (to brew), the cartoon shows a typical beer-barrel. In *Trompetenhelm* the trumpet (Trompete) is really a constitutive part of the helmet, in *Daumenhelm* the two thumbs (Daumen) are decorative additions to the upper part of the helmet. The differences between cartoon and compound nouns are also clear: The picture shows more details. Thus not only the heads and faces are different (even adapted to the helmet), they are a natural background to the helmet, which is absent in the compound. Further details of a prototype helmet appear, like the feather in *Brauhelm* or the tassel on the trumpet in *Trompetenhelm*. In *Daumenhelm* a strange ear-warmer in the shape of a hand is added. Other helmet inventions by Halbritter either use characteristic adjectives (*genitalischer Prunkhelm, Schneckenhauser Kappe*),

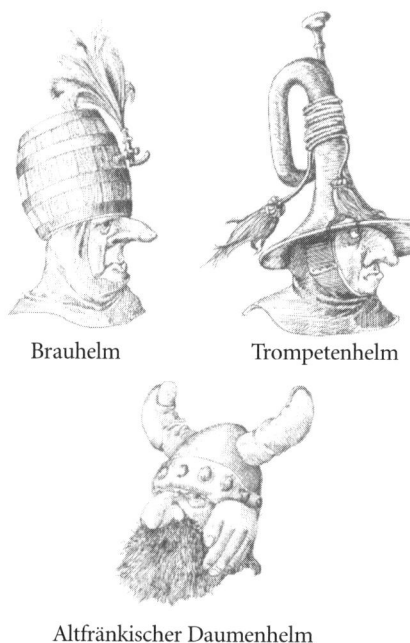

Brauhelm   Trompetenhelm

Altfränkischer Daumenhelm

Figure 6.3 Some of the pseudo-helmets invented by Halbritter (1977)

nonce-derivations (*Watt*aner from Watt = measure of electricity) or give a new meaning to an already existing lexical compound (*Federfuchser*).

The double coding by a nominal compound (respectively an idiomatic expression or a nonce noun-phrase) and a picture gives us a hint as to the manner of imagistic composition. The helmet has two functional parts, the upper and protective (sometimes decorative) part and the cap, which links the upper part to head and neck. In Halbritter's cartoons, the upper part takes the shape of a barrel, a penis, a pen, a trumpet or a snail-shell. In "*Daumenhelm*" and "*Eiserne Jungfrau*" the decorative elements of the upper part are referred to in the determinant of the compound or the noun-phrase. Thus imagistic composition follows a principle of functional and spatial replacement (which is a kind of functional/spatial specification).

This short excursion into picture-word pairs showed that an underlying problem of semantic compositionality concerns the coherence of the resulting imagistic representations. This feature has been neglected in current grammars, which are either only concerned with the compositionality of surface forms as in Chomsky's tradition or with parallel semantic and surface compositionality (Langacker's variant of cognitive semantics). If imagistic composition and the conditions of its coherence and stability is of permanent importance, then the evolution of language must have changed our capacity for imagination, pictorial construction and invention. This fundamental aspect of semantics can be analyzed with reference to the visual arts, which are the topic of the next section.

6.3 Creativity in art and the dynamics of symbolic innovation

The history of art documents periods of stability and decay as well as sudden bursts of creativity and innovation. It is therefore a good example for human creativity in the domain of symbolic behavior and may serve to reveal the social conditions responsible for periods of rise and decay. Moreover, the intellectual struggle of innovative minds, the conditions for their integration or repression can be analyzed using their works, their writings and a variety of other historical materials. I shall analyze three artists representing three distinct periods in the history of European art:

Table 6.5 The three artists and their historical and systematic positions

1. Leonardo da Vinci (1452–1519)	Renaissance	Figural composition
2. William Turner (1775–1851)	Classicism	Landscape painting
3. Henry Moore (1898–1986)	Modern Art	Sculpture (figural/abstract)

If the blending of pictorial and verbal structure has shown how symbolic creativity operates in the spaces of multisensorial imagination, this aspect will be further exemplified in the following. At the same time all artists show that they depend on traditions so that the existing knowledge of art and the iconography of the topic forms the background for the creative act. The artists first take a certain state of the art as given, participate in it, later they introduce changes into their composition, change some principles of figural representation (Leonardo) or modify the level of abstraction (Turner, Moore). In its initial stages, the process of innovation is a kind of "bricolage" of the type Lévi-Strauss describes in the first chapter of "La Pensée Sauvage" (Lévi-Strauss 1962). The painter or sculptor learns a series of techniques and, when confronted with a specific topic, chooses certain elements from this tradition (including ready-made solutions), and then he tries to find his own solution which integrates the ready-made parts with given techniques and standards. Although the act of integration necessary for the formation of a plausible whole is itself a difficult task which requires many "small" inventions, I shall only describe more radical innovations which involve reshaping the organizing schema or rule. The artist breaks with the given convention, *negates* it and seeks a new schema, a new rule. This case of radical innovation necessarily contains an act of rejection, dismissal, destruction, or conflict. This conflict highlights another dimension of innovation already mentioned in the case of nonce-compounds, namely, the stability or instability of the result. The question is: Will the innovative result be rejected or even ignored or will it be appreciated, will it establish a new standard, such that symbolic forms, e.g., paintings, after this innovation look different and have found a new ideal. In the context of (biological and cultural) evolution, the process of acceptance/refusal is crucial; it may push the culture into a rapid cycle of further innovation, perhaps to a cultural climax, or force innovators to leave the society or just to waste their genius, to give up and to surrender to the conservative mainstream. A whole generation of innovators may be lost by emigration or burned out in dependent activities.

But political or economic conditions are not a sufficient explanation because in many times and places there are just not enough innovators showing up or growing up to a sufficient degree of competence and performance in their art or their science. Such a dramatic void of innovation does not only depend on biological chance (i.e., no particular genius is born), there is something like a social or cultural atmosphere, a kind of native soil that allows individuals to let their genius ripen and develop, so that they can find their proper place among friends and rivals. This is probably the most difficult aspect of social creativity. Creativity may show up in childhood and be recognized or overlooked by parents, friends, schools, etc. In the following the individual genesis of creative individuals and the social conditions for their development or their resignation cannot be assessed. I shall concentrate instead on the process of mental reorganization and the creative reshaping of conceptual negation and integration.

6.3.1 Creativity and symbolic innovation in the art of Leonardo da Vinci

In his "Trattato della pittura" Leonardo states that the painter has as his primary aim the representation of two things: man and his mind ("l'uomo e la mente"; Pedretti 1995:§180). The nature of man becomes visible and, therefore, accessible to the eye in the different "accidents", i.e., changes and movements and in the proportions of his body parts (cf. Pedretti 1995:Terza Parte). In order to represent man and his mind the artist must first create a pictorial space, the stage for the topic of the painting. The basic technique rediscovered

Figure 6.4 Leonardo da Vinci's "Last Supper" in Milan

and further developed in the Renaissance is called "linear perspective", i.e., the artist must be able to represent the third dimension with the means of a pictorial plane. Second he must consider light and shadow in human bodies, the gestures of the hands, the postures of the head and facial expression before he distributes the topics of the painting on the surface. Finally landscape, sky, objects, animals, and persons accompanying the topic of the painting (mostly individuals or groups of individuals) must be arranged in space, relative to light and shadow. The central technical concern of the artist, therefore, is the composition of the topic and the choice of those postures that are able to represent the motion and the mind of the central persons.

In the fresco "The Last Supper" Leonardo found a new way to arrange the 13 persons (Jesus and his twelve apostles), such that this grouping is in a state of equilibrium, and corresponds with the meaning of the biblical episode it illustrates (Luca Pacioli offered the interpretation that Christ has just said: "Unus vostrum me traditurus est"). This solution contains a negation of previous traditions as it gives Judas a place among the group of disciples and also creates a new semantic prototype for painting larger groups in interaction around a table. The innovations had consequences for innumerable later paintings, photos, and film-scenes which are evident even in the present (cf. Wildgen 2004a).

The geometrical arrangement of the thirteen actors in the scene has a basic symmetry. Christ versus twelve apostles, six of them are sitting to his left, six to his right. The linear arrangement, which includes Judas, the traitor, is new.

In most paintings which had treated the same topic, Judas was placed on the other side of the table with his back to the viewer.

In one of the preliminary sketches with John resting his head on the table, the grouping of the remaining apostles on Christ's left is two plus three. At his right it is one (Peter) plus two plus two. Leonardo restructures this scene to obtain geometrical symmetry, which may be expressed arithmetically: $13 = 3 + 3 + 1$ (Christ) $+ 3 + 3$. In comparison with this order we may observe that Giotto (1266–1336) painted his "Last Supper" with a central non-homogenous group of three: Christ, John, and Judas on the opposite side of the table plus two groups of five apostles. The arithmetic order is: $13 = 5 + 3 + 5$. Ghirlandajo (1449–1494) also adopts the central group of three persons (with Judas on the opposite side).

Leonardo's proportions are new in relation to the tradition and they define a new cognitive or image-schematic model, which is able to restructure the reading of the biblical story. In an indirect way relevant for the broader public, the story of the Last Supper is a prototype of the interpretation of society and relations in a human group (a family, a group of friends, a group of professionals, a political party with its leader, etc.). Therefore, the innovative organization of the topic in the painting creates a new frame of interpretation not only applicable to spiritual life but also to political and everyday affairs. In this sense, it plays the role of discourse orientation and is able to serve as background knowledge for innumerable situations of communication. This is responsible for the human and social relevance of a piece of art beyond its esthetic function.

The narrative function of the painting is expressed by its dynamics. Christ's utterance: "One of you will betray me", is a force, the effect of which makes a visible and emotional impact on the apostles. Like a shock-wave it hits most strongly the two groups sitting directly to the right and left of Christ and to a lesser degree impacts the exterior groups. If we consider the nearer groups, James is pushed back, whereas John, although displaced relative to Christ, stays calm, and Judas seems to freeze in the moment he reaches for the bread. These two groups are more agitated than the calmer outer groups. Thus the dynamic effect of the words of Christ is represented as a wave with repercussions and vortices. This is also true for the single groups of apostles. If we analyze their postures and gestures, we can further reduce all four groups of apostles into two plus one (center). The central person neutralizes the movement issuing from Jesus and thus brings it to rest, the natural locus of movements in Aristotle's physics. It is as if the impact of the utterance had dynamically shaped the four groups and their subgroups. Dynamically, Judas is clearly separated from the other apostles, he seems to be lost for any positive effect, holds his money in his right hand, stops grasping for a moment at the bread. He shows a closed, sinister face, which is in full contrast to the face of John illuminated by the light from the left.

In relation to the geometry of the painting, we can say that Leonardo tries to organize his composition as an instant in a process which shows the origin of the force, the immediate effects and the multiple structures created by the percussions of the force, which is in and comes from Jesus. As the emotional and intellectual effects of the central force are the main topic of the painting, Leonardo reorganizes the geometry of the scene, in order to arrive at an optimal representation of the percussions in body-postures, gestures and facial expressions.

The second example also refers to the work of Leonardo, but it is closer to linguistic semantics, mainly sentence frames and verbal valence: The thematic composition in Leonardo's paintings of St. Anne. The elaborated cartoon for St. Anne (with Mary and Jesus) was finished in 1498/99, i.e., after the "The Last Supper". It shows a quaternary relation: St. Anne, Mary, Jesus and St. John. The major narrative and topical differences are:

- St. Anne is the mother of Mary.
- In the tradition of this pictorial topic, Mary is sitting on St. Anne's lap and holding Jesus on her own lap.
- The presence of John or the lamb is facultative.

In the elaborated cartoon (now in London) Leonardo avoids a pyramidal construction, or better, he cuts the upper edge of the pyramid such that the heads of Mary and Anne are on one horizontal line. Nevertheless the contours of Mary at left and her line of vision towards Jesus and Jesus' line of vision towards St. John form a triangle.

Dynamically we have a central triad consisting of Mary (holding Jesus), Jesus (blessing St. John) and St. John (receiving the blessing); these are the participants; St. Anne is rather a bystander or part of the background. She supports Mary (on her knees), looks at her and points to the heaven; her pointing hand defines the upper edge of a smaller pyramid with the head of Jesus and St. John forming the base. Figure 6.5 illustrates this analysis.

The lines of vision and hand gestures fit into a triangle; its hypotenuse is the basic force-line, which has Jesus as attractor. The weights of the central groups of adults Anne/Mary are balanced by the body of Jesus, which is a counterpoise to the body of Mary sitting on Anne's knees. The whole composition is, therefore, centered on Jesus (as its centre of weight/force or "bary-center").

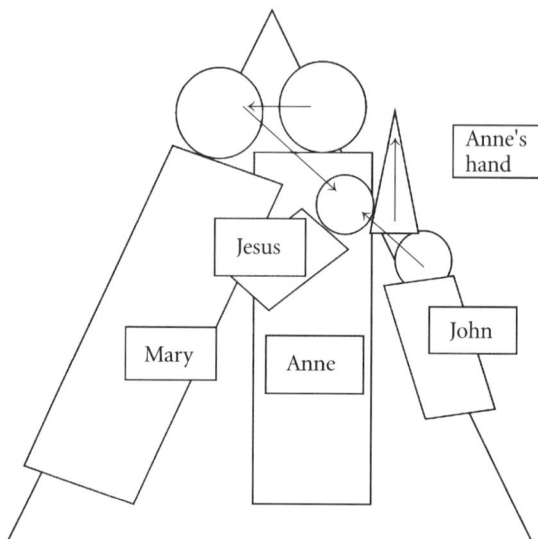

Figure 6.5 Geometrical figures and force-lines in the London cartoon of St. Anne

From 1503 Leonardo attempted different solutions for the representation of the triad: Anne, Mary, Jesus. In one sketch the head of St. Anne in proximity to that of Mary is scratched out and replaced by and a new version where the heads of Mary and St. Anne are at a certain distance and St. Anne does not look at Mary. The final stage (ca. 1510) of St. Anne (now exhibited in the Louvre, Paris) comes back to the asymmetric pyramid with the main force-line at right, placing St. Anne, Mary, Jesus, and the lamb in the same line of vision. However, the dynamics are new. Although Mary is still sitting on St. Anne's lap, she is moving towards the child (Jesus). This complicated decentralization clears the space for a full portrait of St. Anne, who now joins the main line of vision instead of breaking it in two as in the earlier cartoon.

The painting contains a rich geometric and dynamic structure (weights, bary centers, force-lines, lines of vision, etc.) which is used in many of Leonardo's works. A purely static representation would be insufficient for both the pictorial and the narrative aims of the painting. Furthermore, this piece is typical of Leonardo's art, which consistently exemplifies the concept of *dynamic valence.*

In the case of this painting, we have on the surface a quaternary constellation: Anne–Mary–Jesus–lamb. If one considers the force fields and actions, one notices that a basic interaction links three participants: Mary–Jesus – the lamb.

Figure 6.6 Leonardo da Vinci: St. Anne with Mary, Jesus and the lamb (Paris)

- Mary *pulls on* Jesus
- Jesus *pulls on* the lamb
- The lamb *resists*
- Jesus resists being pulled away from the lamb

There is a conflict between Mary who tries to prevent Jesus from seizing the lamb and Jesus who notices this (he looks back to her) but resists against her action. This triad constitutes a force field, which dominates the message of the painting. A first schematic representation introduces two vector-fields with attractors:

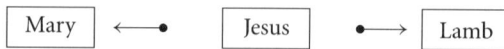

| Mary | ←——• | Jesus | •——→ | Lamb |

Figure 6.7 Two opposed vector-fields with a metastable center (Jesus)

Jesus is in the metastable position between two attractors; the narrative (biblical) content of these attractors is:

- Mary: His mother; she cares for her baby.
- Jesus: He feels the duty to sacrifice and to leave Mary behind (he is attracted by the sacrificial role represented by the lamb).

The cognitive dynamics lying at the heart of the two paintings by Leonardo may be described in the context of dynamical semiotics (cf. Wildgen 1994). The constellation of forces between Mary – Christ – the lamb corresponds to the basic archetype of transfer in Figure 6.8.

As the archetype does not describe all the interactions in the composition one has to add two complications:

- Anne supports/anchors the whole event (physically and genealogically), she is a fourth attractor which does not directly intervene but rather sustains the event (which is happening on her knees).
- The manner of "transfer" is further elaborated in the painting and could be described in a sentence like: *Mary tries to prevent Jesus from seizing the lamb.*

In the painting one sees Mary's hands seizing Jesus and Jesus' hands (and feet) seizing the lamb and we see that Jesus has a stronger grip on the lamb than Mary has on him. The turning of his head creates an opposition to the force-direction of Mary's hands.

In order to go further one needs knowledge, which comes from everyday experience with human interaction. This anchoring domain outside the paint-

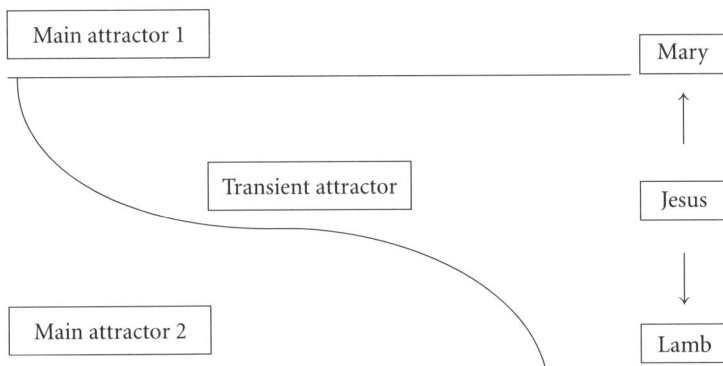

Figure 6.8 The dynamical archetype of transfer (giving) and a fiber on it (with attributed contents)

ing is not linked to knowledge from the Bible. It is rather generic in the sense that the body-centered and enacted schemas are fundamental. The distinction of two levels of analysis is natural because in real-life situations, i.e., when one observes a mother interacting with her child, the first interpretation occurs. In cultural traditions that have elaborated a collective visual or linguistic memory (e.g., of major biblical contents) the more artificial interpretation is superimposed on the routines of the first one. It is typical of art to presuppose cultural knowledge and special "reading" skills; just "perceiving" and recognizing is not enough.

The problem Leonardo faced in the pictorial representation of the two contents: "The Last Supper" and "St. Anne with Mary and Jesus" is a basic semiotic problem. How can a system of dynamic relations and interactions be represented such that a stable sign-structure is created? The elements are not the basic difficulty, although Leonardo worked hard to find models for sketches of the apostles before he began his work in Milan. The basic and really difficult problem was the choice of the central, dynamically representative moment of the scene. This is a basic problem in the evolution of language, which should be able to support narratives. How can a bit of real life experience be caught in a linguistic expression?

In the evolutionary context, one could imagine the first human who tried to speak a sentence which tells someone who has not witnessed it, how a fellow killed the lion with his spear, or his family how he bargained to get a beautiful feather in exchange for a hand axe. Before a permanent proto-type sentence for such complicated interactions could be used, the dynamics of the scene had to be analyzed and reduced to an optimal, stable, image-schema. The creativity of the artist thus throws a light on the cognitive operations of "imagistic" analysis which is presupposed in the evolution of syntax. The child can learn a ready-made language which preserves the results of a similar cognitive analysis in the period of the transition between a protolanguage and a full-fledged language. He/she uses a highly complex instrument, which was invented and designed by others. In the sense of computational models of linguistic evolution she/he "steels" a symbolic tool, he/she would not be able to invent. The creative artist, however, engages with this basic intellectual process again in order to find a pictorial solution beyond that demonstrated in earlier work; he thus re-creates parts of the symbolic solutions which emerged in the evolution of language but which became unconscious because the learning of languages is a holistic process, in which the learners don't need to go through all the difficult processes which lead to the evolution of human languages. Therefore the symbolic creativity of the artist may give us insights into the forces which led to the emergence of language on the background of a more general capacity of symbolic thought (cf. Chapter 9 for a philosophical elaboration of this idea in the line of proposals by Cassirer, Luhmann and Habermas).

6.3.2 Symbolic abstraction and innovation in the art of William Turner

Natural scenes and even actors may fail to be clearly perceptible visually, e.g., a landscape in fog or at twilight, a person under similar conditions, or if the viewer is only allowed a short glimpse, as when passing by in a train. Reduced visual cues for an object or person portrayed in such a way are therefore not necessarily *abstract* but may be *real*. Another example of *abstract* perception occurring in *real* vision may be found in cases in which people half-perceive or only implicitly perceive objects which appear in a repetitive or monotonous context, such as the telephone poles at the side of the road on a long car trip, the contents of a room which one passes through every day, and so on. Although they have the physical ability to perceive the whole situation in a precise manner, people largely ignore the multitude of details and pick up one or two specific features. In such situations our memory is doing something one may call "abstraction". In the same way, the artist may prefer to represent the mental (mnemonic) construal of such scenes out of the selected features and to neglect all predictable and general features. The process of abstraction, division of labor between active memory and actual sign use, was crucial for the evolution of spoken and later written language (cf. Chapter 5). I shall analyze this process in some paintings by William Turner and show that a process observable in the history of art can give us hints towards basic evolutionary mechanisms in the evolution of language and our symbolic capacity in general.

William Turner (1775–1851) stands in the tradition of British landscape painting. Starting in 1729 there was a tradition among aristocratic families of sending their young men on a "Grand Tour" to visit Europe and especially Italy. Paintings of scenes encountered on the tour, mostly in the dominant Italian style, were brought home as souvenirs. In the course of the 18th century painters like Wilson, Gainsborough, Wright of Derby, Cotman, and Gertin, departed from this tradition and Turner radicalized the move away from topographical precision. The loss of referential distinctiveness, the neglect of an identification of specific objects, cities, and landscapes may have been motivated by Turner's preference for vague surfaces under specific (natural) conditions and by his feeling uncomfortable working very long with his materials in the open, i.e., he preferred a more economic or even minimalist method. In a painting of the Castle of Chillon at the Lake of Geneva (1809; British Museum) a precise representation with persons in the foreground, buildings, the lakeshore and mountains is given; in a watercolor painting from 1841 (cf. Figure 6.9) the same lake in Geneva is depicted in a very vague fashion.

Figure 6.9 Geneva: The mole, the lake and the Savoy Hills, 1841 (cf. Wilton 1982:63, Nr. 89)

In the second painting (cf. above) one can still recognize mountains, the shore of the lake, the water surface (blue), ships, and possibly people, but the symphony of colors, the transitions between surfaces and indirectly the emotional values become dominant.

Some of the later paintings reflect very specific, rare and traditionally not represented phenomena like: "Snow storm – Steam boat off a harbor's mouth making signals in shallow water, and going by the lead." Turner gave this precise description to avoid an interpretation of the picture as fantasy or caprice. In a certain sense, some of these paintings are even more realistic than those by Leonardo because they refer to concrete, personal perceptions of the painter. Their objects refer to geographically and historically precise entities that can be identified as parts of the context of the painter's life, episodes of his journey, situations observed and remembered by the painter himself. This subjectivity, which refers to the life, the body of the author is probably the new message which made Turner a precursor of the impressionistic style in the eyes of later generations. Landscape paintings in the style of Turner and later in the impressionistic style manifest the (preliminary) end point of an artistic journey which avoids the dominant urban and industrial areas (in a romantic or postromantic move), and ignores humans who crowd these locations and have shaped them to their economic advantage: It prefers to penetrate the inner realm of perceptual and (later) emotional or intellectual experience.

The neglect of reference to distinct entities in space and time is a feature which marks the deferred reference typical for language, which can easily refer to entities which are not present in the context and must be imagined. The concentration on relevant features and the radical economy in the construction is typical for the lexicon of natural languages and in the syntactic constructions used in utterances. In a sense, Turner, like Leonardo, realizes a technique of symbolic creation in the realm of art, which was brought about in the evolution of language, i.e., we witness basic evolutionary principles responsible for the evolution of language and belonging to the cognitive heritage of humans reappearing in the history of fine arts.

6.3.3 Creativity and radical analysis of human body postures in the art of Henry Moore

In order to restrict the scope of my analysis, I shall only consider the topic of the "Reclining Figure", which is frequent in Moore's oeuvre. In a crayon drawing ("Reclining Nude", red and black crayon, ca. 1923; cf. Mitchinson 1989:96) Moore shows a realistic picture of a "Reclining Nude", where one can easily

Figure 6.10 Henry Moore, "Reclining Figure, Hand", 1979, Bronze (cf. Mitchinson 1989:265)

identify a female body and a historian of art could perhaps identify the person who had posed for this drawing. Ten years later, in 1933, a drawing shows a series of projected sculptures on the same topic. Even if single parts of the drawing may be recognized as belonging to a human body in a reclining position, these figures are like an exercise for variable shapes of persons in the given pose. What is left is the horizontality, and the partial suspension and support of the body typical for a reclining pose (cf. Mitchinson 1989:112).

Henry Moore became famous for his large sculptures, many of which resemble human bodies, but some of which lack any referential support. In Figure 6.10 one of many variants of Henry Moore's treatment of the topic in sculptures is presented and used for further analysis.

If one considers this sculpture as the result of a process of symbolization via abstraction, one can use some of the hypotheses on visual schematization put forward by Marr (1982). The most radical abstraction of a reclining figure would be a curved line with a vertical and a horizontal part, which follows the bary-center of the human body. This (one-dimensional) abstraction can be given a geometrically simplest shape by filling out parts of the line with cylinders (straight parts) and cones, spheres (curved parts). As such basic geometrical shapes cannot be integrated into a continuous spatial form (cones and spheres cannot be fitted to cylinders) a separation of the reclining figure into detached parts is a possible outcome of this kind of analysis. In the sculpture shown below, this radical consequence is still avoided and the iconic relation to a human body in its continuity is still preserved. The conceptual analysis of the reclining figure can be expressed geometrically or linguistically:

- A vertical cylinder – the concept of a *standing* body.
- A horizontal cylinder – the concept of a *reclining* body.
- A bent cylinder or a sphere (as the prototype of bending) – the concept of a *sitting* body.

Figure 6.11 illustrates the type of geometrical decomposition and the correlation with linguistic labels.

The narrative content of a "Reclining Figure" is concentrated in the static verbs: *stand, sit, lie,* with its neighboring motion verbs: *lie down, sit down,* and *stand up, rise.* The viewer of the sculpture may mentally add in masses for the head, the shoulders, the arms, the elbows, the knees, each leg, feet, hair, eyes, nose, mouth, etc. He thus regresses along a path of abstraction analogue to that taken by the sculptor himself (or even engages in a longer "story" of artistic development). This "story" may be understood as the trajectory from a prototype (or a set of prototypes) to our visual representation of a particular human body. This cognitive itinerary is also at the heart of the lexical field: *stand, lie, sit* and lexical field theory should consider the aspect of figural decomposition and the evolution of abstraction in the emergence of the lexicon beyond a protolanguage and the shaping of basic syntactic patterns. The reclining figure is of special interest for Henry Moore because it shows a zone of transition, of instability, and thus focuses on the dynamic aspect in a fashion similar to Leonardo's composition of "The Last Supper".

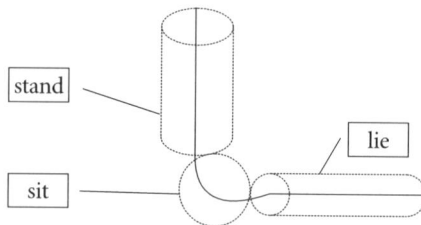

Figure 6.11 Reducing the "Reclining Figure" to cylinder and sphere

A more radical visual analysis of the human body destroys its unitary gestalt, its topological coherence. Three trajectories may be observed in Moore's oeuvre:

1. Instead of one body (from head to feet and hands) several sculptural entities together "represent" the "Reclining Figure". Moore distinguishes two-piece, three-piece, and four-piece reclining figures (cf. Moore 1968, Nr. 10 one-piece, Nr. 11 two-piece, Nr. 40/41 three-piece; the four piece composition (N. 86) is not called "reclining figure" but visibly belongs to the same family of sculptures). The geometrical analysis shown in Figure 6.11 is not sufficient to cover all the variants of the topic; but if one adds cones, bent cylinders, spheres with excavations and others most of his formal inventions may be classified on this basis. The bending of lines, the curves, the concave or convex surfaces refer more specifically to the realm of living, biological entities.

2. Beyond convex and concave limbs and surfaces one can observe gaps. They may appear in a reclining figure, e.g., between arm and body, or arms and legs and the support. These gaps may show up naturally (cf. Moore 1968: Nr. 68, 71 "Reclining figure 1939", and Nr. 73 "Reclining figure (external form) 1953–54"); in other sculptures the title of the sculpture abandons the reference to human bodies, as in: "Three rings, 1966–67" (Sylvester 1968: Nr. 74). The technique of gaps and rings elaborates the topological complexity of the sculpture.

3. Instead of continuous (differentiable) curves, sharp edges ("knife-edge"), pikes and strings attached to bodies appear as in the sculpture: Three points 1939–1940 (cf. Sylvester 1968: 45).

As the cubist precursors of Henry Moore (cf. the work of Picasso in his cubist period) became aware of similar tendencies in primitive art, they realized that their spontaneous artistic inventions participate in a more general and timeless kind of symbolic activity. In fact, as we have seen in Chapter 5, Paleolithic art shows similar tendencies. This means that the principle of symbolic abstraction and decomposition has been part of human symbolic capacity for at least the last 40 ky. As the evolution of language preceded the artistic achievements of Paleolithic art, we can assume that it belongs to the range of symbolic and cognitive capacities elaborated during the evolutionary steps which led from a protolanguage to a full-fledged language. The search for topological and dynamic invariants in the permanent flux of perceptions and actions was the bottomline which enabled simultaneously the reorganization of our lexicon following very general principles, the elaboration of a system of grammatical construction patterns and thus prepared the ground for complex morphology and syntax. In the activity of creative artists the same power of symbolic creativity surfaces and can be analyzed empirically. Artistic creativity is therefore a window to basic symbolic faculties which tend to be hidden by the ready-made products of this faculty like linguistic utterances and linguistic competence. It uncovers the unconscious wealth of symbolic creativity and this establishes the fascination of art for human beings which often tend to overlook the value and depth of their linguistic and cultural heritage.

6.3.4 Remarks on the acceptance of innovation in art

Although radical innovators like Leonardo, Turner and Moore encountered numerous difficulties in the recognition of their work, their success depended on the appreciation of their contribution by contemporaries (be it colleagues, pupils, rich collectors or kings). Until the high Middle Ages European art was primarily commissioned for religious purposes and was functionally embedded in a religious context which provided the necessary appreciation for artistic products. Religious support was linked to support by elite groups with specific privileges; in the time of Leonardo success at the courts of Florence, Milan or Rome was the criterion of selection. Although the rate of individual creativity may be the same statistically in any period, cultural innovation is highly dependent upon the context of acceptance, on the social integration of human creativity. Therefore, artistic innovation is not just a question of individual cognitive achievement. First, the artist stands in a tradition that established a universe of discourse containing certain contents (e.g., biblical or classical themes) and certain techniques of dealing with them. Second, the innovation is rooted in the artist's technical skills which he/she develops further during his/her lifetime. Thus Leonardo was already a gifted painter in Verrochio's workshop, he continued to perform technical experiments, and his technique in "The Last Supper" or the "Mona Lisa" is a secret to modern art experts. His cultural and scientific background are another source of innovation. Leonardo, like Dürer and other Renaissance painters, got their formal training in workshops but also received a humanistic education from friends. Thus they were able to develop a theory or even a philosophy of art and to translate innovation in another sector of culture (e.g., philosophy) into art. Finally political or religious changes (during the Renaissance and later in the time of the Reformation) promoted new values and criteria of excellence. It is the synergetic effect of all these forces and their concentration in the personality of an artist which was able to trigger the radical innovative impulse described above.

In the context of a Semiotics of Art, this means that symbolic innovation needs the mind and body of one or several individuals who integrate the different innovative forces in a given society or culture. These persons are more or less the points of concentration (the "catalysts") of supra-individual forces. They allow for the embodiment of these innovations and their realization in the form of permanent works of art. These can then be referred to, interpreted, elaborated by generations of artists which follow them. This means that innovation in art (in symbolic activity in general) requires the activity of individual personalities; their integration of innovative forces in a culture establishes a stable but new status quo, which can then be read, interpreted or further developed by following generations of artists.

6.4 Creativity in science and the role of mental modeling for the evolution of language

Scientific thinking is one of several modes of human "symbolic forms" (cf. Chapter 9). It takes a clear shape in the first large civilization of Mesopotamia, Egypt and India and reaches a climax in Greek science and philosophy (5th century B. C.) and in Hellenistic science (Euclid and Archimedes). The science of Renaissance (Copernicus, Bruno, Kepler) opened the way for modern science in the 17th century (Galileo, Descartes, and Newton). The great paradigm shifts in physics during the last five centuries may be linked to Copernicus (1543) and Einstein (1905), but many dramatic changes occurred in other disciplines. The question is, how are these dramatic innovations brought about? In the context of the evolution of symbolic capacities one may ask: What are the individual faculties necessary to enable such dramatic innovations? In the context of the evolution of language one may ask: Is science and scientific knowledge a further unfolding of a potential developed in the transition between a (primitive) protolanguage and modern languages? If a positive answer is plausible, one may further ask: Are the principles of scientific creativity good candidates for principles operative in the evolution of language and of its cognitive and cultural preconditions. In the following I shall discuss a paradigmatic case of scientific innovation: the shift from the geocentric to heliocentric astronomy in the work of Copernicus (and further to infinite universes without a centre in the work of Giordano Bruno). The underlying symbolic capacity concerns the fundamental reorganization of a knowledge system under a new perspective, i.e., the insight that a given system of perception and knowledge depends on a perspective and can be globally reinterpreted under a new perspective. In the process of reanalysis of given knowledge, a "natural" or naïve point of view is replaced by a more sophisticated, more artificial point of view. Such global conceptual changes are a test of the flexibility and the freedom of human knowledge systems and thus make the difference against the cognitive abilities of higher primates. They also point to the difference between learning by imitation or emulation and learning by internal modeling, which presupposes a degree of consciousness not yet reached by higher primates.

Nersessian (2002: 140f.) tries to understand creativity in science in terms of "mental modeling". Mental models may contain mental images and they "enable simulative behavior in which models behave in accord with constraints that need not be stated explicitly" (ibidem: 141). The original capacity underlying mental modeling accesses both cognitive abilities linked to perception and to (linguistic) description. Biologically, it was probably developed "as a means of simulating possible ways of maneuvering within the physical environment" as "the ability to anticipate the environment and possible outcomes of action" (ibidem). As soon as linguistic abilities were developed beyond alarm calls and a protolanguage, this mental modeling could be mapped into linguistic expressions and thus integrated into social planning for group activity. The linguistic aspect was furthermore necessary to achieve a level of *expert* reasoning exploiting the facilities of learning accessible through language. Thus mental modeling is a basic strategy that allowed our ancestors to cope with new, rapidly changing ecologies by mentally simulating the consequence their behavior would have under the new conditions. This capacity was probably crucial for the survival of the human species in ecologies which were changing dramatically. At the same time mental modeling constituted a second, imaginary reality in which human actions were represented with their possible outcomes, and which could be elaborated into fantasy and myth.

Mental models characteristically use *modal* symbols "analogous of the perceptual states from which they are extracted" (ibidem: 142) and *amodal* symbols "arbitrary transductions from perceptual states, such as those associated with language" (ibidem). The first may be associated with Peirce's iconic and indexical, the latter with Peirce's symbolic signs. A central operation in mental modeling is abstraction. Nersessian (2002) distinguishes various forms of abstraction, "such as limiting case, idealization, generalization and generic modeling [...] with generic modeling playing a highly significant role in the generation, abstraction and integration of constraints."

If one follows the development of Copernican thought (cf. Wildgen 1998a: 87–128) one can distinguish three major phases. The first one has to do with the biography of Copernicus, who formulated a basic relativistic insight:

Any change of location is either due to a movement of the observed object, to the movement of the observer or to both (Copernicus 1990: 99). Between 1510 (Commentariolus) and 1543, the year of the publication of his major work "De revolutionibus", Copernicus tried to complete his cosmological construction based on a moving earth (observer) and a stationary sun. First he believed his construction would be geometrically simpler, but as he began to consider the different motions in detail, the new system became more complicated than the old one (in terms of number of cycles). This phase is clearly dominated by the perceptually based schema of relativistic motion, which is extrapolated to the earth (on which the observer lives like a sailor on a ship) and the astronomical horizon of the immensely distant stars. In the second phase two divergent lines were followed: a theological line which tried to remove the provocation of the relativistic generalization (or to generalize it, as in the case of Giordano Bruno) and a mathematical/experimental line, which tried to improve the geometrical construction and the quality of the data corpus (cf. Tycho Brahe's technical innovations). The general result of this bifurcation was a theological-political conflict, of which Bruno and Galileo became the victims, and the flourishing of multiple rival if ephemeral models. The third phase began rather silently with Kepler's model of the planet Mars (which moves on an ellipsis) and the two "laws" of Kepler, hidden in his philosophically burdened writings. It found its final expression in Newtonian mechanics. The whole process took 177 years (1510–1687) and even at the beginning of the 19th century some philosophers still argued against a Copernican cosmology. If one includes the Greek precursors of Copernicus, one may even say that this conceptual change took two millennia. Nevertheless, the underlying cognitive operation is extremely simple as it uses analogical reasoning: In everyday human perception, everybody can experience relativity due to motion as perspective changes and with it the set of visible things and their distances. This is very convincing on a ship which approaches or sails along a coast. The analogy with astronomy is that humans are like sailors on a huge ship, the earth, and the coast which changes with the motion of the ship is like the sky and the configuration of celestial bodies on it, including the sun and the moon. This insight was Copernicus' starting point and probably also that of his Greek precursors. The creativity consisted in imagining oneself as an observer at night standing on a huge ship flying through the sky.

Ancient proponents of this idea were laughed at and almost forgotten. Why was Copernicus successful in developing this idea? His efforts to prove the theory mathematically were not really convincing, but his skill and the elegance of his partial solutions (e.g., his theory of the moon which did not depend on his heliocentric universe) convinced a European society of experts that he was not a fool. Although the radically innovative mental modeling persuaded figures like Bruno, Kepler and Galileo, who were already skeptical of the mainstream model, it was not able to persuade the churchmen or the astronomers subordinated to theology, nor mathematicians or technologically oriented astronomers, for whom the "reality" of the universe was just a mathematical fiction. It was also rejected by empiricists (like Petrus Ramus) who refused to consider all global models not reducible to empirically observable facts.

From this brief sketch of the Copernican revolution, one can see that there are very different scenarios of innovation and different reasons to accept or reject an innovation:

–   The analogy seems to be far-fetched as in the case of the metaphor: the earth is a ship, the universe is an ocean.
–   The new paradigm is in conflict with a central conceptual structure. Most European languages cognize an ego-centric frame of spatial orientation: the earth on which we live as centre of the universes fits this frame better than the relativistic view of Copernicus, in which the earth and with it the human observer move around the sun.
–   The agnostic position of most astronomers in Copernicus' time generalizes a nominalistic view of language. Scientific knowledge is just a system of hypotheses (conventions for symbolic representation) and the question of "true" knowledge seems to be irrelevant.

Finally, the convergence of empirical evidence, made possible by the use of telescopes by Galileo and Kepler, and mathematical sophistication led to a new astronomical paradigm in which the major Copernican elements remaining were the basic ideas and the mental image which lay at the root of the paradigm shift. It differed in its technical details which have continued to change until the present. If new techniques of observation and calculation had not been added to Copernicus' innovation, it would perhaps have shared the fate of his Greek predecessors, and remained a strange although fascinating idea.

To return to Paleolithic innovation, this classical example of a paradigm shift shows that the mental modeling of an alternative is *one* aspect of innovation, while experience with its consequences either in practice (by observation) or in an expert system of symbolic representation (mathematics) is the other relevant aspect of the story. Only when both crucial aspects converge can innovation lead to new methodology and new understanding. In the case of the Copernican revolution, two parties fought for the acceptance of the innovation. The first party, who made the early philosophical elaborations of the innovative mental model, could be repressed by the authorities. The party whose role was decisive for the final acceptance and further development of the Copernican model was the European community of astronomers. As a result, the Copernican model in turn triggered further innovations and was established as the ruling paradigm in astronomy.

If we try to apply these observations to creativity and innovation in science to Paleolithic societies, we must distinguish situations in which sub-societies of experts and a global network of expert communication existed from those where innovations only had a limited range of diffusion, and could not be evaluated by and integrated into an expert code. The culture-clash of Cro-Magnon man and Neanderthals in Europe highlights this difference. The population of Cro-Magnon men had probably a loose but global network of intertribal relations which allowed for trafficking not only of goods but also of innovations. In the larger and rather dense cultural networks present in southern France and northern Spain (the Franco-Cantabric culture) they could establish expert networks of art and stone-industry linked to a social stratification with shamans and leaders in the hunting of large mammals or in war-fare. These social groups were the necessary "sounding-board" on which mental creativity and intellectual innovation could be tested and so that new ideas were more likely to develop successfully. The similarities in the style of cave art over long distances (ca. 800 km from the cave Chauvet near Lyon to the cave of Altamira near Santander) and over long periods of time (Chauvet 31 ky BP, Niaux 13 ky BP) witness to the geographical distribution and the stability of the underlying cultural network. Many regional differentiations in the code of abstract signs prove the variation between small communities contributing to the cultural network. The cultural success of these societies and their quick and effective adaptation (in behavior not in bodily constitution) to new ecologies made them survive the severe glacial period in which the rival community of Neanderthals became extinct.

The social management of creativity is therefore the key to evolutionary success or extinction and it is still a strong factor of success in modern societies. The system of experts, of expert knowledge and expert training has become the major factor which decides the welfare and dominance of contemporary societies. In retrospect, the confrontation of men like Bruno, Galileo, and Kepler with the contemporary elite was decisive for the future fate of these societies although the innovators themselves were killed, imprisoned or forced into difficult conditions by just those societies which in the long run profited from the effects of their provocative innovations. There seems to exist a basic dilemma in the relation between individual creativity and society. Insofar as a human group (a family, a clan, a tribe) needs to act collectively, all individual have to contribute to the survival of the group which guarantees their own survival; individual creativity is therefore framed by collective goals. The group tends to repress deviations from a collective norm of behavior. Insofar as the group has to cope with quickly changing conditions (mainly in the case of migration and conflict with other groups) it depends on individual creativity because behavioral routines are insufficient. In this dilemma a compromise, a balance between opposed preferences must be found; the instability of such a balance requires a dynamic equilibrium in which individual deviations are allowed (to a certain degree) and are used to adapt the socially accepted corpus of rules, techniques, and strategies. The transmission and conservation of innovation for a longer time span and a larger geographical area is only possible if a kind of cultural book-keeping is in operation; it supposes an elaborated symbolic system beyond the capacity of a protolanguage.

The evolution of science and mathematics serves the same goal, an effective selection and book-keeping of ongoing innovation in our knowledge system. In the case of expert communities and their specific cultural development a higher degree of coherence and technical know-how was achieved. Languages for special purposes, technical means of symbolization, mathematical calculi and computerized expert systems went beyond the all-round functions found in natural languages but they still presuppose a natural language for discussion, interpretation and semantic stabilization of the specialized symbolic forms. In this sense science and scientific creativity develop the potential of symbolic forms which is implicit in the evolution of human language.

6.5 The evolutionary dynamics of symbolic innovation

An artist reacts subjectively to landscapes, persons, or to topics found in other paintings, to the practice of colleagues every day, every hour. His "translation" of this input into a picture is subject to various factors such as his mood, his materials and various chance circumstances. The many degrees of freedom in these processes contribute to art's *stochastic* character. The memory of the artist, the routines he has learned, a set of goals he has already achieved or has observed others achieving define the (small) set of "slaving parameters" (deterministic controls of a stochastic flow), which break down the dimensionality of relevant forces and allow a structured response to the stochastic input the painter is exposed to. This may be called the component "necessity" or the deterministic component (cf. Haken 1983: Chapter 5). In extreme cases, a bad painter will reproduce the same type of schematically enforced picture under any conditions; he is simply insensitive to the variable input. Thus a portrait painter or a painter of female nudes whose paintings show female faces which are all alike, such that one recognizes a large family of twins, has successfully learned to paint *one* face, but he/she cannot represent an individual personality or cannot represent the variability of female faces. Innovation in symbolic systems has a stochastic component (chance) and a deterministic component (necessity) and it fits the complex cooperative systems described in Haken's "Synergetics" (cf. Haken 1983). The chance component is constantly fuelled by situated components in actual symbol use, i.e., every symbolic activity, be it monological or multilogical, incorporates elements and is subject to the effects of external situations which are practically uncontrollable. This constitutes a huge and permanent dynamical flow with a very high degree of freedom (innumerable dimensions of variation). The fact of creative innovation is therefore caught in a dilemma:

–   One reacts specifically to the variability in the input which is potentially infinite. In this case the reactions are chaotic as they are without repetition (period, rhythm) and order; the outcome is like *noise*.
–   One finds an aesthetically optimal form of representation by mapping every input on one of a few archetypes. In this case one looses the specificity of the input; the reaction is *blind*.

In this field of conflict only dynamic equilibria are possible; i.e., the conflict scenario necessitates a permanent search for new solutions and thus symbolic creativity. In a short time interval the evaluation of innovation in symbolic behavior is difficult if not impossible; a stable evaluation can only be achieved by a kind of *evolutionary selection*. This "selection" is the sum of millions of single decisions and the statistical flow they trigger generally has a non-linear character. If an innovation has not achieved a minimal amount of recognition after a period of time, it will be forgotten and lost. Even if this innovation would have achieved a high selective value in the long run, it cannot be chosen, because it has disappeared from the choice "table" before the process of long-term selection could be applied to it. In this situation collective memory in ritual, mythical form or in a continuous line of transmission between father and son / mother and daughter / teacher and pupil, in modern time by libraries, museums, and schools are like a store (memory) of symbolic innovation. They enable the recovery of former innovations if properly used. The individual innovator must be able to accumulate an amount of innovative force *and* to have it perceived and accepted, in order to have a non-zero effect on the cultural dynamics in his society. As the cultural memory reacts primarily to contemporary forces (supported by living innovators and their surrounding social field), the chance of going beyond the critical point of acceptance diminishes with time. Final integration into the canon, say of artwork, thus depends on a super-critical effect in the lifetime of the artist *and* a major (permanent) effect on the long-term memory of the culture in which he lived. If this culture undergoes dramatic or even catastrophic changes, these innovations are often lost temporarily or forever. Thus, the Renaissance rediscovered classical philosophy, architecture, literature, etc., and defined a new measure of evaluation depending on this rediscovery.

Linguistic innovation is a much more collective process than innovation in art, but it also depends statistically on individual innovators. There are three major differences:

1. Almost everybody in a linguistic community contributes to linguistic innovation, as everybody speaks and makes spontaneous adaptations of the socially accepted system in the situation of use. However, Labov (2001: Part C) has shown, that there are groups of innovators, leaders of linguistic change. The community is mostly not aware of the effect and the role of innovators and therefore linguistic change seems to be governed by some mysterious "hidden hand".

2. Linguistic innovations are not rewarded or punished by the group in the same way that scientific or artistic innovations are. Nevertheless, they result in a certain amount of prestige, as when someone exploits an innovative capacity to be entertaining in conversation, convincing in commerce or politics, argumentatively dominating in court or in other decision-making bodies. In these cases, language use becomes a rhetorical skill, a (verbal) art and linguistic creativity is "paying".

3. On an evolutionary timescale (say of 100 ky) what counts are the global changes which are produced. Thus, an increase in the lexicon from 3 or 4 referentially stable calls (for apes) to a set of 50 calls with internal structure (basic compositionality) is a dramatic step. If instead of 50 calls, 5,000 basic lexemes, and a resultant huge number of possible sentences are in use, this constitutes another dramatic shift. This means that there are quantitative thresholds typical for any type of symbolic form (language, art, science, etc.). Further research should specify the thresholds typical for the single symbolic forms. In order to cross such a threshold, a new type of organization must emerge, which often requires a new level of cognitive ability,

e.g., a higher level of consciousness and new techniques of stability control (in order to avoid the chaotic effects of higher levels of self-organization).

In large civilizations, a corpus of memorized myths, stories and rituals may be assembled and literate civilizations can fix this repertoire permanently. This leads to a new level at which not the lexicon but the canon of texts incorporates the major results of cultural dynamics (together with art, law, and technology). In the 21st century, human rights, monetary equivalences, global markets, the language of science, and massentertainment are candidates for a further level on the hierarchy of symbolic forms or global media of communication (cf. Chapter 9). Any symbolic innovation must be analyzed in this context, because there are clear dependencies that may in the simplest (linear) case look like those illustrated in Table 6.6.

The innovations on level A may or may not be relevant for level B; thus written languages and literary traditions can shape the cultural canon in B, without reaching the global level C. Innovation in art, music, or science may contribute to a "world civilization" by selecting features from a set of civilizations while rejecting others (at level B). From A to B to C the amount of pluralism will normally increase, i.e., rather incoherent pieces must be integrated to new wholes (at the levels B and C). This requires a loss of specificity in terms of information and aesthetic value such that only basic innovations can achieve global acceptance, because coherence and gestalt-integration is easier to achieve for rather elementary symbolic patterns which control the dynamics of complex dynamical systems (otherwise these systems tend to become fractal and devolve into chaos).

For the same reason, linguistic innovations in *one* of the written languages and *a fortiori* in unwritten languages as well have only a minimal effect on level B and C. Innovations in world-languages and, even more so, in the universal

Table 6.6 Hierarchy of innovation

		C
		Innovation in the global symbolic flow (global world)
	B	
	Innovation in the corpus of cultural texts (civilization)	
A		
Linguistic innovation (language community)		

"language" of the natural sciences and technology, in mathematics and information technology, have a deeper impact on level C. Therefore innovations in natural science and technology, which have clear-cut standards of evaluation (selection), tend to be transmitted more easily to levels B and C than linguistic innovation. The hierarchy A>B>C in Table 6.6 illustrates an ongoing evolutionary process which has the evolution of language as its baseline and increases the complexity and globalization achieved by natural languages in the late Paleolithic period. The proper understanding of language evolution may help us to guess further steps and possibly to evaluate (perhaps modify) ongoing processes in the globalization of human communication.

"Fossils" of evolution in the lexicon of HAND and EYE (mainly in German, English and French)

7.1 Preliminary remarks on morphological continuity, linguistic "fossils" and conceptual development

A direct path to an understanding of the evolution of language can be laid by uncovering the steps in the process through which it passed between 7 my, when our evolutionary line bifurcated from the "tree" of primates, and the current situation. The anatomical and behavioral changes, the context of selection and major functions and adaptations must be determined with a view to reconstructing a continuous path of evolution compatible with the principles of evolutionary biology and modern genetics. On this thorny path many sources have to be assessed, many lacunas to be filled by reconstruction and reassessed where new data are available. Still it is, methodologically speaking, the straightest path to take and so I have exploited all relevant data in the Chapters 2 to 5 in order to provide a maximally coherent picture.

In Chapter 6 I made a detour from this direct path and considered historical information (in the history of art and of science) and synchronic research on lexical innovation in order to find basic principles of symbolic creativity relevant for our understanding of evolutionary innovation.

In this chapter the lexicon (and basic syntax) of living languages is the background for reflections on the evolution of language. This strategy of research presupposes a continuity in the evolution of language such that effects of it show up in actual language use and in their grammars. Jackendoff (2002: 206) calls the corresponding phenomena "fossils" of linguistic evolution:

> But in addition – and I take this to be a major innovation – in some instances, I will be able to show, not just that these earlier stages are still present in the brain, but that their "fossils" are present in the grammar of modern language itself, offering a new source of evidence on this issue. (Jackendoff 2002: 236)

As a consequence Jackendoff breaks the "grammar box" of UG (universal grammar) into constituents that may have evolved in different periods and under different constraints. In this line of thought (cf. also Chapter 8), the lexicon becomes a parallel component rather independent from, and possibly more basic than syntax. The third parallel layer would be a phonological one (cf. Jackendoff 2002: 12). The lexical component serves as an interface between phonology and syntax and it consists mainly "of a collection of skeletal fragments of l-rules (lexicalized rules, the author) built into lexical memory" (ibidem: 191).

Any grammar of a natural language is therefore not only a possible result of evolution, but it also contains an implicit record of major principles operative in human evolution. Insofar as analogies resulting from evolutionary processes in nature are accessible to common human experience they should reappear in human language (as the treasure trove of human knowledge). From this perspective one has to look at contemporary languages in order to uncover morphological principles which have been operative throughout the evolutionary process and which in a sense surface in the organization of language.[1]

Some physical analogies between humans, apes, mammals, animals in general and even plants are so obvious that they are also encoded in the lexicon of human languages, mainly appearing in the lexicon of terms for body-parts (nouns) and bodily activities (verbs). One could say that by encoding such analogies, the lexicon of human languages also encodes a naïve "theory" of evolution. The first semanticist who explicitly included an evolutionary dimension in his work on lexical semantics was probably Thomas Ballmer (cf. Ballmer 1982; Ballmer & Brennenstuhl 1986). He related the classification of verbs, mainly their complexity in terms of valence (or argument structure) to the evolution of behaviors from single-cell organisms to humans.[2] Our view in this chapter is less ambitious: Humans perceive basic relations between entities and processes which are the result of evolution as they have an intuition of the fundamental unity of the existing world. In some cases this intuition may even be called a folk-theory of evolution. This basic knowledge is expressed in the semantics of natural languages. The following Sections 7.2 and 7.3 unfold this intuition, whereas Section 7.4 draws some theoretical consequences. Syntactic patterns which may be derived from the lexicon of HAND and EYE are considered in the Sections 7.5 and 7.6.

A further remark concerns the conceptual development of children that prepares and guides the transition to language acquisition. Piaget showed in 1926 that in the first developmental phase, which he called *sensorimotor*, the child perceives an object such as a ball in the context of actions, like rolling the ball, looking at it, or grasping it. In the first stage, the object 'ball' ceases to exist in the consciousness of the child as soon as the act ends (or if the child's attention moves elsewhere). The object-schema begins to exist when this dependence on the immediate action-scheme decreases; the child in this stage of development may then be observed to come back to the object, continue to interact with it; or to search for the object if it is hidden, etc. Nevertheless, the link between action-schema and object-schema is not completely lost after further developmental steps have been taken. Parallel to the separation of object-schema and action-schema the "symbol" (in Piaget's use of the term) is created when the child is able to handle her/his representation of the object or action by imitation in a game and he/she learns words, which allow the expression and social communication of the symbol. In his analysis of mental images, Piaget makes a sharp distinction between verbal signs, which signify concepts, and (mental) images, which signify objects (cf. Piaget 1966). The images remain polyvalent and highly individual whereas the verbal signs have a quasi-objective character because they are regulated by social rules, which eliminate or minimize individual variations. Some of Piaget's ideas may be reformulated in the context of ecological semantics (cf. Gibson 1966; Wildgen 1994). The objects in our environment have specific valences ("affordances"), which are discovered in the process of the child's cognitive development. As Kurt Lewin (cf. Lewin 1936) showed, the "significance" of the child's environment changes dramatically for a child who can grasp, crawl or walk. Cognitive development has, therefore, a basis in the affordances of the environment relative to the state of bodily development. In Piaget's terms, the child cognitively assimilates the affordances of the environment and accommodates his or her cognitive faculties to it. In a similar vein, the evolution of languages depended on the features of an environment, which changed in the course of human evolution and to a lower degree as an effect of human evolution (this effect was rather small before large populations appeared). Linguistic categories and devices had to cope with the expansion and differentiation of environmental perception and action. As many of these affordances are still existent, the internal logic of the evolutionary process is itself within the reach of human perception and categorization and language may represent indirectly evolutionary processes.

In the following sections, I will give an "evolutionary" account of a lexical field centered in terms like: hand, eye (Engl.), *Hand, Auge* (German) and *main, oeil* (French). "Evolutionary" will mean in this context that the users of these languages refer to a folk-knowledge of the evolutionary links between the referents of different readings of these words, i.e., they implicitly refer to analogies and homologies which presuppose an evolutionary connection between the named entities. Between the referents, e.g., body parts and the specific lexical meanings of *eye, oeil* and *Auge* etc I assume a tertium comparationis, called the concept EYE (capital letters indicate this abstract level, which refers neither to a lexical entity in a given language nor to specific ontological entities like body parts).

7.2 A comparative analysis of the object-category HAND in different languages

The historical development of the lexical labels for HAND and the polysemy of their readings can tell us a story about the underlying categorical perception of the complex field of objects and events linked to HAND. In order to uncover the order hidden behind this lexical field I must first review its etymology and the paths of morphological derivation starting from the concept of HAND.

Although the object <hand> is a universal one, different groups of Indo-European languages have different etyma: The English and German: hand/Hand have correspondent forms in older languages: Middle German/Old German: hant; Old Saxonian: hond; Old Nordic: hond; Gothic: handus. Specific relations exist to verbs like Gothic: hinÞan = to catch; and to English: hunt; German: Hund (dog).

The French word *main* is related to Latin *manus*; and the same etymon appears in Italian/Spanish mano; Rumanian: mina; Catalan: ma; Portuguese: mão. Some words with the component *manus* had already been shaped in Latin and were then transferred to Romance languages. Example: French: demain (meaning: tomorrow; from oldfr.: demaneis) < Lat.: de manu ipsu (directly at hand, immediate). Other words were adapted later from Latin roots, like French: manette, manier, maniable, remanier, manière, menotte. From Latin derivations other words have been developed in French:

> manica → manche; mendare → demander, commander, mandat
> mancers → émanciper; mancus → manquer; manualis → manuel, etc.

In English and German, we find words derived from Latin manus. Thus we have in German: Manifest, Maniküre, Manipulation, Manual, manuell, Manuskript; in English: mandate, maneuver, manicure, manifest, manipulate. Words from the Latin root like *manage* (manager) sometimes appear in contexts contrasted with words from the Germanic root like *handle, handling*. Some of these derivations are more complicated and involve several stages. In total, one can observe a rather broad field of historical developments based on the two roots: Latin = manus and Germanic (e.g., Gothic) = handus.

In order to show the synchronic values of *main* I will sketch the range of uses current in French. These examples are mainly based on the dictionary "Petit Robert" which distinguishes three major classes of usage:

I. As a part of the human body. This first and largest group I is further subdivided into four basic subgroups:

   1. The human hand in specific functions such as: (1) touching, (2) grasping, (3) pointing and other gestured movements, (4) taking and giving, (5) working, (6) hitting.
   2. The human hand used to differentiate positions, i.e., for local prepositions: à main, de main (morte), en main, entre les mains, sous main.
   3. Abstractions expressed through a symbolic connection to the concept hand: action, liberty, possession, authority, marriage, work (oeuvre).
   4. Terms connected with card games and board games.

II. Similar body-parts in vertebrates and even in plants.

III. Analogical usages of a more general kind.

In German and English, many of these types reappear. Of specific interest are prepositional and adverbial locutions, because by means of these one may observe the lexical item "hand" in the process of grammaticalization, which means that rather general, abstract features are extracted from current use of the term "hand". In Merriam Webster's Dictionary of English, we find the "meanings" enumerated in Table 7.1.

In German some readings of HAND are on their way to a purely grammatical function, i.e., they are part of an adverbial or prepositional entity and have lost the basic (nominal) meaning of "Hand".

In order to achieve a comprehensive picture of these usages one has to start from a basic gestalt which relates spatial forms (our own hand which we can see and control by our movements in space) and the typical and important functions such as: touch, grasp, gestural communication, exchange (take, give), hit, and manufacture, manipulate etc. Irrespective of the external objects <hands> and their dynamics, one observes two lines in the evolution of multiple readings.

First, *contexts* of use are "caught" into phrasal locutions, which tend to confer a specific contextual meaning on the concept HAND. This evolution is

Table 7.1 Sixteen different adverbial readings of hand in Merriam Webster's Dictionary

at hand (1)	near in time or place within reach	at hand (2)	currently receiving attention
by hand (1)	hand-worked implement	by hand (2)	from one individual directly to another
in hand 1 in hand 3	in one's possession under consideration	in hand 2	in preparation
on hand 1 on hand 3	in present possession or readily available in attendance: present	on hand 2	about to appear: pending
out of hand 1 out of hand 3	without delay or deliberation out of control	out of hand 2 out of hand 4	done with: finished with the hands (eat)
to hand 1	into possession	to hand 2	within reach

Table 7.2 Adverbial and pronominal readings of German Hand

German reading	Translation	German reading	Translation
linker Hand:	on the left	rechter Hand:	on the right
von der Hand (gehen):	easily	vor der Hand:	now
Hand in Hand:	co-operatively		
anhand von:	on the basis of		
zu Händen von:	to the attention of (used in business correspondence)	zur Hand:	at hand

evident in the use of HAND for specific purposes. Thus Webster's Unabridged Dictionary mentions very specific, technical readings of HAND:

> 25. Mach. The deviation of a screw or gear, as seen from one end looking away towards the other. 26. Building Trades. A. The position of the hinges of a door, in terms of right and left, as seen from outside the building, room, closet, etc., to which the doorway leads. B. The position of the hinges of a casement sash, in terms of right and left, from inside the window.   (Webster 1989:641c)

In French, one finds specific uses in the context of games: avoir/faire la main, être à la main. This means in the game called "baccarat": deal the cards, have the bank. In German, die *tote Hand* means in a juridical context that some institution does not have the right to sell or to leave its property. This process may be called "context extraction". A specific contextual meaning is "frozen" into a lexical reading.

Another process is *grammaticalization*. The choice of lexical readings is concentrated into some adverbial or prepositional usage. On the one hand, lexical specificity is lost in this process, while on the other hand the stereotypical small expressions created may be used in many different contexts and thus achieve a high level of frequency. From a diachronic perspective, they may even be integrated into a morphological paradigm.

The fact that the prototypical and basic referents of HAND occupy a prominent place in the *evolution* of human beings and of their semiotic capacities seems to enable a rich network of readings which organize many areas of human knowledge from body parts of animals and parts of plants to social activities, technical relations, games etc. The implicit evolutionary knowledge coded in the lexicon helps to optimize our lexicalized knowledge base.

At the phenomenological level, the gestalt, with its *shape and dynamics*, plays a dominant role. The shape-component may be easily observed if we compare the transition between: human hand, the hand of primates, apes, the "hands" of horses, and to the technical variants, e.g., the hands of a clock. The domain of biological variance may be modeled by a topological transformation of the contours of <hand>, as shown in Figure 7.1 (the zoological classification is not centered in the human hands as the lexical field is).

A second major phenomenological field concerns *parts and wholes*. Thus <hand> is a part of <arm>, <body> and has as proper parts <finger>, <thumb>, <middle finger>, <nail>, etc. (cf. Wilkins 1996; Wildgen 1999b: 50–55). The phenomenological field of the referents of *hand, Hand, main* is the domain in which the object-schema is defined. It has general features based on the objective appearance of <hands> and the natural part-whole relationships. It may also have a cultural/linguistic profile consisting of an emphasis on certain aspects of the object-schema, which in turn serve as the basis for conceptual constructs and figures of speech particular to a certain language. Thus we must distinguish the general object-schema of <hand> and the culturally specific object-schema. The linguistic consequences of culturally specific object-schemata show up in typical metonymies and metaphors used in a language community (or even in a multilingual area, which shares cultural object-schemata). The analyses of metaphors proposed by Lakoff & Johnson (1980) may be understood as a contribution to cultural semantics in this sense.

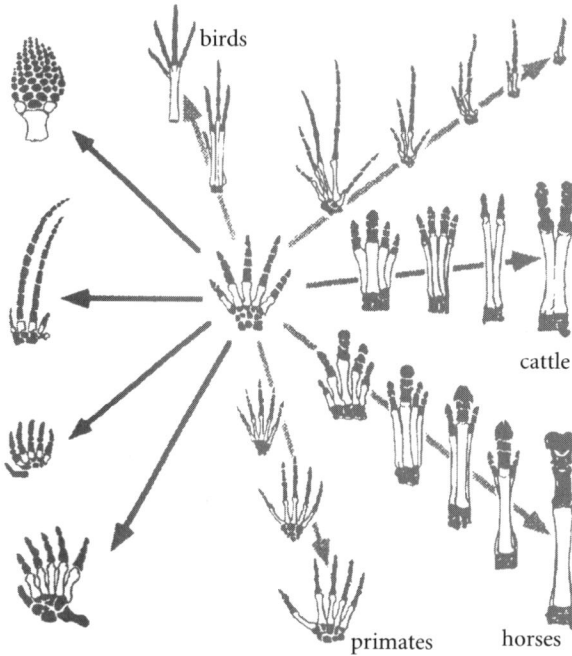

Figure 7.1 Different evolutionary lines of <hands> related to an archetype (in the center), and the specific line of primates (cf. Riedl 1980)

7.3 A comparative analysis of the object category EYE

The <hand> is part of a limb, i.e., of the body periphery. It is a point of contact with the environment and therefore highly adapted to the dynamics of its environment. The <eye> (with its concept: EYE realized as: eye, Auge, oeil) has a different bodily context; it is located in the face, where sensory and communicative "windows" of the body have been concentrated in mammal and primate evolution. It may even be seen as part of the brain, insofar as the first layers of the retina and the projection fibers to the occipital visual centers perform classificatory and organizational tasks typical for the brain. The visual perception of depth is already a kind of internal simulation of an external fact, so that David Marr (1982) has called human vision $2\frac{1}{2}$ dimensional. These basic facts make clear that <eyes> have a different bodily embedding and different functions than <hands>, and this difference should show up in the lexical organization of the concept EYE.

The hands have a dynamically associated pair of limbs, the feet; in locomotion their rhythm is coordinated, although they do not serve the same functions.[3] The eyes are associated with the pair of ears, which are also highly integrated into the brain. The two systems: hands–feet and eyes–ears are again linked in the sensomotoric system, i.e., they manage intentional mobility in space.

If <hand> links the body to its environment, <eye> links the body (and its environment) to the mind. Together the two pairs of body parts constitute the functional "skeleton" of human ecological adaptation. The prominent role of hands and eyes for primate cognition is evolutionarily very old. Together they allow an almost complete model of the external world at short and long distance. The ear and the vocal system cover the medium range and are thus a kind of compromise or overlapping zone, whereas olfaction and taste allow only for partial and specialized models of the environment (in humans); cf. Quiatt and Reynolds (1993: 120ff.). I shall analyze the semasiological and the phenomenological (often called "onomasiological") field of EYE and its consequences for verbal frames in the same fashion as I did for HAND.

All three lexical items, *eye, Auge, oeil,* have a common root in the group of Indo-European languages. In contrast to the etymological situation of HAND, the families of Indo-European languages share the same etymon for EYE. In the Germanic languages we find: Gothic: augô; Old Nordic: auga; Anglo-Saxon: éage; Middle English: eie, ýe. In contemporary Germanic languages the corresponding items are: English: eye; German: Auge; Dutch: oog; Danish: oje; Norwegian: oye.

In other Indo-European language families we have: Latin: oculus; Greek: *oγγε*; Old Slavonic: oko; Lithuanian: akís; Sanskrit: aksi (the Indo-European root is: *ok). The French *oeil* is derived from Latin: *oculus* (acc. oculum). Other Romance languages, including Rumanian, Italian, Catalan, Spanish and Portuguese, have derivations from the same root. Many of the readings illustrated by the usage of modern French are also observable in Latin and Greek. The lexical field shows a high degree of diachronic stability, which may be explained by the naturalness of the basic dimensions of its organization (see below). Other concepts for body parts with common roots in Indo-European languages are: HEART, FOOT, KNEE, ARM, etc.

On the synchronic level, the three languages used for comparison here show a similar organization of the field and I shall summarize the basic structure.

In French (Petit Robert), four groups of readings are distinguished (oeil, sg., yeux, pl.):

I. A basic and large group with meanings linked to the human (animal) <eye>. Six subdivisions of group I concern:

The perceptual organ	In a medical context the Latin and Greek roots lead to: oculaire, ophthalmologie, ophtalmoscopie.
Vision in general	Avoir une chose devant ses yeux (to have something in the eyes, i.e., in the mind); by extension: Jeter le mauvais oeil (lit. 'throw a bad eye', i.e., put the evil eye on someone).
Rapid perception/understanding	Un coup d'oeil (a stroke of the eye; i.e., a moment).
Attention	Ce qui frappe et attire l'oeil (What strikes and attracts the eye).
Attitude, judgment	D'un oeil critique (With a critical eye).

Other types of idiomatic expressions

II. Technical objects may be called *oeil* for their similarity with shape and function of <eye>.

oeil de verre	glass eye
oeil électrique	photoelectric cell
oeil magique	magical eye in radio

III. A whole range of readings is connected to group I by an analogy of shape:

oeil d'une aiguille	*« eye » of a needle*
oeil poussant	*bud*
oeil de la lettre	*technical term in printing*
oeil du cyclone, and others	*meteorological term, eye of the storm*

In group III, some of the readings are distinguished by forming a regular plural: *oeil–oeils*, whereas the main group of readings has the irregular plural *oeil–yeux*.

Considering the German and English examples could further differentiate this list. In general, it shows a rather simple organization. There is one basic function: *vision*. From vision, secondary functions like perception, attention, attitude, judgment, emotion, and emotional signaling are derived. This type of organization is shown in Group I. The readings in Group II exploit the analogies of shape and appearance. We can summarize the analysis so far by proposing two basic scales.

The prominent function of vision is unfolded into one basic dimension reaching from external perception (direction of the look), becoming aware of or attentive to something, to conscious actions like: perceiving, recognizing, understanding, evoking attitudes and emotions, communicating emotional reactions. The different readings seem to be more coherent than in the case of HAND and this has to do with the compactness of the body-part <eye>, i.e., it cannot be divided conceptually into different parts as obviously as can the <hand>.

A second dimension concerns the shape and appearance of <eye>, its parts and bodily neighbors. This dimension will be further analyzed in the following. The <eye> is a highly specified organ, which is the result of evolutionary adaptations over many millions of years. The functional analogies inherent in a lexical usage allow application of the concept EYE simultaneously to humans, mammals, vertebrates, fishes, and insects. These analogies seem to exclude distributed quasi-visual capacities of organisms like bacteria and algae, which allows for the conclusion that a concentrated, extremely sensitive organ of vision is the functional basis. This line includes organs like that of the cuttlefish which are not evolutionarily related to our eye, but do realize a similar solution to the same problem of how an organism can concentrate vision in one or two central organs, with extremely high sensitivity and recognition power.

In the domain of the human eye the central part, the eyeball, is very small and light (depth: 24 mm; weight: 7 g; volume: 6, 5 ml). Most of it is hidden in the cranium. The visible parts are: the pupil, the iris, the cornea (internal parts), the eyelid, the eyelash, and the surrounding parts of the face (external parts). Some of the readings of EYE refer to a hole. The pupil, which is the entrance of light into the inner eye, realizes the schema of a hole. In some cases, the oblong shape of the open eye is taken as reference as in the following readings:

- a hole through the head of a needle,
- a loop or catch to receive a hook,
- an undeveloped bud (as in a potato),
- a triangular piece of beef cut from between the top and the bottom of a round.

Both geometrical shapes (circular opening/oblong opening) may be further generalized as in: 'the eye of the problem'. In the case of the "evil eye", the stationary pupil in a longer and stable glance without motion of the pupil is thought to establish a connection of force and magical power.

7.4 The synergetics of hand and eye, ear and mouth as dynamic threshold for higher symbolic behavior

The eyes and hands (feet) had to be coordinated in monkey locomotion in the trees (e.g., for three-dimensionally exact grasping). The ear and the mouth were coordinated for calls in the whole evolutionary line of hominoids. Nevertheless, this coordination reached a new level, when motor-learning was further elaborated through the evolution of mirror-neurons and enhanced motor-learning and when acoustic discrimination and categorization was coordinated with the control of oral motor-behavior. In both cases the precise perceptual categorization (eyes, ears) is linked to a quick and precise motor planning (hands, mouth). The motor-skills of the hands were freed from locomotion functions since the evolution of up-rise-locomotion and the mouth was freed from heavy biting in attack/defense or in the mastication of hard plant food with little energy concentration (which enforced hours of intensive mastication). In both cases the loss of functional load of motor-organs left space for new, in this case communicative functions. In a parallel, perhaps causally linked evolution, the growth of the brain gave space for more highly specified perceptual and motoric processing. In a general rule, the capacity of sensorimotor control and performance was dramatically increased in the evolution of man.

If we concentrate on the feature "coordination of different subsystems" we enter the theoretical field of "synergetics": "Basic to this idea is the concept that by the cooperation of individual parts, new qualities emerge via self-organization" (cf. Haken 1996:33). Simple physiological synergetic systems are those systems, which show motor-system internal coordination such as phase transitions in finger movements (cf. Haken 1996; Chapter 6.2) or animal gaits and their transitions (ibidem:Chapter 9). In these cases, two fingers of the hands (of the same body) or the four legs of a horse or another animal moving with four legs are "slaved" by forces which make that two, three or four different rhythms appear regularly depending on the level of energy (speed). They may be modified by learning/training and even acquire new emerging modes or repress others. In general they have a very low level of order (number of different stable solutions) in spite of the enormous number of possible intermediate orders, semi-orders or of the permanent danger of chaos (infinite periods of order).

There is a related question as to how perceptual categorization and motor-programs which inherently coordinate a large number of muscles are synergetically coupled. It is much more complex because the two systems, perceptual categorization and modes of motion, respond to physiologically different organizations which are not per se governed by similar principles. It is only *coevolution*, i.e., an evolutionary pressure to cooperate, that could link these dynamic subsystems. As we have shown, the two systems <hands> and <eyes>, manual motor-programs vs. visual perception have a place on a behavioral scale from: thought/will, imagination, perception (sight) → towards interaction with other agents (i.e., in the act of giving/taking), action on objects, prehension, motion. This pragmatic scale causes the different fields on this scale to respond to a unitary pragmatic goal: *Respond quickly and exactly to an environment by acting with the help of the hands controlled by the eyes.* As the evolution of tools since 2 my BP shows, the coordination and learning/teaching of a high coordination level of hand and eye was the earlier stage; only later, when this level of synergetic organization had stabilized did the second system of mouth/ear evolve further and transform the call-systems into something we call a protolanguage. The necessary condition was an integrated quick (learned) recognition of sound (syllable) sequences and their precise enactment by the articulatory organs. In a sense which has to be analyzed further, the advance in self-organization of the synergetic system <hand> / <eye> had to be transferred to the domain of communication centered on the physiological system <mouth> / <ear>. In a further step the symbolic capacity was further transferred to the old and very proficient system <hand> / <eye> in body painting, stone-engraving and finally cave-art. In the Neolithic period with the rise of highly organized civilization and higher density of population (and thus of communication) a system of book-keeping and conservation of texts was developed which led to the (cultural) evolution of writing. Although writing is such a recent cultural technique that it could not shape our biological disposition for it (cf. the many difficulties encountered in counteracting illiteracy in large populations and phenomena like dyslexia), it combines the older system of the synergetic coordination of <hand> and <eye> with the more recent one of articulated language (<mouth> / <ear>). Today almost any kind of cerebrally controlled motion-behavior (even blinking with the eyes) can be used to support a linguistically organized communication. Thus linguistic performance seems to be independent from the modes of sign production and reception. But this is neither statistically true, as verbal communication (<mouth> / <ear>) still dominates the field of human communication nor is it true in an evolutionary sense, because the basic bodily predispositions for linguistic communication have been refined by the synergetic system <mouth> / <ear> in coevolution with the prior system <hand> / <eye>. The dispute about a priority of gestured language over phonic language could be resolved by saying that even if no comparable gestured language existed before the phonic protolanguage evolved, still the synergetic system of <hand> / <eye> which evolved earlier was a physiological/cerebral precondition for the transition between simple call systems to a phonetically complex protolanguage.

The highly elaborated lexicon for the body parts <hand> and <eyes> reflects the functional relevance and proximity of the two systems to the linguistic system in which they are encoded. In this sense the lexicon "refers" to the evolution of human language (indexically) as it contains traces of an evolutionary hierarchy translated into a relevance hierarchy, which then shapes the level of lexical elaboration and metaphorical exploitation.

7.5   The lexicon of HAND and EYE as a starting point for syntactic deep structures

From a phenomenological perspective, the concept HAND is associated by most language users with something moved by the will (in newborns by inborn motor programs) and which has an intentional vector. It presupposes an outside object which is touchable, graspable, and may be given or taken. That object should afford certain actions being performed upon it. The intentional vectors open a range of process-scenarios, which link the basic (evolutionary shaped) capacities of <hand> and certain elements of the environment which are afforded by their size, stiffness, etc., being objects of the activity of <hand>. This phenomenological and intentional context defines a gestalt constituted by an agent (centre of the will, starting point of the intentional vector), and an object which by its size and consistency (perceptual attractiveness) allows for being touched, grasped, thrown, given, taken, shown.

In a second step, <hand> is perceived as a mediating force between the agent and the object; therefore it is conceptually connected to the role of an instrument. If a culturally shaped instrument replaces some operation of the <hand>, e.g., a hammer, the intentional vector is extended towards a noninstrumental object. Thus the stable role which we call INSTRUMENT enters the grammatical system. It shares features of <hand> and of its objects. This process of dynamic/intentional unfolding can be repeated. In Table 7.3 the unfolding process is schematized.

This unfolding of the dynamics and intentionality of <hand> can be linked to syntactic devices like morphological case, thematic hierarchies (e.g., subject prominence), and word-order regularities. If we take syntactic patterns, we can

Table 7.3 The emergence of semantic roles out of the concept of HAND

First Stage:	HAND is an autonomous entity (driven by an inborn mechanism).
Second Stage:	Emergence of the dynamic vector: AGENT – HAND (movable at will)
Third Stage:	Emergence of the intentional vector, which elaborates the dynamic one by attributing Source (self) and Goal (object) to it: AGENT (self) – HAND – OBJECT (goal)
Fourth Stage:	Prominence of the instrumental function by merging some features of HAND and some of its objects: AGENT–HAND–INSTRUMENT–OBJECT (goal) (self) (inalienable) (alienable) (alienable) (source of intention) $\rightarrow$ $\rightarrow$ (goal of intention)
Fifth Stage and further stages:	The primary instrument may unfold into a series of instruments, which allow for the transition of the initial intentional energy to the intentional object, its final goal.

compare sentences of different quantitative complexity (distributed over the subject, the verbal phrase and the nominal phrase) as in:

Hands up!
Put your hands up! (you – hands)
Take the hot bread in your hand! (you – bread – hand)
You should cut the bread with the knife in your hand! (you – bread – hand – knife)

I will consider the typical verbal frames into which the object-schema of EYE is fitted. It has, as I said, two basic dimensions: the perceptual–cognitive–emotional function and the contours of different parts of <eye>. The three languages considered show the following idiomatic locutions with EYE as constituent:

Table 7.4 Idiomatic locutions in English (Unabridged Webster)

have an eye for (appreciate)	have eyes only for (admire)
keep one's eye open (alert)	keep an eye out for (be vigilant)
lay, clap, set eyes on (see)	make eyes at (gaze amorously at)
open one's eyes (become aware)	pipe one's eyes (weep)
run one's eyes over (examine quickly)	shut one's eyes to (refuse to see)

In this short list, EYE stands syntactically in the object position and has as implicit or explicit background the self (cf. one's). The German lexicon (Duden, CD-ROM) lists a few constructions with EYE in subject-position: die *Augen waren größer als der Magen* (someone's eyes were bigger than their stomach), *da bleibt kein Auge trocken* (there wasn't a dry eye in the place), *jmdm. gehen die Augen auf/über* (someone's eyes were opened to...), *jmds. Augen brechen* (some one has died). These constructions imply an agent (who has eyes) as background. The other examples show EYE in object position (N = 30) or in a prepositional phrase (N = 22). The examples where EYE appears in a prepositional phrase use the following prepositions:

Prepositional head: *in* (number of items N = 10): jmdm. stehen die Tränen im Auge (the tears stand in someone's eyes); etwas springt/fällt ins Auge (something springs/falls into the eye)

Prepositional head: *mit (N = 7)*: etwas mit bloßem Auge sehen können (*to see something with the naked eye*); etwas mit den Augen verfolgen/verschlingen (*to follow/eat something with the eyes*); mit offenen Augen schlafen (*to sleep with open eyes*).

Prepositional head: *aus (N = 2)*: jmdn. nicht aus den Augen lassen/verlieren (not letting someone or something get out of sight); jmdn. aus den Augen verlieren (lit. to loose someone out of the eyes, i.e., get out of touch, loose track of someone).

Prepositional head: *um–willen (N = 1)*: etwas nicht um jmds. schöner blauer Augen willen tun (lit. to do something not just because of his/her pretty blue eyes, i.e., used ironically to assert that one can't be expected to do something for nothing).

In prepositional phrases which are not governed by the valence of the verb the following idiomatic expressions were found: *in*: Aug in Aug (eye to eye); *um*: Auge um Auge (an eye for an eye); *unter*: unter vier Augen (lit. under four eyes, i.e., between two people only, privately); *vor*: vor aller Augen (lit. in front of every eye, i.e., publicly, openly). The prepositions *in* and *aus* use the image of a ray (of vision) which comes out of the eye or enters it, i.e., they illustrate a folk-view of vision, which corresponds to the classical theory still accepted by Descartes. The preposition *mit* is either instrumental, or it is comitative/ornative. The last example with *um–willen* (in favor of) exemplifies a benefactive use. In French some of these idiomatic expressions reappear (e.g., pour les beaux yeux de qqn, avoir l' oeil sur qqn, faire de l'oeil à qqn).

If we compare the translations of German idiomatic expressions with EYE into French and vice versa (based on Harrap's Weiss Mattutat 1981), we can distinguish four types of correlations: direct mapping: *oeil/yeux–Auge/n*;

derivations from *oeil* or *Auge*, abstracta like *vue*, *Blick*, etc. (vision), metonymic correlates like *pupil*, *eyelid* or *face*. The results of the comparison are shown in Table 7.5.

Although the direct correlates make up only 29,5% respectively 15% of the sample, we see that in the case: GERMAN→FRENCH 22,7% items are lexically different, in the other case (FRENCH→GERMAN) 50% show an independent lexical choice. The low percentages in French–German translation probably have their source in a specific idiomatic use in French EYE (*oeil*), where emotional meanings are coded based on the vulnerability of the <eye>. This is illustrated in Table 7.6.

In German the expression *etwas/jmdn. wie seinen Augapfel hüten* (to guard something or some one as the apple of your eye) exploits the same aspect, but the corresponding negative perspective is not used in the way it is in French.

Table 7.5 The correlation between German and French locutions with EYE

1. GERMAN EXPRESSIONS TRANSLATED INTO FRENCH		
a. directly correlated	13	29,5%
b. derived correlates	1	2,3%
c. abstract correlates (vision)	15	34,1%
d. metonymical correlates	5	11,4
e. totally different lexical choices	10	22,7
Total:	44	100%
2. FRENCH EXPRESSIONS TRANSLATED INTO GERMAN		
a. directly correlated	6	15%
b. derived correlates	1	2,5%
c. abstract correlates	12	30%
d. metonymical correlates	1	2,5%
e. totally different lexical choices	20	50%
Total:	40	100%

Table 7.6 Comparison of some idiomatic expressions in German, English and French

French idiomatic expression	English expression	German idiomatic expression
je m'en bats l'oeil	it doesn't concern me	das ist mir schnuppe
se mettre le doigt dans l'oeil	to be mistaken	sich irren
se fourrer le doigt dans l'oeil	to put your foot in your mouth	sich gewaltig in die Finger schneiden
coûter les yeux de la tête	to cost an arm and a leg	ein Heidengeld kosten

In this section we have focused on an analysis of idiomatic expressions as they belong like the nominal compounds described in Chapter 6.2 to a zone of transition between lexical items (prototypically simplex words with or without flexional affixes) and *online constructions* (cf. Jackendoff 2002). From an evolutionary perspective, which assumes (cf. Chapter 8) that the protolanguage was basically a system of an economically organized and growing lexicon and pragmatic principles for its contextually adequate use, these quasi-syntactic structures are a point of departure for understanding the emergence of syntax. They still belong to long-term memory (and thus are akin to the lexicon) but have a rich compositional architecture.

7.6 The emergence of a syntactic "machinery"

In the examples treated above (which are far from representative for idiomatic constructions), one observes the unfolding of the referentially motivated valences/affordances of a lexical item (for HAND, EYE) into a construction of the type verb phrase or even (basic) sentence. As the comparison between German and French showed, there are tendencies in common for different languages, but there is also an important drift in the direction of differentiation and specificity. This specificity is even more obvious in the case of idiomatic expressions not related to body parts, i.e., the evolution of constructional complexity even at the level of idioms tends to abolish general, species specific forces and bifurcates into many directions thus blurring the footprints of evolution. We can summarize this point in a further principle:

First post-bifurcation principle
The dynamics underlying lexical compounds (cf. Chapter 6.2) and idiomatic phrases (this chapter) give us hints at the line of linguistic evolution in the period which enlarged the lexicon and evolved a rich compositionality.
     A final question I want to assess has been asked by Jackendoff:

> When did homo sapiens elaborate the 'syntactic tricks' such as long-distance dependencies (the relation between a wh-phrase or topicalized phrase at the front of a clause and its trace elsewhere in the sentence) and the other major types of violation of the Head Constraint ... "   (cf. Jackendoff 2002: 193)

When did all the machinery evolve which has been put into the centre of linguistic research by grammarians in Chomsky's line? If our guess at a possible time scale of linguistic evolution was correct, these features which more or less surface in all existing languages should have been in place when the new species spread over all continents, i.e., at least 100 ky BP. Comparative analysis of syntax could perhaps find further evolutionary steps which arose in different continents (in Australia after 50 or 40 ky BP, in the Americas after 30 or 15 ky BP), but they do not allow us to reconstruct a situation 100 or 200 ky BP. As we have shown that even the first steps towards compositionality in compounds and idioms open the Pandora's box of typological differences, it is rather plausible that something like a universal grammar (basic for complex syntax) never existed. As ongoing comparative work tends to show, one finds almost a kind of "anything goes" in terms of word-classes and grammatical devices and this is not at all astonishing if one considers the migration of modern humans in the last 100 ky and the separation of a basic linguistic community at 200 ky BP, if it ever existed. Nevertheless, I will risk a further hypothesis linked to ideas to be discussed in the next chapter.

Second post-bifurcation principle
Languages after 100 ky BP became less biologically determined (they began to overcome a stricter determination with the rise of learned and culturally transmitted behavior) and are more like social institutions.

In the terminology of Chapter 9, they became like generalized media of communication integrated to a corpus of social rules, rituals, belief-systems, which silently "slave" the social structure of a group, a clan, a network of interacting groups. Only if we reconstruct this life-space (life-form), can we understand the conditions which shaped a specific set of mythic beliefs, ethical principles, law-like rules and grammatical patterns. As a consequence, the explanation of this late stage in the evolution of language is beyond the scope of this book with its basically biological, post-Darwinian perspective and it can only be further advanced if the social ecology of human groups and networks between 200 ky and 10 ky BP are better understood. In Chapter 5 I have touched this zone with reference to Paleolithic art and the cultural evolution leading to writing. These analyses should be deepened in order to find plausible hypotheses for the evolution of the late complexities in the syntax of human languages, which probably exploit the potential inherent in post-protolanguages under the circumstances of a more global network of cultural communication and the institutionalization of discourse, narrative and argument in the beginning civilizations. The effect of this social evolution created those long lasting imprints we were able to analyze in Chapter 5.

7.7 Some methodological conclusions

This analysis of EYE and HAND in English, German and French has demonstrated the existence of different dimensions of the synchronic field (the diachronic aspect has only been sketched) controlled by object-schemata, which include typical dynamic and intentional vectors. The object-schemata select syntactic constructions which have been analyzed on the level of semantic roles and syntactic functions. The analysis has shown that although different roles are realized, the object-schema (with its dimensions and variants) constitutes the basis on which the choice of role-vectors and syntactic constructions can be made. A more complete analysis of syntactic frames and verb valences would have to include other object-schemata co-occurring in the sentence. The object-schemata for body-parts like <eye> and<hand> assume the relevance of several factors:

– The whole body or larger parts of it (the face, the head, the arm, the shoulder).
– The ego as the centre of intentionality (the mind, will, emotion, imagination, memory, etc.).
– The alter ego to which interaction is directed.
– The external objects, which are manipulated, as in the case of HAND, or perceived, as in the case of EYE.
– General contexts of the processes mentioned above such as space-time, society or history.

The examples analyzed in this chapter show that the evolutionary dimension is relevant even for a proper synchronic analysis of the lexicon of natural languages. A fortiori, it is basic for diachronic analyses of meaning shifts and large-scale reanalysis of lexical fields in different families of languages.

This chapter has pointed to the fact that the languages of the world contain in themselves "fossils" of the evolutionary processes which have unfolded and formed the human capacity for the learning, elaboration/change of languages and for their integration into the practical and social life of the community. Implicitly, lexical semantics incorporates folk-theories of the analogy/homology between humans, animals, plants and nonliving entities. Although these folk-theories depend on traditions which are much more short-lived than the evolutionary processes themselves, they mirror the common consciousness of a continuity which unites the whole sensible world humans live in. Thus the study of living languages can contribute to hypotheses on the origin of language. If the methods of linguistic analysis develop further, we may be able to separate different layers of fossilization in the grammars of languages. Our analysis has shown that a good working hypothesis would separate:

- Lexical semantics and inside the lexicon a core which contains terms for body parts (possibly other basic lexical fields).
- Lexical compositionality as shown for compounds (in Chapter 6) and idiomatic phrases as shown in the case of idioms with HAND and EYE.
- Online syntax rooted in valence patterns up to valence three or four.
- Global manner, place and time complements (the TMA component found by Bickerton in Pidgins and Creoles; cf. Chapter 8).

Phonological structures haven't been treated at any length for two reasons:

- Our direct method using the traces of human evolution to derive hypotheses on the symbolic and cognitive steps responsible for the evolution of language did not give access to phonological structures. One must remember that a (poorly) reliable indication of pronunciation was only possible when phonologically based writing systems came into use and technically only with the invention of phonography.
- The basic forces underlying human phonetics and phonology probably reach very far. As Calvin and Bickerton (2000: 110ff.) remarked, the emergence of superior auditive capacities paid off even in the first period when our predecessors began to live in the savannah surrounded by dangerous carnivores. The sophistication of motor control for hand/fingers and memory for complicated sequences of movements was inherited by the system ear/mouth and has its roots beyond the bifurcation at 7 my BP.

On this physiological and cerebral basis a process of self-organization could have formed quasi-automatically the phonetic/phonological capacities children use in order to learn their mother tongue(s) (cf. Chapter 8 for more details). It seems therefore methodologically coherent to separate the phonetic/phonological capacity from the cognitive/semantic capacity and to treat their relative evolutions separately. Moreover, phonology emerges from the basic capacity of (categorical) hearing and quick motor-programs for articulation by way of self-organization and the selective stabilization of its results. Therefore it does not make sense to retain the deep barrier between phonetics and phonology; the latter is just a restriction on the possibilities given by the first; i.e., both form one organizational gestalt. This return to a pre-structuralist position (in fact only the Copenhagen-school followed the axiom of a totally abstract phonology) will allow a more naturalistic view of language and facilitate the application to linguistics of results obtained in the natural sciences.

A future theory of the evolution of complex syntax should probably sooner consider the principles of self-organization inherent in hearing/uttering than the mysterious inborn universal grammar with its strangely sophisticated ad hoc machinery (cf. also Chapter 8.2).

The form of a "protolanguage" and the contours of a theory of language evolution

The idea of a "protolanguage" is as old as are reflections on language. One encounters it in the concept of the "adamic" language, i.e., the language God gave to Adam and by which Adam was able to give names to all beings. In the pre-Darwinian theories of the origin of language, which were not creationist (Condillac, Rousseau, Maupertuis, Herder, a.o.), some basic capability, a language of action and gestures (Condillac), a musical form of expression for passions (Rousseau), the imitation of natural sounds in onomatopoetic words and the capability of reflection (Herder) constituted a point of departure from which specific human forms of communication and language could be further elaborated. Since Darwin's theory of evolution (theoretically even since Lyell's "transformationalism" against Cuvier's "catastrophism") the basic idea behind descriptions of a protolanguage has been that of a continuous evolution (i.e., moving by infinitesimal steps). Applied to language, it derives linguistic capacities in a continuous series of steps from communicational habits and intellectual capacities of mammals (and animals in general). In this perspective, the concept of a protolanguage looses its theoretical foundation, as no specific and stable intermediate level can be assumed. After Darwin, the "protolanguage" can only be a construct for an intermediate stage which helps to fill the gap between animal communication/cognition and human communication/cognition. All hypotheses, even contemporary ones, which assume a sudden "creation" of human language by some mutation popping up risk falling short of the Darwinian revolution.

Recently Derek Bickerton has made proposals for understanding protolanguage. I shall shortly comment on Bickerton's proposal from a methodological perspective. He assumes an internal stratification of human language capacity, which recapitulates (and thus indicates) an evolutionary stratification (cf. Haeckel's law of a recapitulation of evolution in ontogenesis). Basically he presupposes an additive effect of evolution, i.e., early developed forms of behavior persist and constitute the stable platform on which later forms rest. This assumption is roughly plausible for brain architecture but it neglects the (relative) loss of older structures, the interaction between neural structures and change of functions. He formulates his methodology as follows:

> If there indeed exists a more primitive variety of language alongside fully developed human language, then the task of accounting for the origins of language is made much easier. No longer do we have to hypothesize some gargantuan leap from speechlessness to full language, a leap so vast and abrupt that evolutionary theory would be hard to put to account for it.
>
> (Bickerton 1990:128)

The author uses data from Pidgin- and Creole studies (cf. his bioprogram-hypothesis developed in earlier work, e.g., Bickerton 1981; Bickerton et al. 1984), data in primate and child language acquisition and the Kaspar Hauser cases (he discusses the case of Genie, a thirteen year old girl from California, who was "found to be incapable of speech"; Bickerton 1990:115).

Although such a comparative analysis can give interesting insights, I shall not adopt it here. Basically the analysis of human evolution is not harder to account for than other cases of morphological and behavioral evolution (cf. Bickerton's argument above) and any analysis of the evolution of language should strictly follow the general strategy and methodology of post-Darwinian theories (as they are the only theories which survived the progress in this field). In Chapters 4 and 5 I have considered the traces of semiotic activity of hominids and early man until the emergence of writing systems as data for the reconstruction of intermediate forms of human language. This direct strategy has two consequences:

–   Insofar as the contours of early semiotic capacities can be reconstructed from artifacts and art, one can only infer the semantics (perhaps the pragmatics) of an earlier language capacity, not its lexicon or syntax.
–   As the artifacts point rather to the cognitive level than to the level of linguistic expression, the reconstructed semantics must be a type of cognitive semantics (although it differs from those cognitive theories which have no evolutionary dimension; evolutionary question are only discussed in the "blending"-theories of Fauconnier & Turner 2002).

The term: "protolanguage" has under this methodology a different profile (and content). As the evolutionary process is in principle continuous, the term designates a zone between the linguistic capacities of early hominids and modern humans (whose language is documented). In any case we do not assume that a small zone (say some 10 ky) of "synchrony" existed in which a specific "protolanguage" was used. If discrete steps separating one or more proto-levels show up in the data, they should be explained either by the dying out of intermediate species or by rather sudden ecological changes which triggered the realization of some genetic reserve in the chain which reads out, realizes the genetic information of a species. In general the existing empirical evidence is used to make an informed guess for one possible intermediate stage. (The derivation of language capacity directly from physical or chemical base structures without the impact of Darwinian principles as favored by Chomsky is rejected by biologists; cf. Maynard Smith & Szathmáry 1996.) The assumption of one stage is purely methodological; it follows from the fact that the empirical evidence is too scarce to separate a series of intermediate states (for the general scenarios of language evolution and the dating of intermediate stages cf. Chapter 2).

8.1   An informed guess at the form of protolanguage

I shall try to respond to the following questions:

- What is the most plausible evolutionary era in which a protolanguage existed or which may be represented by an (idealized) protolanguage?
- Can artifacts such as stone tools, engravings, paintings tell us something about the cognitive basis of a protolanguage (i.e., as *one* semiotic form among others)?
- Does the anatomical change of hominids give hints as to the shape of a protolanguage?

8.1.1   The plausible time span of a protolanguage

In a classical analysis of mitochondrial DNA by Stoneking and Cann (1989), two lines were distinguished: one leading to genetic variability inside Africa and one leading to all other populations of humans outside Africa. The common ancestor was dated between 142,5 ky and 285 ky BP (assuming a divergence of 2% to 4% per million years), making 200 ky BP a good guess at a plausible time span.[1] This guess fits well with the archeological data. Bräuer (1992) sees the beginning of the line of anatomically modern man around 200 ky BP. As the linguistic capacity is a common heritage of all existing human populations, the date of 200 ky BP could be the date at which the capacity for *language* in modern man had been evolved. An earlier stage and thus a candidate for populations with a *protolanguage* is the Homo erectus: early African Homo erectus is dated around 1,6 my; the separation of African and Asian Homo erectus may be dated to 1,0 my.[2] In one of the evolutionary scenarios the Neanderthals, the archaic Chinese and the Archaic SE-Asian Homo erectus died out and were replaced by modern man.

These considerations leave us with two candidates of populations equipped with a capacity for *language* or *protolanguage*:

1. Ancestors of modern man ($\sim$ 200 ky).
2. Homo erectus populations distributed in Africa, Europe and Asia ($\sim$ 1 my)

The first could be too near to modern man to show significant differences, the second could be too far from humans to have had a comparable language capacity. It is plausible that the ancestor population ($\sim$ 200 ky) was genetically near to modern humans and only a kind of genetic assimilation (cf. the concept of 'Baldwinian evolution' in Bickerton 2000: 264) could have produced changes in language capacity. If the ancestor population is too modern to fit the idea of a protolanguage intermediate between the separation of chimpanzees and humans (a minimum of 5 to 6 my) then the populations of early and advanced Homo erectus (1,6–1,0 my) is a better candidate.[3] If one goes further down to Homo ergaster and Homo habilis, one reaches roughly a period of 2,0 my and one is in the middle of the evolutionary period since earliest hominids ($\sim$ 4,0 my). A basic argument for the language capacity of Homo erectus populations refers to his usage of tools and fire. Therefore, I shall first assess the second of the questions mentioned in the beginning of this chapter, keeping in mind that such a protolanguage could have existed 1 my BP.

8.1.2 Can artifacts tell us something about a protolanguage?

The first stone axes were produced around 2 my, they make up the so-called pebble culture.[4] The pebble culture requires the use of a stone or bone to chock (another) stone, in order to produce a sharp edge on the pebble, i.e., the tool is used to produce a specific shape and is fitted to a large number of uses. Probably other materials (bone, wood, and fur) were again shaped using the primitive stone axes (cf. Chapter 4).

If fire had to be conserved (as in populations found in Tasmania and Australia which rather conserved than reproduced fire), the process of fire had to be controlled. In both cases a control of causation and instrument use (with an iteration of processes of cause-effect control) and as its precondition a *representation* of possible effects, possible shapes and functions had to be mastered. The "Homo Faber", as Bergson called man at this stage, had the cognitive abilities for symbolic representations. The question is: Did he use phonetic language to express these representations or gestures, or neither of these? Some authors favor a motor origin of language, and thus stand in the tradition of Condillac's "langage d'action" (cf. Hewes 1977, who distinguishes a gestural/semantic and a full vocal language, and Quiatt & Reynolds 1993: 266ff.). In this perspective the protolanguage of Homo erectus populations would have been gestural (with holistic phonation as supplement). Lieberman (1989: 409) argues that the rapid evolution of the supra-laryngeal tract in Homo erectus makes an "entirely gestural language unlikely".

Artifacts are not only hints at the cognitive level of humans, they are also linked to social life. In order to produce artifacts and to keep fire, a socially organized exploitation of the environment, a division of labor and a mode of social distribution of products must be in place. This requires rules of collective behavior, and language is the prototype of rule-governed social behavior; it not only helps to represent and enact social behavior, it is *the central* symbolic representation of social behavior (cf. also Habermas' "theory of communicative action" in Habermas 1982).

8.1.3 Anatomical evolution and the shape of a protolanguage

The classical measure, brain size normalized by body weight, reached a critical level necessary for higher cognition with Homo habilis. Brain size is correlated with the size of social groups (cf. Dunbar 1992). Social cognition is linked to a degree of self-other distinction, to a theory of mind, to the possibility of strategic control of action, and control of the social perception of oneself by others. Such an evolution creates the pragmatic capacities which can be worked out and represented in language. The control of a larger area, the use of centers for communal life, the systematic expansion into new areas presupposes high ecological flexibility and a global spatial orientation. It seems therefore highly plausible that the advanced Homo erectus who migrated to Europe and Asia had the cognitive and social capacity for symbol use, i.e., for a language which probably was organized vocally with gestural cues. The power of motor imitation in the learning of techniques, gestures and phonations was already given to higher primates (as the existence of mirror neurons in some primates including man shows; cf. Rizzolatti & Arbib 1998). Thus the cognitive, social and behavioral requirements for language were given. The basic question: "Did they speak a language?" can only be answered probabilistically: As all conditions were given, they probably did. Foley (1977: 70f.) concludes from a set of studies that "protolanguage was already well established with Homo habilis".

He assumes that with the Homo erectus "the lexical resources of protolanguage continued to increase up to several hundred words" (ibidem:71), that the length of sequences of sign units, i.e., containing something like protophonemes, appeared with Homo erectus (ibidem). In the next section I shall argue in a less informal way and make use of dynamic system theory to propose a specific format for an evolutionary grammar.

8.2 The format of an evolutionary grammar

An "evolutionary grammar" necessarily has a temporal dimension, i.e., the proper dimension of the evolutionary processes. The question of the adequate format of such a grammar encounters similar problems as developmental grammars (cf. Klein & Dittmar 1979), grammars for linguistic change (cf. the work of Labov), diachronic grammars or models of grammaticalization and grammar-genesis. A system of rules and even one with basic categories, modules and principles is not able to map the inherent (and not just parasitic) developmental, historical and evolutionary processes. The same is true for interlanguages, Pidgin and Creole languages, contact varieties, social varieties, and their context dependent registers. The grammatical tradition of normative grammars, school grammars, competence grammars, falls short of these demands, but no adequate alternative, in which changes and the forces which control them were fully integrated, has been forthcoming.[5]

8.2.1 The semantics of space and time in a protolanguage

One can distinguish two sub-aspects: processes in space, such as spatial orientation and navigation, and temporal classifications and rhythmical patterns.

The representation of *space* has to do with frontiers (their transition) and perspectives. A first perspective is centrifugal, i.e., starting from the self and its basic bodily motions an *experienced* three dimensional space is cognized: in front of – behind (go), above – below (climb, fall), left – right (grasp with the left hand or the right hand). This space of bodily motion with feet and arms defines the immediate space, where objects may be approached, reached and manipulated. The intermediate space depends on man's ecology; it can be the housing (the cave, abri) or the village; the distal space contains roughly all possible itineraries (of hunting/gathering). The second perspective is centripetal, i.e., the self is seen as the place of effects triggered by external causes. The sky, the horizon (typical points where the sun sets or rises), the favored direction

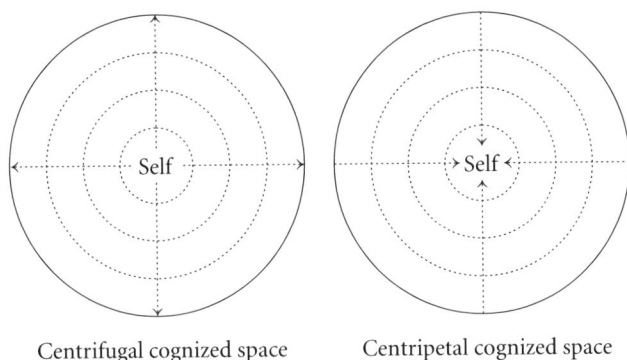

Centrifugal cognized space   Centripetal cognized space

Figure 8.1 Force fields of centrifugal versus centripetal orientation

of winds, the ridge of mountains may be the external locus of orientation for the self, who is at the center of a force field or gradient implicit in these delimitations. Many myths and religions refer to this extreme locus of orientation as they interpret the fate of humans as standing under the control of such distant (and often invisible) forces. In Figure 8.1 the topology and dynamics of such a cognized space are illustrated (cf. also Chapter 5.2 for the opposition of a space of hunting and a space of shelter).

The cognizing of such schemata for orientation may only show up in behavior (as it does in many animals), it may be gestured or it can be deictically organized in a phonic language (cf. Levinson 2001: 317ff.). For the Homo erectus the cognized space seems clear. The inner space is defined by the use of hands and instruments, the medium space by the choice or construction of dwelling-places (to which the group could return). The centripetal organization is involved in long-range excursions and migration. As the orientation system cannot be genetically coded (as in bees after millions of years of evolution) it has to be learnt, adapted to changing contexts and socially shared. Language is one possible solution to this problem, be it gestural (behavioral) or phonic and as humans have chosen the path of phonation it is plausible that our ancestors began to proceed further into this direction. (This is an application of the principle of continuity in evolution.)

The representation of *time* is rooted in the classification of multimodal sensory inputs using specific temporal rhythms (clocks). Pöppel (1994, 1997) proposed two temporal windows for multimodal integration:

- The window of 30 msec. Only after a stability of 30 msec does an event become an object of (multimodal) perception; it can be classified, labeled, compared, i.e., further processed.
- The window of 3 sec. A sequence of events can be understood as a structure. In this window the smaller units (30 msec) are correlated as: before – after, cause – effect, etc. This is the point where a notion of structured temporality is born.

In a similar vein (but without reference to neurobiology) Bickerton (2000: 275) refers to a "higher level signal coherence" as a precondition for hierarchical structuring and tries to explain the "catastrophic" transition to syntax along this line. A protolanguage must categorize events and actions (by proto-verbs) and must discriminate stable entities (by proto-nouns). The question arises as to whether temporal, dynamic, quantitative, qualitative *relations* between them can be mastered and if so, to what degree. This question brings us to the two basic delimitations of a protolanguage discussed by Bickerton: phrase structure (X-bar-structures) and government (case-frames). I will argue in the next sections that there are intrinsic complexity barriers which could have blocked the further elaboration of a protolanguage for a long (evolutionary) time-span.

8.2.2 Representation of actions and events

In order to have access to a complexity measure I shall introduce a model of event-schemata using catastrophe theory (which is a classificatory subfield of dynamic systems theory). One can take grasping (with the hand) as the basic scenario (cf. Chapter 7). The action-concept GRASP involves two stable entities: the body (the hand) and the object. Every point on the lines in Figure 8.2 is an attractor, i.e., the perception of a stable entity in the 30 msec window (cf. above). The whole schema should fit into the 3 sec window, e.g., in the sentence:

The father took the book (from the table)
A   B

Early humans (e.g., Homo habilis) already had a hand with the opposition of thumb and fingers, but some features are still linked to climbing (as in gorillas and chimpanzees). The Homo erectus had a hand which was adapted to strong grasping (as places on the bones, where muscles are attached, show, cf. Piveteau 1991: 74f.). This was still true for Neanderthals but even in humans, bushmen

The book

The father   The father (having the book)

Catastrophe of capture

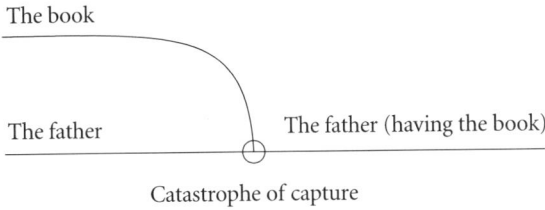

Figure 8.2 Catastrophe schema of GRASP

(San) and Australian aborigines have a shape of the finger deviant in the same direction from the statistical average of modern humans.

One may distinguish three ways of grasping:

– the force grip (e.g., of a branch)
– the precision grip (e.g., of a small tool)[6]
– the refined grip (e.g., of a needle; Cf. Piveteau 1991:29, who calls it: « préhension de délicatesse »)

The refinement refers to the topology of the capture. In Figure 8.3 the first two modes are geometrically abstracted.

These distinctions which have a long evolutionary history constitute a kind of manner specification in relation to the schema in Figure 8.2. This leads to a first principle of a protolanguage.

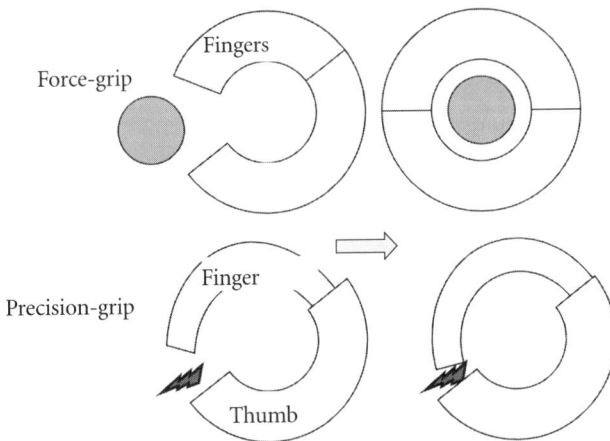

Fingers

Force-grip

Finger

Precision-grip

Thumb

Figure 8.3 Topological difference between power grip and precision grip

First principle of a protolanguage
The GRASP schema constitutes a structured (bivalent) action schema with a long evolutionary history and includes a manner specification categorized on topological cues.

As the distinction between several types of grips shows, more elaboration appears as soon as more precise manipulations on objects and instruments are developed. The fact that a cognitive bivalent schema and a manner component can be cognized does not necessarily mean that it could be transformed into phonic signals. One could even argue that the teaching of hand skills does not call for linguistic instruction. If we assume a frequent vocalization (inferred from the evolution of the sub-laryngeal tract; cf. Lieberman 1989) and a steady increase of memory (due to the growth of the brain) linked to an advance in social cognition it becomes clear that this cognitive schema and subsequent ones are a preadaptation for the evolution of verbal phrases or valence patterns in sentences. Thus, in order to verbally represent important and recurrent actions in a protolanguage the cognitive schema of grasping could be used as a kind of ground for iconic/metaphorical transfer to all kinds of manipulations on objects. As soon as instruments were used this schema could be iterated.

- The father (A) takes a hand-axe (B) to move/change/kill ... object (C).
- The father (A) takes a stone/bone (B_1) to hit/shape the pebble (B_2) which should later kill the animal (C).

Second principle of a protolanguage
The topologico-dynamical schema of grasping assembles causal/enabling/intentional meaning components, which are necessarily present in the purposeful shaping of a tool and it also lays the groundwork for force-dynamics (cf. Talmy 1988) in human language.

In this development a first barrier of complexity appears. While the schema shown in Figure 8.2 is dynamically and topologically simple (it can be derived from an elementary catastrophe of the type cusp), the composition of such schemata is not simple (in a mathematical sense). One needs a specific topology/geometry to restrict the degrees of freedom for such a composition.

First restriction (valence complexity)
The iteration of basic action schemata presents a barrier of complexity as the composition is not dynamically stable. It calls for specific controls of stability.

A second restriction concerns the manner component. The evolutionary old distinctions between forms of grip and manners of locomotion (related to the dynamics of the legs) are topologically basic (cf. Figure 8.3) and could belong to the basic constituents of a protolanguage.

Second restriction (manner component)
Further elaborations related to type of object, motion and rhythm of objects, their resistance, etc., require very specific techniques of categorization and it is likely that they were therefore not yet part of the semantics (and the lexicon) of a protolanguage.

A set of rather abstract specifications which are often grouped together in Pidgin and Creole languages can be called (after Bickerton 1981) the TMA-component (T = Time, M = Mode, A = Aspect). They are the next step which could have "evolved" in the protolanguage (made possible by different evolutionary changes).

Third restriction (TMA-component)
The TMA-component of sentences lies at the transition line between protolanguage and true "grammatical" languages.

The order of emergence of grammatical features transcending these restrictions could have been:

– elaboration of valence patterns (up to valence 3 or even 4)
– elaboration of the manner component
– elaboration of the TMA-component

I have started from the grasp schema, but there are simpler schemata. The dynamically simplest schema is that of stable existence. If we apply the 3 sec-window, any entity not changing in this window is a candidate. As the inputs of classification or labeling-reaction are not only spatio-temporal events but also qualities, one can assume the slow increase of quasi nominal/adjectival labels as soon as memory capacities and social demands increased. One could imagine that labels for other people, animals, plants, and artifacts were the first candidates for a growing lexicon. This development is also the natural continuation of classificatory capabilities of other mammals (even birds and fishes) and the differentiated warning calls of specific apes.[7] The cries of alarm, disturbance and food constitute a basic lexicon with reference to specific situations and they have distinctive pragmatic values, e.g., as asking for, responding to, informing about, etc.

Between the bivalent schema of grasping and pure existence the dynamic hierarchy predicts the first type of catastrophe: birth (appearance) and death (disappearance). Therefore, labels of temporal sequence and transition through non-symmetric barriers: begin/end; enter/leave; come/go could show-up before the grasp scenario is managed linguistically. I presume that the grasp-scenario is already the transition point between a protolanguage and the pathway towards a full-fledged language.

Third principle of a protolanguage
The *inchoative, progressive, terminal* aspects of action were probably represented in a protolanguage, e.g., by intonation or gestured modification.

8.2.3 Beyond the grasp scenario

The manufacturing of stone tools (and *a fortiori* of tools shaped with the help of stone tools) goes cognitively beyond the grasp scenario as I have shown in Chapter 4. One hand (or one foot) must fix the pebble, the other hand grasps the stone or bone which hits the stone. Finally the planned breaking off subtracts material from the chosen stone and after several strokes the desired sharp edge of the pebble is produced. This scenario involves two objects, two hands and a change in shape of the pebble (the separation of parts from it). René Thom (1983:182) proposed the *excision* schema which is presented in a modified version in Figure 8.4.

This schema contains four symmetric "grasping/emitting" sub-schemata (simple instrumental action) and one further "emitting" schema (grey circle). The first four are integrated in the (double) transfer-schema. The integration of the shaping by the tool is on a higher level of complexity (it has two force dimensions) and has structural stability only under very specific conditions (cf. for a mathematical analysis of these schemata called "semantic archetypes" Wildgen 1982a:67–78 and for the schema above Wildgen 1985:215f.; in German). In fact a linguistic description of the action normally requires more than one basic sentence pattern in actual languages.

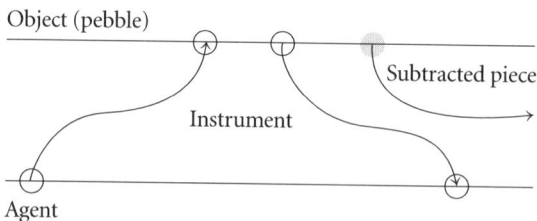

Figure 8.4 Schema of shaping an object with an instrument via excision

Fourth restriction (of modern languages)
Schemata with three and more (not linearly arranged) stability centers are at the limit of complexity of human sentence patterns.

8.2.4 The complexity of (nominal) phrases

Bickerton (1990: 195) suggests that in order to organize a descriptive (nominal) language one needs three structural layers:

(a) a generic class, X; (b) the properties peculiar to particular members of that class (large, with a dark red cover, of Mary's) and (c) the specification of the complete individual in terms of abstract relations such as quantity, proximity, familiarity, and so on (a, this, there).

His proposal reflects again a position typical of generative grammar (in 1990); in Chomsky (1995) many of the specific features of the Principles & Parameters-model are abandoned, because they "appear to be computationally irrelevant" (ibidem: 389). I think that there is no need to follow the traditional X-bar-schema in an "evolutionary grammar". The primary reason is that the determiners (a, this, there) refer to a different function than other specifiers (attributes), i.e., deixis or the anchoring of an utterance in the context. This function may be called indexical and it has another evolution linked to traces and to effective binding between language and non-linguistic action. The evolution of the indexical function, although it lies beyond the scope of this chapter, represents a vital aspect of *evolutionary grammar* and is a worthy field for further research (cf. van Heusden 1999).

The head and its attribute (or non-determiner specifier) are of the same basic type (nominal/adjectival) and the restriction is primarily concerned with the risk of blending two or more semantic spaces.[8] If every noun or adjective is associated with a place in a semantic space, then the mapping of one place in space A to one place in space B is a problem insofar as the spaces are different and may not be easily transformed into a conjunct space A x B. This is possible if A is *father* and B is *old*; in this case *old + father* has a new, well-defined place, insofar as *age* is an implicit feature of humans. It is not the case if one tries to combine *father* with adjectives like: *narrow, deep,* or *fluid* and *quadratic.* Moreover if A has n dimensions and B has m, then A x B has n + m dimensions and any increase in dimensionality creates instabilities (cf. on the dimensionality of texts and pictures, Wildgen, forthcoming 2004c). Another danger is that the mapping of a space A to another space B under deformation (insecurity, vagueness, variation) easily produces chaotic results as experiments with video feedback have shown (cf. for chaos theory in semantics: Wildgen 1998b). Thus classical X-bar-theory and its application by Bickerton (1990) underestimate the problem of (iterated) attributes to nouns. On the basis of these considerations, a fifth restriction may here be formulated.

Fifth restriction
The semantics of complex noun + attribute combinations leads to complex mapping problems and creates the risk of a chaotic product.

8.2.5 The self-organization of a grammatical system

Pinker and Bloom (1990) think that the central human feature of language is syntax and that therefore an evolutionary theory of language should explain the selection criteria for the syntactic abilities of modern humans. Contrary to them, Kirby (2000) argues that compositionality (and thus syntax) may emerge if the size of the lexicon (meanings associated with linguistic expression) increases and if individuals learn from utterances. In a computer simulation he shows that after a stage of random invention (and noise) a sudden change appears, after which: "The number of meanings covered increases dramatically as does the size of the grammar" (ibidem: 313f.). A further stable state emerges when the number of meanings increases and the size of the grammar drops. The resulting grammar is not only compositional but it "groups all the objects (…) under one syntactic category (…) and all the actions (…) under a second category" (ibidem). Hurford (2000) devised experiments in the line of Kirby's simulations, which showed that less general rules (idiomatic expressions) tend to be replaced by more general rules in the learning and transmission sequence between users, i.e., given a certain size of the lexicon and a dynamics of transmission (learning) languages tend to evolve a rather general syntax without any Darwinian selection being necessary. Nevertheless the biologically determined capacity of learning may co-evolve with elaborated languages as "the evolved, more general communal grammars provide a human made environment, which selects for individuals with greater aptitude for learning just these grammars" (ibidem: 348). Computer models of language evolution based on game theory come to a similar result (cf. Cangelosi, Greco, & Harnad 2002). In search of further answers one may turn to the mechanics of sign production, i.e., to phonetic evolution. MacNeilage (1998) proposed in his "frame/content theory" of the evolution of speech production a mechanism also applying to higher order organization in language. Studdert-Kennedy (2000: 171) states in his comment to it: "Both short- and long-term phonetic memory were also essential preadaptations for syntax [...] Without a preadapted system for storing phonetic structure independently from its meaning, syntax could not have begun to evolve" (cf. also Wildgen 1998c; de Boër 1999; Studdert-Kennedy 2000).

The purely syntactic problem of chaining elements of an existent vocabulary does not therefore require a specific endowment and evolutionary processes enabling it. The deeper problem is that of semantic compositionality, because the mapping/blending of spaces with different topology and the account of the dynamics inherent in verbs is crucial for sentential units. This is the tremendous problem, which has to be resolved in order to allow for a stable and reliable communication via phrases and sentences. In order to arrive at a conventionalized system of syntactic behavior early humans had to consider two major factors:

– The cognitive demands for a stable solution of semantic compositionality. The basic conditions have been described in the last section. One could call this the *cost* of higher order language capacity.
– The communicative and social demand for a compositional level of referentiality. This could be called the *gain* of the evolutionary game.

Even if the cognitive capacity was given, and I have described the pathway of cognitive evolution since the Homo erectus in Chapter 2, human society must still have a strong demand for higher order communication. Probably rewarding situations often arose by chance and the evolving species spontaneously used the "dormant" capacity. I am sure that with the increase of population density and networks of supra-regional communication and exchange in modern humans, such a system became necessary. As soon as it was developed, it brought about long traditions of language usage up until modern times. As language is deeply grounded in human biological constitution, the turning point in the use of cognition for language must lie before the rise of modern man, i.e., before at least 100 ky BP and probably even before 200 ky BP. Thus, the central question is not how syntax came about, but what made it rewarding to use the available cognitive potential for syntax. The pay-off can be a social or an individual one (which again can lead to higher social competence and thus to social gain).

In the line of Dunbar's argument, where language continues and replaces other activities of social care and contact, like grooming (in chimpanzees) or sex (in bonobos) a higher level of phonetic, lexical and syntactic complexity can only bring further gains if the relationships themselves become more complex and ask for a highly differential social behavior. This could be the case if partnership between males and females, child rearing, the teaching of technical and cultural skills etc. become much more complicated then in chimpanzees and bonobos. A plausible model for such higher communicative demands due to social evolution is missing.

Another line of functional explanation could take the role of language in (silent) thinking as point of departure (thus following the ideas introduced by Vygotzky (1962) into psycholinguistics). If thinking is a kind if silent speaking learned in early childhood, the complexity of an internalized language could bring gains for silent deliberation and planning even if it is not (always) uttered or even repressed by social communication. The intellectual advance would indirectly lead to advantages for the community having (and listening to) individuals able to act strategically and to plan effectively (or to solve other difficult problems). These communities could be selected for their excellence in situations of competition. The role of specialists (technicians, artists and scientists) is highlighted by the first large civilizations like the Egyptian one; possibly the artists which created Palaeolithic paintings and sculptures belonged to such groups marked by their intellectual and practical excellence; cf. also Chapter 5. This line of thought, which seems promising, is sketched in Foley (1997:73).

8.2.6 Major levels of an evolutionary (biological) grammar and the transition towards a culturally based grammar

From the hypotheses (principles) and the restrictions here proposed, a first sketch of the grammar of a protolanguage may be given. It specifies three hierarchically scaled levels of primary categorization:

1. *Stable* entities: no change in the perceptual and classificatory time window and recurrence as pattern (statistical relevance).
2. *Dynamic aspects* of *entities* in change and motion ("force-dynamics").
3. The *bivalent* GRASP-schema (capture or emission).

This allows for the accumulation of a lexicon of proto-nouns/-adjectives and proto-verbs. The combinatorial possibilities depend on context (in a similar way as many ad hoc noun + noun compounds depend on the valence of their constituents and on the context of use; cf. Chapter 6.2). The grammar of the protolanguage is based on these proto-classes and their implicit dynamical binding forces (linked to force dynamics).

The restriction principles may explain why further conditions of control on the combinatorial/mapping/blending semantics had to evolve in order to arrive at a more complex and less context-dependent grammar. I mentioned three basic restrictions, which apply to proto-manner adverbials, to a compact TMA-component and to recursive constructions of specifier phrases with a proto-nominal head. The restriction on higher valences shows that modern languages are still restricted and can overcome those restrictions only by building larger periphrastic and textual structures.

In the next section, I shall discuss some proposals for a theory of language evolution, which consider analogies between language and genetic code, between selection in language change and biological selection, etc. This access to the problem can be called *external* because one observes two different types of structures and tries to find common laws or tendencies, which correlate both. The strategy followed in the last sections may be called *internal*. As language capacity and the capacity to learn language are the product of evolution, they show traces of the process of evolution in their organization; i.e., we assumed a type of continuity between the process of evolution and the products of evolution. This continuity is obvious in our bodies and their stages of development; it is still plausible for behaviors (K. Lorenz was the first to shift the comparison from anatomy to behavior), but less obvious for languages and other symbolic behaviors. Nevertheless, as the analyses of the last chapters have shown, this is a line of research, which comes near to the center of human language capacity and the underlying capacity for symbolic behavior.

8.3   The contours of a theory of language evolution

A theory of language evolution may focus primarily on biological processes, which induce genetic, anatomic and (basic) behavioral changes. As social selection becomes more important because of higher population density and larger networks of exchange and communication, the selective pressure shifts from biological features to the quality of socio-communicative networks and their consequences for overall fitness. The species Homo sapiens gradually redefines its own environment, relative to which it is optimally adapted. This self-referential fitness is a specific quality of human evolution, which gives more weight and impetus to cultural development. Cultures or civilizations competing for survival, dominance or expansion may or may not affect the biological outfit because populations confronted with other populations which have cultural advantages may adapt culturally to them (learn their techniques) without changing their pattern or profile of biological reproduction. In other cases, a biological mixture is the result of cultural contact (even when initial contact resulted in conflict). In extreme cases, a population may be enslaved and even biologically controlled by a dominant population, which tries to avoid mixture. Thus, cultural dynamics may have biological consequences but many other outcomes are possible. The last chapters have amply demonstrated the effect of cultural dynamics and how they continue, unfold and diversify the results of more fundamental processes due to (Darwinian) mutation/variation and selection.

If cultural dynamics do explain the rather quick development of late tool industries and "art" in the Paleolithic period, the Neolithic revolution witnessed even quicker dynamics and brought about the historically documented languages, art in historical times and the current processes of globalization in many parts of the world. Nevertheless early civilizations and the rise of writing, mathematics, science, and philosophy are still correlated with external, e.g., climatic, economic and political factors. Thus the Nile valley, which could feed a large population and was isolated/protected by extended deserts on both sides, enabled easy transport of goods, people and ideas on the river, functioned like an experimental box for the development of a complex society. In other areas less rich and/or less protected, no such evolution could take place. In the present period, human societies are much less dependent on the availability of resources locally, and one can consider their dynamics as primarily controlled by symbolically coded information. It is in this context that one could assume that only the dynamics of "memes", that is of information which has been coded, memorized, transmitted by humans, counts, that the action of "evolution" may be reduced to the flow of information. An even narrower view reduces the flow of information (cf. Dretske 1981) to the flow of "linguemes". These new entities are defined by Croft (2000: 239) as:

> a unit of linguistic structure, as embodied in particular utterances, that can be inherited in replication; the replicator is the basic linguistic selection process; the linguistic equivalent of a gene.

Parallel to the gene pool, Croft (ibidem) defines a "lingueme pool", i.e.:

> the total number of linguemes (including all variants) found in a population of utterances; the linguistic equivalent to a gene pool.

In the following, I shall review several pathways, which try to link evolutionary biology and the dynamics of languages and formulate the major features, which a theory of the evolution of language should cover at the end.

8.3.1 The genetic code and human grammar. What is the relevant analogy, if there is one?

Any analogy is by definition mistaken. An analogy points to isolated features, which make two entities seem similar. The choice of these features out of a large and possibly infinite set makes the analogy in a certain sense arbitrary so that any entity may be considered similar to any other if the proper level or point of comparison is chosen. What counts are the consequences, which may be misleading or may function effectively.

In López-Garcia (2002, Chapter 7) different types of analogies between the sequence of bases in the DNA and language are discussed and evaluated. The following correlation is a false analogy in his view:

Table 8.1 Analogies between DNA and language.

Nuclear bases of DNA.	→	Letters/phonemes of a written/spoken language.
Triplets of bases.	→	Morphemes or words of a language.
Sequences of bases in the DNA.	→	Sentences of a language.

This comparison was suggested by Jakobson and later used by Crick and Watson, i.e., by a famous linguist and two famous biologists. A closer look shows some misleading consequences of this analogy.

– Words and sentences of a language represent something; they have a referential or a functional meaning. This cannot be said for molecules in the DNA. Even if their control over the production of specific proteins and the role of these proteins is interpreted as "meaning", the problem remains, as large parts of the sequence do not control the anatomy or physiology of the animal in question, i.e., they have no "meaning".

– The bases are abbreviations of chemical structures, which have a rich spatial and dynamic structure; thus the atomic nature of these units is just a convention (abbreviation).

– Typical for base-sequences are long repetitions of the same base; although reduplication of syllables is possible in language, this feature constitutes a mismatch. Thus, the codons of the DNA are not similar to morphemes or words in natural languages.

– The combinatory freedom of sentences in human language is superior to that of the genetic code, i.e., their syntax is not comparable.

Thus the simplest possible basis of an evolutionary theory of language, a structural parallelism between the genetic code and human languages, fails.

López-Garcia (2002) advocates another analogy, which is more abstract and thus less amenable to falsification. He imagines a stranger who analyses an unknown language and who segments the utterance using pauses, which (often) indicate functional transitions. He proposes an analogy between the third, second and first base of a codon of genes and the functional categories in a sentence, which he calls complement, nucleus and specificator (ibidem: 108). This proposal leads to a much smaller set of combinations of these functions into sentences and thus to a closer analogy with the sequences of bases in a codon. Therefore this structural analogy could, as the author suggests (ibidem: 143), explain the innate capacity for language advocated by Chomsky.

The major problem of this and similar proposals is that the transmission of the structural pattern from the genome to a historically evolved and individually learned language cannot be explained and seems impossible within the framework of this model. The transmission of structural patterns through all the categorically divergent intermediate states would be a miracle.

8.3.2 Darwinian principles of language change as a basis of an evolutionary theory of language

The pitfalls of a direct parallelism between language and biological structures and the dangers of such an explanation by structural analogy between entities in very different domains (genes and languages) are evident. A less dangerous strategy of metaphorical transfer avoids a parallelism between phenomena (genes and languages) and compares major principles of their dynamics. Darwin introduced two basic principles: mutation (variation by chance) and selection (fitness in relation to external forces). Why does one not apply these two principles not only to biological entities (species in the botanical and zoological sphere) but also to symbolic entities? The transfer of genes in animals is due to reproduction (in higher animals through sexual reproduction); learning is a correspondent mechanism of transfer and the entities transferred (or selected) are bits of information. The memory traces and elements in a flow of information may be compared to genes. Dawkins coined the term "memes" (in analogy to "genes", "mimetics" and "memory"). Blackmore (1999) elaborated this rather speculative proposal. I have already mentioned the parallel notion of "lingueme" introduced by Croft (2000).

- The basic Darwinian principles are redefined in the context of language change. Linguistic replication in the chain of tradition produces variation, i.e., "mutation"; it pertains to the classical field of sociolinguistics.
- In his "Theory of Utterance Selection" William Croft defines the "selection" of linguistic features (cf. Croft 2000: 30). The speaker may conform or not conform to the conventions for the language he/she uses. "The reasons for nonconformity are the causal mechanisms of altered replication" (ibidem: 30).

The (terminological) innovations allow Croft to reformulate the results of sociolinguistics, language contact research and research in language change in term of his "evolutionary approach" (cf. the title of his book). The basic question is whether individual decisions to use language in a nonconforming way is in fact a possible source of language evolution in its proper sense, which covers the last 200 ky or possibly the last 2 million years. If one takes into consideration the collective dynamics which spread or suppress individual innovations, individual choices may explain change in progress as exemplified in Labov's work (cf. Labov 2001). However, can it explain long-range historical change, e.g., the divergence of Romance languages during the last two thousand years or even the difference between the language of Cro-Magnon man and modern humans? A general feature of language changes as analyzed in the context of sociolinguists is their neutrality in relation to content (a postulate inherited from neo-grammarian linguistics in the 19th century).

The direction of change may be furthered by specific groups of persons (innovators) who occupy key positions in the social network. However, the system of grammar, lexicon, and phonology does not become worse or better. This means language change is just an unconscious drift, which prefers some easier channels and major trends in specific sub-societies. If social forces apply, they are rarely goal oriented and persistent. If Croft (2000: 180–183) uses the term "selective advantage of a variant", he means the furthering of social functions like "social identity" or "prestige". In no way do the selected variants improve the language in question; they may stabilize the social coherence of a group, foster social stratifications, etc. One of the basic dogmas of sociolinguistic in Labov's style is that idioms which are different cannot be evaluated on a functional scale as worse or better (for the controversy with sociolinguistic analyses in the style of Basil Bernstein; cf. Wildgen, 1977a, b). Now, this attitude may have a positive effect in eliminating racist arguments and it may even hold for societies at the same level of development. If it is applied to large-scale changes (say 200 ky or 2 my BP), it forbids any increase in expressive and functional power of a human language, which could make them so different from the ways of communication in other mammals. If the sociolinguistic dogma is correct with regard to change in progress or language change on a scale of decennia or centuries, then one must find other mechanisms, which operate on a scale of thousands, ten thousands and hundred thousands of years.

8.3.3 Long range selective advantages of linguistic features

Bichakjian (2002) dares to contradict the opinion held by most linguists that all languages are functionally equivalent, i.e., that no language has a substantial advantage over another language. He provides a new definition for the concept of "advantage" in language and uses the history of Indo-European languages and the history of writing as test cases for his hypotheses. "Advantage" in linguistics is based on lower costs and increased functional capacity:

> Language evolution will therefore be a process that replaces an existing feature with a new one that requires a smaller expenditure of energy while providing at least equal and preferably better functional capabilities. It is this characteristic two–prong quest – that of finding implements that perform better and cost less to operate – that underlies the purely biological and cultural evolution of humans, and the evolution of their languages.   (Ibidem: 94f.)

Bichakjian considers three major types of advantages:

1. Greater neuromuscular simplicity (example [s] or [f] is simpler than [θ]).
2. Early acquired linguistic features are advantageous, making the time of language acquisition shorter and are of consequence for the mental and cultural development of an individual. There is an advantage not only for early (easily) acquired linguistic features; an early language acquisition is itself an advantage, because other cognitive and social processes can be made earlier and more easily as a result.
3. Greater functionality. "If the operational area of an item is greater than that of another, one may safely conclude that its functional capabilities are greater." (ibidem: 100)

It is clear that the exact measurement of "neuromuscular simplicity" and "operational area of an item" is difficult, but in the perspective of a Darwinian model of linguistic evolution, the definition of "advantages" is the crucial point; without such a measure, no evolutionary theory of language compatible with modern evolutionary biology can be developed.

I cannot comment in detail on Bichakjian's analysis of the test-case "Indo-European languages". He discusses the "advantages" of modern obstruents against glottalized consonants, long and short vowels against a system with laryngeals, the advantage of an elimination of the dual and the regression of gender, the higher cost of morphological markings by vowel alternation (as in the Ablaut in German), the advantage of temporal distinctions against aspectual ones, the advantages of a subject function and a passive voice, the advantage of a shift from head-last to head-first structures (cf. ibidem: Chapter 5, where they are described and discussed in detail). The general consequence is not that some languages are better, others worse, but that reorganizations are made in language change over long periods (millennia). They occur possibly under the pressure of a more intensive use of language in dense populations whose methods of communication change and require new functional adaptations, or under the impact of intensive language contact which opens a space of choice to bilingual speakers. These reorganizations have a preferred direction and thus accumulate major advantages (given a functional grid to evaluate them, which may also develop in time). Such dynamics are able to describe cultural changes, which affect the functional capacity and the economy of a linguistic system dramatically but cannot explain such fundamental differences as between animals and man, because all the accumulated "advantages" depend on cultural transmission, learning, acquisition contexts and do not affect the inherited capacity of language and language acquisition.

8.3.4 Selective advantage through "symbolic theft" and the exploitation of the "mirror system"

In the last section, the possibility that humans succeeded in speaking more easily (with less energy) and covered more domains that are functional was discussed. But even if in the 6 ky or 7 ky years of language change in the family of Indo-European languages such changes occurred and brought about a communicative "advantage", all other languages can still be learned and practiced by humans, i.e., the human capacity for language was not basically changed by these developments. In order to explain the dramatic changes which separate humans from chimpanzees, other types of "advantages" which have more dramatic consequences for biological selection must be found. These advantages must go beyond that of symbolic systems; they must refer to the transition between the non-symbolic and the symbolic. Non-symbolic representations are "analogue sensorimotor (iconic) in the first instance and then categorical representations" (Cangelosi, Greco, & Harnad 2002: 196). One can assume that non-symbolic representations are already present in animals; they are indexical and require the co-presence of the representing sign (call, gesture) and the represented object (cf. Deacon 1997). The transition to symbolic representations has to be explained by a dramatic advantage of symbolic versus non-symbolic representations and it should specify the zone of transition and intermediate stages.

Cangelosi, Greco and Harnad (2002) tested a computer model in which representations were first adapted to "sensory inputs" yielding a kind of categorical perception (this was technically realized by a neural network). They call these representations "grounded" as they relate effectively to a world (in the simulation an extremely reduced mini-world). In the sequel, two strategies are tested (against one another): the *toil* and the *theft* strategy. In the sensorimotor *toil* strategy categories are acquired by trial and error, are corrected by feedback, and occur in real time (ibidem: 203). In the *theft* strategy, uttered labels of the category are used to learn the category; the symbolic (categorical) information is "stolen" from others who either have acquired it by the toil strategy or have "stolen" it themselves. The authors demonstrate that in competitive simulations the symbolic thieves outnumber the symbolic toilers after several generations. This means that a subspecies capable of using the symbolic theft strategy is selected and replaces a population of toilers. Steels (2002) proposed an integration of the two processes of learning grounded representations and associating symbols (which may be "stolen"). His models accomplish a "structural coupling" (ibidem: 215). For him "communication through symbols provides important feedback to representational learning" (ibidem) and he points to the fact that "often there is more than one possible way to cluster the data depending on the dimensions that are considered or the parameter settings of the clustering algorithm" (ibidem). This means that already at the level of category formation and even more if hierarchies of categories are derived, symbol-use is necessary to stabilize a common standard of categorical perception, and hierarchical structuring. His hypothesis is again tested by a computer-device, in which two robot players (talking heads) play an "evolutionary game" ("A game is evolutionary if the players change their internal states in order to be more successful in the future"; ibidem: 216). The establishment of a coherent system of conventions in a discrimination game (for color) is much better if it is associated with a naming game (ibidem: 224, Figure 10.5). Although the experiments were done with robots and in an extremely reduced universe of discourse, the results show the primary advantage of language (at the level of simple naming):

- Individual categorical perception and hierarchical structuring of knowledge is furthered by the use of symbols (theft strategy).
- Collective perception, categorization, hierarchically organized knowledge become coherent by the use of symbols.

This means that the introduction of language brought relevant individual and collective advantages to a sub-species capable of implementing it; hence such populations were fitter in an environment demanding in terms of individual and collective cognitive competence.

In Arbib (2002; same volume) the basic ability of sensorimotor learning (cf. the toil strategy) is related to the mirror system (mirror neurons) discovered by Rizzolatti et alii (1995) which gives rise to new qualities of behavioral learning (ibidem: 236):

- Self-correction: based on the discrepancy between intended and observed self action.
- Social interaction. By anticipating what action another monkey has begun, a monkey can determine how best to compete or cooperate with the other monkey.
- Learning by imitation at the level of a single action.

The second stage is interpreted by Arbib as a byproduct of the first one; the third stage is not at all developed in monkeys (ibidem), but it was "a major step on the way to developing a language-ready brain in the hominids" (ibidem).

As the mirror neurons are associated with hands and grasping in the brain, the GRASP scenario with its sub-schemas: precision pinch, power grip and side opposition is adapted to the shape and volume of an object. This basic action schema was probably at the origin of the evolution of a larger set (architecture) of action and object frames (cf. Chapter 7, and Wildgen 1999b). These pre-linguistic frames were already "well established in the primate life; supporting a variety of complex behaviors and social relations" (Rizzolatti et al. 1995: 249). Based on these frames which could be communicated via enactment and observation (made possible by the mirror system) a verb-argument structure could be derived as soon as naming and symbolic theft mechanisms operated on a broad level.

> A grammar for a language is then a specific mechanism (whether explicit or implicit) for converting verb-argument structures in particular, and more complex structures based on marked compounds of verb-argument structures more generally, into strings of words. (Ibidem: 249.)

The major result of this section is that it seems possible and plausible to define and experimentally evaluate large-scale advantages of the symbolic mode in communication and to apply the Darwinian principle of selection without metaphorical bleaching.

8.3.5 Conclusions for a theory of the evolution of language

Contributions to a theory of the evolution of language have been made throughout this book and it has become clear that, although many proposals exist and a body of relevant empirical facts is at hand, a theory in the proper sense with a formal (mathematical) core and testable hypotheses, which are derived from it, is not yet in our reach. The following constituents seem necessary in order to arrive at such a theory:

- A theory of biological evolution, specified to the brain, the ear and the articulatory organs and covering the stages of hominization.
- The genetic information relevant for linguistic capacities of living and extinct hominids must be found, such that the genetic heritage relevant for the human language capacity can be defined.
- The functional and selective effect of language in different evolutionary periods must be assessed more precisely; the different dimensions, e.g., the cognitive versus the social effects should be further investigated (possibly their interaction or coevolution).
- Prelinguistic or protolinguistic evolutions in human communication have to be reconstructed using the results of paleontology, e.g., mainly the remains of technical and artistic production.
- Finally advances in the description of language change and language typology should help to reconstruct the protolanguage in the time of the Neolithic revolution and possibly even of Paleolithic populations (ca. 40–12 ky BP).
- The history of writing systems may be used as a guide to the cultural dynamics of symbolic systems. The same is true for cultural innovation in technique and art.

In general, all these sources of information and reconstructions of evolutionary lines based on them are insufficient to determine a clear and unambiguous explanation of language origin and we have to wait for more data from paleontology, genetics, comparative ethnology and general/typological linguistics in order to narrow down the possibilities still left open by current reflections in this field.

CHAPTER 9

Symbolic forms, generalized media, and their evolution

The place of language in the context of general semiotics

The terms "symbolic form", "symbolic behavior", "semiotics" (theory of signs and symbols) presuppose that signs and symbols belong to a field of phenomena which can be separated from physical phenomena or purely psychological or social ones. The term "symbol" may adopt different meanings. In one sense, it is just a synonym of "sign", in another it designates a special type of sign, which is based on conventional use (and not on iconic or indexical cues). In others, it is contrasted with signals and stands for signs typical of humans whereas signals are typical of animals (and for technical devices). It is clear that the latter reading does not fit into our evolutionary framework; therefore "symbol" and "symbolic" shall here be used to cover at least all sign-behaviors which evolved parallel to language (including language), and cover the period of transition between a purely context-dependent, ad hoc referential behavior based on instinctive (built-in) mechanisms and modern symbolic media. As the transition must be continuous, symbolic behavior is an emerging category with fuzzy boundaries, i.e., behavior is symbolic to a certain degree. This is linked to criteria like deferred reference, representation rather than presentation, degree of consciousness (level of "theory of mind" attained) and others. The discipline which has symbol- and sign-use (its evolution, its structures, its functions) as a major subject of research is called "semiotics" (or "semeiotics" as coined by Peirce), "semiology" (in the tradition of de Saussure) or "philosophy of symbolic forms" (in the tradition of Cassirer). The differences between these historical denominations and characterizations should not bother us too much because none of them explains the evolution of "symbolic or sign-behavior" corresponding to the state of the art in evolutionary biology.[1]

A system of semiotic *genres* gives a first tableau of such a discipline. Semiotic genres may be compared to literary genres or discourse genres in two ways. First literary and discourse genres establish a fundamental categorization and, therefore, a rough description of the field called literary studies or discourse studies, second literary genres and discourse genres are semiotic categories and are, therefore, genres of second or third order related to semiotic genres. Thus, if spoken/written language is a semiotic genre, then literature and discourse are sub-genres (second order) and their major types are again sub-genres (third order). The basic problem known since antiquity is the same for semiotic, discourse (media) or literary genres:

- Do genres exist in the phenomena (realistic position) or are they just conventions to talk about the phenomena (nominalistic position)?
- Are genres based on temporary boundaries, i.e., historical *styles*, modes that come and go or are they trans-historic?
- Is there a natural (biological/cultural) evolution of genres (which would justify the etymological root "gen-" in "genre")?

It is clear that a purely nominalistic answer to (a) confounds *genres* with *styles* (b) and makes question (c) irrelevant. I shall assume that there is something in the phenomena to which *genres* refer in a natural way and that question (c) has some relevance (restricted by historically contingent boundaries, cf. question [b]). If, finally, this assumption should fail, then the socio-historical question (b) would become the only relevant one.

9.1 Symbol formation and symbolic forms (in Cassirer's philosophy of symbolic forms)

For Ernst Cassirer the symbolic is by definition an activity of creative form giving. In his programmatic article on "The concept of symbolic form in the constitution of the humanities" ("Der Begriff der symbolischen Form im Aufbau der Geisteswissenschaften", written in 1921, cf. Cassirer 1994) Cassirer defines the symbolic forms as:

> ... that energy of the mind [...], which maps meaningful content in the mind to a concrete sign and is internally appropriated by this sign.
> (Cassirer 1994: 175; translation by the author.)

The symbolic forms are manifested in the areas of phonetic language, myth, art, technology and pure knowledge (reine Erkenntnis). This plurality of types of symbolic forms functions as a kind of medium (Medium, Vermittlung) between the objects and ourselves (ibidem: 176).

> ... they designate thereby not only negatively the distance, into which the object moves relative to us, but they also create the only possible, adequate mediation and the medium, by which any kind of intellectual being may be seized and understood.   (Translation by the author.)

The symbolic forms establish an intermediate domain, subdivided by different types, in a field between the ego and the outer world. The typical character of the *symbolic* form is defined by a vector in this field, which transforms passive "pictures" received by the senses into something, which is actively formed by the mind. The force of this formative process transforms the perceptual content into a symbolic content.

> In it the image has ceased to be just something received from outside; it has become something shaped from within, in which a basic principle of free form-giving has been efficient.   (Ibidem: 177; translation by the author.)

The basic polarity between *self* (consciousness) and *object* is further complicated by the fact that the rather static objects are "represented" by a steady flow of processes in consciousness. This basic difference precludes any kind of mapping or pictorial representation between the two extremes of the field.

If the formation of symbols is the general type of symbolic activity, the diverse "symbolic forms" are the genres. The set of genres is neither invariant in time nor does it strictly follow an evolutionary scale. Thus, the basic symbolic forms, which Cassirer treats in the first two volumes of his "Philosophy of Symbolic Forms", i.e., language and myth, are the first genres of symbolic behavior. If we start from a flow of thought, from a continuum between the subject (of experience) and the object, then rituals and mythical beliefs create a symbolic organization of this continuum without cutting it into pieces. The symbolic form "myth" does not represent, it presents. Thus, the name or picture of a god, the magical or ritual formula does not stand for something named, it calls it into presence, has a causal impact on it, is a proper part of it, by which humans are able to control it. Expressivity is not separated from the body, which is a natural support of quasi-physiognomic signs and these signs cannot be manipulated at will, are not variable, not reflexive in their usage. Cassirer links mythical thought and symbolism with the function called "Ausdruck" (expression).[2] The reference of linguistic symbols (to something ontologically different), the variability (arbitrariness) of the attribution of sign and referent and the "ability to isolate relations – to consider them in their abstract meaning" (Cassirer 1944: 38) is (still) absent.

Although the transition between expression alone (Ausdruck) to representation (Darstellung) is considered by Cassirer to be constitutive for the transition between animal and man, he does not consider there to be a strict evolutionary hierarchy relating the symbolic forms myth and language. This becomes most clear in his late book: "The Myth of the State" (1946) where he analyses the role of modern, politically instrumentalized myths in the context of the Nazi regime in Germany.

The third volume of Cassirer's "Philosophie der symbolischen Formen" treats the phenomenology of knowledge and more specifically of scientific knowledge, which is considered not as the negation but as a higher quality (Steigerung) on the scale which separates language and myth. A further loss of the materiality (Entstofflichung) of the sign, a poorer link to sensual memories (Anschauung) and a higher degree of separation (Ablösbarkeit) from the (real) objects leads to the field of formal logic, mathematics and mathematical physics and may stand for the scientific revolution initiated by Einstein's theory of relativity and modern quantum mechanics. As a first result, we may consider the following scale:

Table 9.1 The scale, which organizes the three "symbolic forms": Myth, language and science

Expression (animals/humans)	Myth < language < science	Abstract meaning (in logics and mathematics)

The specific symbolic forms can migrate on this scale, thus modern myths may be technically produced like war machines, which apply scientific results, and language is relevant not only for the transmission of myth but also for communication between scientists.

The symbolic form called "art" (poetry, music, painting, sculpture) does not have a place or a typical range on the scale mentioned above. Referring to the basic functions, expression and representation, aesthetic forms aim at an equilibrium of these functions. In two manuscripts on language and art (cf. Cassirer 1979: 145–195) Cassirer shows that the symbolic form "art" takes another route than language, although it is, in many respects, comparable with it.

> But art and the artist have to confront and solve quite a different problem. They do not live in a world of concepts; nor do they live in a world of sense perceptions. They have a realm of their own. ... It is a world not of concepts but of intuitions, not of sense-experience, but of contemplation. ... This aesthetic contemplation is a new and decisive step in the general process of objectivation.   (Ibidem: 186.)

The creation of art depends by its nature on the medium:

> Art is not only expression in general, in an unspecified manner, but expression in a specific medium. A great artist does not choose his medium as a mere external and indifferent material.   (Ibidem)

In the case of poetry and other types of art which use language as medium, the different functions of language, namely the emotional, descriptive/narrative or enacting (as in speech-acts) define separate media and thus sub-genres. These functionally defined genres cannot be classified by structural criteria (see above); rather, they realize functions which depend on contexts of use (changing traditions, roles of authors and audience, etc.). If these contexts are properly defined, we may arrive at such traditional notions as poetry, narrative and didactic prose, and drama. As these functions are both cognitively and pragmatically (socially) interdependent, their boundaries are fluid in time and cultural space.

To summarize: The general purpose of symbols to objectivize thought and emotion leads to different symbolic forms which have their proper range of variation, and which may intersect and combine. Nevertheless a fundamental diversity is created. To a certain extent cultural evolution may be understood as a change between symbolic forms and as an internal complexification of symbolic forms.

We can derive an evolutionary hypothesis on the basis of Cassirer's analysis:

First hypothesis on the evolution of symbolic forms
Between emotional expression (in animal and man) and perfectly abstract meanings (in mathematics), we observe an overlapping sequence of semiotic genres:

- myth (ritual and magical thinking)
- language (referring, descriptive, narrative)
- science (optimized control of reference, relational architecture and inference hierarchies)

Therefore we can expect that myth has a minor but still basic role in social communication and that natural language has a strong impact on the artificial languages of the sciences.

9.2 Sociological models of semiotic genres (Luhmann, Habermas)

In the following I shall consider a vein of ideas rooted in Husserl's phenomenology and leading to a philosophy of "Lebenswelt" (world of life) or of culture (Kultur). For every human in a human society there exists a horizon of understanding, interpretation and action which he or she takes (implicitly) for granted and which cannot easily be transgressed. It has been constituted by historical and cultural processes beyond the life-space of the individual and is thus transcendental, although the individual may (mostly in a minimal way) contribute to its further development. In this sense, the "Lebenswelt" is semi-transcendental (cf. Habermas 1982:190). Every thing which may be said or acted is contained in this horizon; the "Lebenswelt" is thus a closed world of semiosis. For humans one may assume that the system of possible meanings has been symbolically reorganized, i.e., "meanings" which were *functionally* closed in the system of animal behavior have been reorganized into a *semiotically* closed system of meanings in the evolution of man. *Semiotically closed* means that the "Lebenswelt" is almost closed, i.e., the changes individuals make are either ad hoc and transient or statistically irrelevant. Still, in the addition (and reinforcing interactions) of billions of actions a statistical flow of the "Lebenswelt" is made possible. This is similar to the temporal stability of linguistic systems which seems to have absolute validity for the speakers of a linguistic community, although the system changes in a historical dimension. These long-range developments will be discussed in the next section.

The proposals for a classification of basic genres in the symbolic organization by Luhmann take as their starting point the "symbolic interactionism" developed by T. Parsons and H. Mead. The systems of "meanings" in symbolic interactionism neither come from the ontic structures themselves (the world) nor from cognitive processes in the individual mind; rather, they are the product of interactions between individuals. If simple interactions in the domain of simple animals, e.g., the exchange of resources and the compensation of mutual needs may be regulated ad hoc (or by instincts), this is no more the case for humans who for reasons of complexity need a common system of meanings which regulate the exchange or the interaction in general. The analogy of money and language points to the semiotic nature of every social interaction.

In Luhmann's (1975) theory of symbolically generalized media of communication, a square table of basic types, i.e., genres of media, is proposed. Social interaction is reduced to the pair (EGO–ALTER), and the resources exchanged in interaction and symbolically categorized (they are called *codes*) are:

- exchange of values/judgments (truth/language)
- exchange of love/care/empathy (love)
- exchange of property/money/valued objects (possession/art)
- exchange of power/rights (power/law)

ALTER and EGO have two basic types of reactions: experience (passive) and action (active) and they have selective/determining power ($\rightarrow$) on each other. Luhmann distinguishes:

- the experience of EGO/ALTER
- the action of EGO/ALTER

The table of social interactions and of social coordination defines the proper place (locus) of four genres (media, codes in Luhmann's terms).

The interaction (represented by $\rightarrow$ in Table 9.2) is a selection of ALTER on EGO and vice versa. The media are specialized codes, which help to resolve conflicts in these interactions and which have been developed in a process of cultural evolution; they allow more complex but still stable forms of interaction. The differentiation and further specification creates a divergence, which requires repair systems; religions are such meta-codes, which try to integrate the divergent media into an imaginary holistic system. Such a meta-medium can only be meta-stable as the media evolve with the societies and their ecologies and thus change the demands for integration to the meta-medium.

The four genres (media) may be described as follows:

- The medium, which correlates the experience of ALTER and EGO, selects experiences and classifies them dichotomously as true/false. In the interaction between ALTER and EGO, experiences, which EGO did not make personally, can be *learned* (cf. the "symbolic theft hypothesis" discussed in Chapter 8). Thus, both the dichotomous selection on the scale "true/false" and the transmission of foreign experience govern this genre. *Language/information* is the specific symbolic form, which codes

Table 9.2 The four generalized media based on interactions between ALTER and EGO

	Experience of EGO (Ee)	Action of EGO (Ea)
Experience of ALTER (A_e)	Ae $\rightarrow$ Ee Truth / language	Ae $\rightarrow$ Ea Love
Action of ALTER (A_a)	Aa $\rightarrow$ Ee Possession / art	Aa $\rightarrow$ Ea Power / law

these categorizations (true/false), and their transmission. Discourse genres are the different ways to do this; i.e., they are sub-genres of the semiotic/communicative genre language/information. I will come back to the evolution of this genre in the next section.

– The medium *friendship/love* (philia/amicitia) regulates the action of EGO (E_a) in order to select a positive experience of ALTER (A_e). It tends to isolate subsystems (pairs) from the anonymity of the group (society) and thus to constitute stable social islands (couples, families, groups of friends, etc.). Language may help to establish such bonds and, therefore, a further function of language is its socio-emotional function.

The next two media are basic for sociology and their link to language is rather indirect.

– The third medium causes the activity of ALTER (A_a) to be accepted or indulged by the experience of EGO (E_e), insofar as he/she accepts, e.g., the use of restricted resources by ALTER. A system of accepted rules allows possession and with it the asymmetry of possession. The flow in this system (its dynamics) may be regulated by generalized goods or money. This genre is basic for the evolution of economic systems beginning with simple exchange systems, which presuppose that rare goods exist and are objects of solicitation. Thus, in very simple (stone age) societies rare but beautiful objects (shells from the sea, feathers of rare birds in the mountains) are exchanged along specific routes, involving a whole chain of social groups. (This is still the case in inner New Guinea.) It is astonishing at first sight that art is placed in the category of rare and valuable objects, because in the modern forms of this medium money and contemporary art seem to belong to different media; art may have an economic value but for most artistic products this is not the case, they just please the artist and some of his/her friends.

– Finally, the action of ALTER may select the action of EGO, e.g., ALTER has the opportunity to decide on the action of EGO, either by enforcing it or by taking the action which ALTER prefers also as preferred one for EGO. In a social system, this kind of asymmetry has to be regulated by a kind of consensus in order to be stable and reliable. Norms of expected behavior or formal rules and laws are the symbolic forms typical for this medium. Again language is an instrument to fix the consensus and it is in itself a system of rules and norms, which may be used as the blueprint for social rules and laws. (This is obvious in the case of rules for greeting, speech acts and discourse organization and can be generalized to rules of grammar.)

The classification gains plausibility if we consider first the diagonal which opposes the experience of ALTER and EGO and the actions of both; it opposes social experience and social action. On one side language elaborates social experience and enables the coordination of distributed experience and a complex awareness of the other (its internal status, its mind). On the other side the medium power/law is the major control medium of social action.

The other diagonal is characterized by the impact of experience on action and vice versa and it opposes two asymmetric media: love versus possession/art. The coordination of EGO's action with the evaluative process in ALTER enables the constitution of a social code of evaluated action (called *love* by Luhmann). In a similar way, the access to resources produces stable possession and perceivable attributes of wealth (symbolically represented by the possession of rare objects, e.g., gold). The two diagonals of Luhmann's table are different. Truth/language and power/law went through a process of objectivation and (almost) became a neutral medium beyond individual differences, whereas art and love remained subjective and therefore unstable. The structure hidden in Luhmann's table is shown in Table 9.3.

Language seems to be a medium beyond Luhmann's classification insofar as it not only is implied in the medium truth/language/value and power/law but also has specific sub-functions which contribute to the media love (emotional function), and possession/art (language as social stigma and the esthetic function of language). In the case of art one may add that although language may resemble law insofar as its grammar has rules which must be followed, it tends to go beyond rules, to explore new fields of meaning, to move into domains not yet codified by rules. In situations where no common linguistic code exists, e.g., in communication with infants and foreigners who don't share a language with the speaker, basic linguistic capacity still enables a larger amount of emotional, social and (partially) referential communication.

The non-linguistic codes: love, possession and power/law had evolutionary precursors related to sexual choice, access to food-supply/water/protection and status in animal groups (with territorial control). A code could only develop after the symbolic capacity had evolved and a degree of consciousness had been reached. Language is the prototype of any such code, although the full range of linguistic functions and the actual shape of human linguistic capacity only

Table 9.3 A possible semi-order of Luhmann's generalized media

$$\text{Law} \begin{array}{c} \nearrow \text{Love} \searrow \\ \searrow \text{Art} \nearrow \end{array} \text{Language}$$

emerged with the different media which had to be socially encoded in order to achieve a higher degree of complexity and stability. The trans-medial character of language allows a second evolutionary hypothesis.

Second hypothesis on the evolution of symbolic forms:
Before language (in an elaborated form) emerged, the precursors of the media love, possession/art and law had existed in a non-symbolic form. As they were socially codified, symbolic forms evolved and elaborated the precursor media to socially codified, behaviorally complex and stable generalized media. Language evolved as a trans-medial tool for the organization of these media, it was the condition for their evolution and was itself formed in order to fulfill its generalized organizational function.

In conclusion, we may say that language (discourse) has different functions corresponding to basic media of social interaction. Further differentiations of media/genres are possible and may interact. Thus, in the choice of a lover/friend economical aspects may be relevant, status (power) may be sexually attractive and information status (education) may be a criterion of partner choice or give access to wealth (possession). Information (truth/falseness) may depend on beliefs (religion) and these on power (cf. the principle "cuius regio, eius religio"). In general, a set of prohibitions can limit the convertibility of semiotic genres. What is basic are the functions which are fulfilled and the complexity/stability of social systems enabled by a differentiated system of semiotic genres.[3]

Habermas (1982), who distinguishes different routes of reproduction and their disturbances, addressed the central dynamical problem of social systems, namely their reproduction (cf. Table 9.4).

Primary language acquisition and in certain contexts also secondary language acquisition are filtered by the conditions of the medium "language", as the reproductive process selects for regular, coherent linguistic structures (more strictly in second language acquisition than in primary language acquisition, cf. the results of research on Pidgins and Creoles). Social systems are controlled via social reproduction, i.e., incoherent or incomplete social systems tend to disappear under the effect of reproduction, if the new generation does not understand and, therefore, not reproduce them. In analogy to grammars, which fit the conditions of language learning, generalized media and symbolic forms must be stable under reproduction. If codes for love, art or power management cannot be learned by the next generation (either because its attitudes have changed or because the codes elaborated by the adults have become in-

Table 9.4   Social reproduction and disturbances (cf. Habermas 1982, Vol. 2: Fig. 21, 22, 23)

Routes of reproduction	Disturbances in the reproduction
Cultural reproduction (the tradition of cultural knowledge).	Loss of meaning ("Sinnverlust"), i.e., the cultural framework in which meanings have to anchor in order to be communicated, is destroyed.
Social integration (the coordination of actions with accepted norms).	Social anomia or social disintegration.
Socialization (the formation of a personal identity in a social context).	Personal psychopathologies resulting from the impossibility to create a stable personality which has its place in a social context.

coherent), they are replaced by new codes. This process points to a central capacity of humans and human societies to *create* semiotic genres.

Although I could not discuss the theories of Habermas and Luhmann in detail, it has become clear that a system of semiotic genres and their possible variation and migration depends on basic social mechanisms, their ability to manage complexity and the conditions of their evolution and stability.

9.3 The evolution of symbolic forms and generalized media

In his "Essay on Man", Cassirer argues on the basis of contemporary results on the "mentality of apes" (cf. Köhler 1921) that in animal behavior we find only signals but not symbols, that the animal possesses a practical imagination and intelligence, whereas man alone has developed a new form: *"a symbolic imagination and intelligence"* (Cassirer 1944:33). The major developments in zoo-semiotics came after Köhler (1921) and have shown that under the specific conditions created by man, higher apes can learn to communicate symbolically at the level of a two or even three year old child whom we would consider to have language. Even birds are able to categorize different objects, to learn songs, to create variable codes (dialects), etc. Consequently, the range of symbolic forms and genres has to include zoosemiotic systems. On the other end of the evolutionary scale one finds the development of mathematics and scientific knowledge in the first civilizations of the Near East, in India and in China. One could therefore propose the following scale:

Table 9.5 Hierarchy of symbolic behaviors in their possible order of emergence

Before 7 my BP	Simple ad hoc instruments and communication at the level of apes (with isolated referentiality in the calls of some species).	Level of communication of primates (beside the line leading to homo sapiens) and (probably) before the bifurcation.
Until 2 my BP	Evolution of a repertoire of referential signs, evolution of technical skills, dominance of phonic communication for social bonding and orientation in space.	Evolutionary steps towards a protolanguage, stage of pre-protolanguage.
2 my until 1 my BP	Stabilization and elaboration of "protolanguages"; establishment of "industries" of stone manufacturing.	Stage of protolanguages.
0,7–0,2 my	Differentiation and rivalry between primary "cultures".	Stage of post-protolanguages.
After 200 ky BP	Evolution of the complete repertoire of symbolic forms, biologically based on a full language capacity.	Stage of (complete) language capacity (in the sense of actual human capacities).
After 40 ky BP	Evolution of large networks of exchange (rare goods, women, innovations); art of caves, portable art, and the use of abstract graphical symbols.	Geographical networks of local cultures supported by symbolic organization.
After 7 ky BP	Cultural evolution, complex economic networks, elaborated writing system, global religious systems.	Phase of globalization (until today).

Mythical codes (belief systems, rituals, dances) could have existed before or at the same period as phonetic language. As we can only infer the existence of myths from art or mythical texts, the position of myth is the most questionable one.

There is an apparent relation between art/objects of value (e.g., rare objects) and money, which was not mentioned by Cassirer but was emphasized by Luhmann. Economic and artistic values may in fact be opposed to language on another scale, which separates the rules and procedures valid inside a community and those which allow for interaction and communication beyond the community. The exchange of goods which required a system of common values and which ultimately led to the appearance of money as an economic medium was necessary for interactions with neighboring or foreign communities. The same is true for art (and rare objects) which may be accepted at least in much larger areas than those covering a dialect or local language. In a similar vein, "love" is a medium, which tends to go beyond established frontiers. This could explain why the media in the first diagonal: law/language of Luhman's table (cf. Table 9.2) and the extreme position in Table 9.3 are locally more restricted and more stable (as they are valid for a more coherent community), whereas the media: love/art are less restricted and less stable. All media tend in the course of cultural evolution to loose their local restriction. This is true for languages, which tend to become fewer in number (although the number of speakers increases dramatically) and to have larger areas of distribution and for laws, which are adapted to international standards. The same is true for money and art. These common dynamics point to the fact that all these phenomena are members of one big family of phenomena which can be called "symbolic forms" and that they should be analyzed in the framework of one integrated theory of symbolism.

The differentiation of generalized media of communication starts (if we follow Luhmann 1975) with the first civilizations (e.g., the Mesopotamian and the Egyptian). It is, however, obvious that the media called love, power, possession, truth must have existed before the classical civilizations, although their complexity probably did not require the institutional stabilization of specific codes. Even a socially organized group of bonobos shows bondages (coalitions) of friends, levels of power, privileged access to resources and standards of communication. If one considers the very general system of interactions and selections in Luhmann's system, one wonders if it could not be applied to any socially organized group of living animals having an awareness of the other; i.e., which are able to distinguish categorically between EGO and ALTER, i.e., which reaches the basic level of social consciousness (cf. Chapter 10).

Luhmann's hypothesis that large civilizations after the Neolithic revolution created specific "media of generalized communication" controlled by new institutions can be integrated into a theory of language evolution as a step which goes beyond the evolution of spoken (natural) languages. It inaugurated a first post-language evolution stage, in which more abstract and more global, partially artificial systems came forward. They were able to integrate a number of divergent mythical traditions into a coherent corpus of beliefs and to fix this synthesis in the form of monuments and in written documents (a religion). As this further stage of symbolic evolution needed institutions and specialists for its realization and transmission, it only concerned a small subgroup inside large societies (e.g., the "scribes", the specialized geometers, engineers and artists in ancient Egypt and the astronomers in Mesopotamia). The mass of the population in these civilizations and all populations outside them were not specifically concerned by this development.

The intuition of Luhmann that larger civilizations (after the Neolithic period) create a specific level of generalized media can be used to conceive a future level of human (cultural) evolution. The largest part of the global population remained unaware of the post-language developments until general literacy and schooling in the 19th and 20th centuries contributed to the global diffusion of these codes and the corresponding social institutions. Economic and political globalization during and after the Second World War continued and deepened this new stage of human (cultural) evolution and will reshape the symbolic forms and generalized media in use. This means that the evolution of the symbolic capacity is continuing and we are now only witnessing a transient stage far from some (final) stability. As these developments are too quick to be fixed in our biological equipment but depend on instruction and corresponding institutions, they can be easily destroyed and may disappear one day. What will be left is the basic capacity to invent, develop and use language and this heritage will only be lost with the extinction of the human species. The pursuit of these ideas would lead to another book dealing with the future of human communication and not with its history and prehistory

In both Cassirer's and Luhmann's system language is relevant but not central (it is one of several alternatives). It seems, however, that with hominization a centralization of semiotic capacities has occurred which is supported by the face on the one hand and the hands on the other. With the evolution of phonetic languages, the more technical functions were taken over by the hands (including pointing and spatial gestures) and the more general (abstract) semiotic functions by the system of speaking/hearing (mouth/ear). In a much later stage, the cognitive complexity of the subsystem eye/hand could reorganize linguistic competences in writing and reading.

Chapter 10

Consciousness, linguistic universals, and the methodology of linguistics

Symbol formation as designed by Cassirer can only emerge in perception if stable gestalts and schemata for recognition and memory retrieval are evolved. But this level of sensory experience, attention and memory coding is only the background on which specific symbolic forms, e.g., language emerge; it does not yet contain symbolic forms. A *self-referential* loop by means of which results of symbol formation in the individual mind gain stability and are materialized such that they can be perceived and achieve social relevance is necessary. In this process the *sign*, i.e., an object/event that can be sensorially experienced does necessarily reenter the self-referential cycle of symbol-formation, and thus at least achieves implicit consciousness. Mediated by the public character of the sign individual concepts, images and memory contents become objects of collective perception, and shape the collectively recognized "symbolic forms" such as language, myth and art.

The emergence of *signs* which accomplish complete semiotic gestalts with the aspects mentioned by Peirce: iconicity, indexicality and the (conventional) symbolic, requires a self-referential dynamic organization. Self-reference is by itself a basic feature of consciousness; therefore implicit or explicit consciousness of the contents of perceptions, of the mind which performs perception, imagination, memory, and of the other mind must be presupposed if a full-fledged symbolic form is to evolve. Some results of consciousness research are therefore discussed in the first section. Levels in the evolution of consciousness are related to a stratified system of linguistic universals. A first proposal for such a stratification is made in section two. Finally the new profile of linguistic research gained by the systematic consideration of the evolution of human language requires new linguistic methodology. The contours of such a methodology are sketched in the last section. In general, the reflections in this final chapter can only invite the reader to complete the argumentative network presented in this book. A systematic answer to the questions of human consciousness, language universals and a new methodology of linguistics is clearly beyond the scope of this book.

10.1 Consciousness and linguistic signs

Consciousness is itself a graduated faculty. Implicit consciousness of the effect of communication on other members of the family or group can be assumed in the case of the alarm calls by apes and the food-calls of chickens and other animals; cf. Hauser (1996:567–586). The next stage in complexity could be either active (a false signal is given) or passive (no signal is given) intentional deception. In both cases the other can be manipulated for the profit of the animal in question. In many cases it is not clear whether such behavior is truly intentional (in the human sense) or just the result of inborn behavior properly selected in the evolution of a species.

The human child needs several years to run through a series of grades of consciousness, but:

> Infants are born with the requisite ingredients for a theory of mind in that they are sensitive to an object's goal directedness, are aware that self-propelled objects are driven by internal mechanisms, and are aware that an individual's direction of gaze or attention provides important hints as to what he or she thinks or feels.   (Hauser 1996:651.)

In the sequence of the development of explicit consciousness, language is crucial, because the child can make utterances and thus materialize states of consciousness in a pronoun like "I, you" or in verbal phrases like : "I think, I believe, you think, you believe".

By means of signs man became aware of the contents of cognition, namely, the concepts and schemata in his mind. He can thus react to semiotic objects both by perceiving the external stimulus and by connecting it to an internal category which could not be assessed without the sign being perceived as a link to it. Thus, sign-use triggers the emergence of cognitive self-consciousness. This evolution presupposes the prior evolution of (implicit) consciousness of the body and the body's movement, of the self as such and of individual action. This consciousness is indirectly a precondition of human action, human will and intention. As a preliminary proposal one may consider the following hierarchy of consciousness in individual cognition.

a. Consciousness of one's *body* (e.g., of one's hands).
b. Consciousness of one's *action* (implicitly one's intentions, one's will, as a vague force behind Ego's action).
c. Consciousness of the *entity* subjected to one's action (implicitly of forces underlying its/his/her motion/action).
d. Consciousness of the *other* as a perceived entity, one may act upon (as on an object) but which also acts on its own and has its own intentionality.
e. Consciousness of the sign as different from external objects/events and the body (own or other).
f. Consciousness of the double nature of the sign as sensation and as reference to external object/events and/or internal states (in oneself and the other).

The social dimension of sign-use requires collective consciousness and collective knowledge. It presupposes consciousness of the other and of his "alterity". The other ("alter") has been highlighted in the discussion of Luhmann's theory of generalized media (cf. Chapter 9); the generalized media are only accessible if a theory of mind has evolved. Basic features of a theory of mind may exist in higher animals, but for the rise and stabilization of a system of signs more is presupposed. It is not sufficient to understand the other as different or similar to oneself, Ego and Alter must be analyzed, understood as members of a society, a social class, a group, i.e., as parts of a coordinated system of sub-systems with individual members. Thus *social consciousness* is a necessary precondition for effective human sign-communication. Possibly, the complexity barrier for valence patterns discussed in Chapter 8 is linked to social consciousness, because the three-valent (and central) scenario corresponds structurally to social exchange, and it implies equilibrium between the needs of Ego and Alter. For this purpose, a stable reference system of values attached to objects and events must have been established. Such a value system is again a sign system because specific objects: shells, feathers, stones, bones, and later gold and silver are given a symbolic meaning as a standard, a *tertium comparationis* of social value in the exchange of goods. As soon as multilingual and multiethnic communities (with high and low languages) arise, the knowledge of a specific (high) language may itself become a "good" which has its value in a "linguistic market" (cf. Bourdieu 1970).

10.2 Linguistic universals based on evolutionary principles

It has become clear in the last chapters that human language did not appear suddenly, due to some supernatural genetic reorganization,[1] but has evolved in a process of continuous evolution driven by the internal logic of growth (morphogenesis) and external changes/catastrophes which necessarily resulted in either adaptation or extinction. The different stages in this process of evolution are separated either by internal barriers of growth and self-organization or by ecological catastrophes. The resultant language capacity is, despite its internal coherence, stratified such that features which evolved earlier have a different place in the cerebral (bodily) architecture and are functionally presupposed by more recent strata. The boundaries between each layer may become fuzzy as a result of later reorganizations, but this does not necessarily mean that more primitive developments have been completely eliminated. If we recapitulate the results of the chapters in this book, we may postulate the following stratification:

Basic level: This most basic cognitive level contains the capacity of efficient locomotion, for causal impact on the environment and action. If consciousness is added one obtains a set of dynamic scenarios which control intentional behavior and the understanding of causality. It already shows up in tool usage and has had consequences for human cultures for 2 my BP (cf. Chapter 4).

Emergence of performing vocal articulation and auditive perception: At this stage highly performant perceptual and motor faculties for vocal communication evolve. One presupposition for elaborated motor learning becomes present very early with the evolution of mirror-neurons, but with the prominence of vocal communication for social comfort and control this capacity is further elaborated and was well established in the time of the worldwide expansion of Homo erectus (ca. 1,6–1,0 my BP). The basic principles of phonology may have evolved in this period.

A protolanguage based on a compositionally enriched lexicon: The underlying capacity characteristic of this stage of development is a very systematic exploitation of the affordances of the ambient and changing ecology. It can still be observed in the tremendous knowledge about the flora and fauna and their use for nutrition, medicine, etc., about weather and the seasons in hunter-gatherer societies. This capacity was amplified by continuously profiting from the growth of associative areas in the cortex. It probably evolved continuously in a long period between the migration of Homo erectus and the reign of late Homo neanderthalensis and Cro-Magnon man, when it finally reached the complexity of our current languages before 100 ky BP.

The evolution of syntactically and textually complex languages: This step is certainly linked strongly to the last stage and emerges with the mastering of stable valence patterns and the use of verbal art (narratives, rhetoric, song, myth). It allows the establishment of a canon of myth and other text-based cultural traditions. Probably this level was not accessible to Homo erectus, but emerged with archaic Homo sapiens and was fully evolved and functionally exploited in Cro-Magnon populations, which created the first large cultural networks in Europe, Africa, Asia, and America. The first civilizations presuppose a full unfolding of this capacity.

Modern and future phases on the evolution of human communication: The current period began with the foundation of towns and with socially stratified civilizations in the later Neolithic period. In this phase farming, cattle breeding, pottery, and writing were developed; specific symbolic codes for large-scale communication were created (cf. Chapter 9). On the basis of these developments one could conjecture the future evolution of mankind (if it survives the next 100 or 200 ky).

Linguistic universals, like those projected in Chomsky's Universal Grammar (UG), should respect the evolutionary stratification of the linguistic capacity of humans. It should predict universals on the levels of:

a. action/motion perception and planning (dynamic archetypes);
b. phonetic/phonological principles and routines, such as basic feature distinctions, syllable structures, rhythmic and euphonic constraints (i.e., phonetic universals and principles of phonological self-organization);
c. universals of lexical fields, polysemy, metaphor, and compositionality principles for word like gestalts;
d. syntactic and textual principles for the organization of larger linguistic gestalts;
e. generalized codes for globalized communication in writing and other media.

It would be premature to design a new variant for the "market" of modular architectures for grammars (cf. Jackendoff 2002, for proposals in this line). The list of stages mentioned above could however be useful for a discovery-strategy. In the following I shall discuss some consequences for linguistic methodology.

10.3 Consequences for linguistic methodology

The integration of the evolutionary dimension into linguistics is a fundamental challenge to current linguistic theories. It involves a demand for a new defini- tion of language studies in general. The relevant timeframe for consideration of the symbolic and linguistic (phonic) capacities of humans now stretches back to the emergence of the species Homo (which begins at least with Homo ha- bilis, perhaps with Paranthropus). In this larger frame fundamental changes in the basic capacity of human cognition (via symbols) and language have to be considered, i.e., "language" in this framework is not neutral as to the cogni- tive capacity it enables or presupposes. If one takes an evolutionary approach to language, it is necessary to investigate interactions between evolutionary bi- ology and linguistic skill. That is, changes in the social and communicative functions of language can be traced to biological and cultural evolution, and found in turn to enable or even prefigure such developments.

If the chronological scope of this approach is compared with those of Jakob Grimm and Ferdinand de Saussure, the reversal of the trend in the discipline becomes evident. Jakob Grimm considered (in 1822) the documented history of a specific language, e.g., German, and the not yet documented rise of this language as the proper field of linguistic/philological analysis. Thus "German Grammar" had a temporal scale of 2,000 years, based on the first Germanic consonantal shift, which separated the West-Germanic languages from the main stem of Germanic languages (roughly between the 2nd century B.C. and the 6th century A.C.). The shift towards synchronic analysis introduced by F. de Saussure reduced the temporal scale more or less to one generation of language users (30–50 years); this was a reduction of 70:1. A linguistic theory based on an evolutionary time scale reverses this trend as it expands Grimm's time span of 2 ky to 200 ky or even 2 my years, which means an amplification of 1:100 or 1:1,000. This change in the temporal scale has dramatic consequences in other domains.

The context of use and the social background of language change dra- matically insofar as the conditions of life and the density and extension of populations in communicative contact change. Migrant hunting populations of the species Homo erectus (and Homo neanderthalensis) have different social organizations (in smaller groups) than the Cro-Magnon societies in the Franco-Cantabric area with stable places or stable itineraries returning to important places. This social organization changes dramatically again af- ter the Neolithic revolution. With the rise of the civilizations in Egypt and Mesopotamia, with the foundation of towns, of states with central power, armies and administration the type of social organization which still persists was created. This means that the communicative conditions of a sedentary and hierarchically structured society have been in place for almost 9,000 years. Thus it is evident that the social conditions for symbol and language use were radically different in the periods of the out-of-Africa migration, in the period of coexistence with Homo neanderthalensis (and possibly late descendants of other species descendant from Homo erectus in Asia and Africa). Because of these significant and long-lasting changes in social and evolutionary conditions for language use before written language appeared, conclusions drawn only from the period of linguistic history since the development of writing are probably not valid for language on another evolutionary scale (e.g., of 200 ky or 2 my).

Although the Homo sapiens living side by side with Homo neanderthalensis in the Near East (90 ky BP) were biologically almost identical with modern humans (cf. Chapter 2), this was probably not the case in the time-span of speciation (species separation) from some predecessor species (500 to 200 ky BP). Because of the biological differences from modern humans at the time of speciation, any protolanguage appearing in that period (such as that discussed in Chapter 8) would have had to function within the limitations of a smaller brain, smaller groups, simpler stone-technologies, less developed systems of religious beliefs, rituals, myths, etc.

An immediate consequence of the large scale theory of language concerns the role of other not dominantly phonic means of communication: gestures, spatially mediated communication, tool-industries and the presupposed techniques of teaching and learning, symbolic creativity in art and ritual play, belief systems and mythically motivated social distinctions (leadership, gender roles, etc.). An outline of such a semiotic theory which places language in the field of other symbolic forms and generalized media was developed in the last chapter.

For current linguistic methodology, the semiotic aspects dealt with in some of the chapters of this book may seem too far removed from the central concerns of linguistic theory to justify a demand for major modifications in linguistic methodology. However, the lexico-semantic analyses of Chapter 7 have shown that even current lexicology has an (implicit) evolutionary dimension and incorporates a folk-theory of human evolution (in the domain of instrumentality and symbolic transfer). In Chapter 8, the cognitive-semantic principles and restrictions of a protolanguage in the period of emergence of modern humans were formulated and a critical review of current proposals for the format of a theory of language evolution was given. The facts and arguments accumulated point to a new program for future language studies and to the proper format of a new type of language theory and a new methodology of linguistic research. I will first state what such future theories should *not* be. They should not follow the tradition of rationalistic reconstruction (cf. the Cartesian program) or the utopia of perfect languages searched for by language theorists in the 17th century. Furthermore, syntactic competence is not the first and major feature of language which has to be explained. As the complexities of syntax are probably latecomers in the evolution of human language, their explanation has to be grounded on principles of phonetic production/memory and lexical semantics.

The fundamental evolutionary layers of language require different types of methodology:

a. As I have shown in many chapters, there are fundamental action-schemata based on motor control. They were first applied in the invention, manufacturing, and specific instrumental use of tools. The tool-industries (cf. Chapter 4) are manifestations of this basic layer of human symbol use. A methodology for the analysis of this layer should develop a *cognitive* reanalysis of the artifacts in their reconstructed usages and major functions. As such an empirical enterprise has only a restricted precision and concreteness, the theoretical lacunas can be filled either by experiments with tools in proper contexts or by theoretical models for stable action patterns which produce and use these tools. The topologico-dynamic semantics proposed by René Thom and elaborated in Wildgen (1982a, 1994) were a first step in this direction. As the mathematical background of this new type of semantics would have burdened the major lines of argument in this book, I have argued in favor of the plausibility of such a basis in different chapters of this book. As in Piaget's phase-model of individual language development, specific levels in the evolution can be explained by (long-range) equilibriums between the assessment of a cognitive level and the communicative (cultural) profit derived from it. Together with different paybacks in different ecological niches, any advance in cognitive-semantic capacity may have taken millennia to stabilize and to reach populations which did not participate actively in its development. Therefore, the overall evolution of the cognitive-semiotic capacity could have been rather smooth even if thresholds existed and prefigured the direction evolution would take under proper conditions. Our theoretical emphasis on complexity levels does not therefore necessarily imply catastrophic transitions.[2]

b. Any theory of language evolution which reaches back beyond the period of a documented cultural evolution has to take into account the biological changes of the human species and ecological changes which determined or restricted the use of phonic language and its cultural functions. Basically, it must investigate the separation of the human from the ape-line (chimpanzees, gorillas, orangutans). In this context, comparative ethological analyses become crucial. This work is mainly done by anthropologists and geneticists. Linguists can only help in this research field in the context of joint ventures.

c. On the lower level of the evolutionary scale leading to modern languages, the prehistoric documents have to be reassessed from a cognitive-semantic perspective. This question was addressed in Chapters 4 and 5, which analyzed the semantic categorizations underlying the instrumentality (causal control) of tool manufacturing and tool use and the cognitive-semantic background of cave-paintings/drawings, early sculptures, and artistic creativity in general. As Chapter 6 has shown, a proper understanding of human creativity is the key to the historical understanding of cultural development.

d. The complexity of all languages currently in use, especially their phonological, morphological, syntactic, and textual complexity should be explained by a process of cultural accumulation enabled by the learning capacity of children. Crises in the transmission of these complexities as in Pidgin-Creole transitions, language acquisition by the hearing impaired or other disabled people, and linguistic recovery after brain lesions (aphasia), all give insights into the process of language creation and the conditions, which enable, restrict or promote it. Therefore even in the case of living languages it is insufficient by far to describe the competence of fully developed, healthy people. Rather, we must try to assess the forces of memory, imagination, learning, etc, which enable and shape the language humans speak.

Beyond individual learning, the density of populations and the fertility of the ecology they create and exploit add a social dimension which is crucial for language evolution. Further consequences of population density are culture-clashes, the migration of symbolic sub-systems such as forms of kinghood, ceremonies of burial and the diffusion of technologies. They are able to reshape communication, communicative functions and the symbolic means of communication. Studies of linguistic and cultural contact can contribute an answer to these questions. The methodology developed should be further elaborated in order to cover temporally and geographically more global influences and to find general principles underlying linguistic and cultural contacts, conflicts and their results.

At first sight, evolutionary aspects of language may seem to be empirically inaccessible because no (written) record has survived; a closer look reveals that any explanatory endeavor in linguistics depends heavily not only on the analysis of language acquisition and language change but also on a proper understanding of language evolution. If one adopts the easy gesture "Ignorabismus" (we never shall know), one gives up explanation in linguistics. As Carnap and other empiricists have shown, any description which does not have an explanatory value is more or less worthless. The proper selection among rival descriptions, the decision on the basic principles of description and model building depend on the explanatory value they have. Therefore, the search for a proper and in the long run successful description of language must always start with explanatory hypotheses and must argue in favor of or against such hypotheses. They are the sources of meaning and relevance in the scientific study of language. They cannot be the last step following a purely technical methodology be it inductive, as the discovery procedures of American descriptivism, or deductive and falsifying like the methodology of generative grammar. If the explanatory power of linguistic theories and models cannot be increased significantly one would be forced to give up linguistics as a scientific enterprise.

Notes

Chapter 1

1. Currently one distinguishes the African line reaching up to the Homo rudolfiensis, which had a brain of less than 1000 cc and the Indonesian, Chinese and European Homo erectus with a brain volume bigger than 1000 cc. The African link to all Homo erectus out of Africa could be the Homo ergaster (e.g., the KNM ER 993 found in the Turkana area). The oldest specimens of Homo erectus in Java have the age of 1,8 my (the youngest could have lived until 50 ky BP). The Homo erectus found in Georgia (Dmanisi) has an age of 1,7 my.

Chapter 2

1. Even if the brain weight can be computed on the basis of archeological skulls (mostly parts of them), it is still difficult to compute the body weight of the analyzed species. The statistics for an extrapolation may be either based on living primates, e.g., chimpanzees or humans; moreover the degree of sexual dimorphism can change and if the sex of the analyzed item is not known further uncertainties are added.

2. In comparison with higher primates humans have chosen the strategy of giving birth to mentally immature children; this is a strategy also chosen in other mammalian lineages and is not restricted to humans (cf. Jablonski 1998). Neoteny and the raising of physically and mentally rather immature children raised important questions of the use of resources, which relate the metabolism of the mother during gestation, the amount of energy necessary during weaning, gestation time and birth giving rhythms. Cf. the "maternal energy hypothesis" put forward by Martin (1998).

3. The nursing baby can still breathe and drink simultaneously because both pathways are independent. A subvelar position of the epiglottis has also been observed in other primates (cf. Starck 1981:586).

4. In the case of fossils where only parts of the skull are conserved it is difficult to reconstruct those parts of the line towards the neck and below the (lost) brain. Daniel Laitmann (contribution to the conference in Leipzig 2nd of June 2002) showed that two major forces govern this evolution: the expansion of the parietal lobe, which inflects the line, and facial retraction probably due to lesser force necessary for mastication.

5. Ambrose (1998) discusses a series of bottleneck scenarios. He refers specifically to the explosion of the volcano Toba in Sumatra around 70 ky BP, which lead to a volcanic winter of

several years and brought about the coldest period in the Later Pleistocene. As this very cold period persisted for almost 1000 years, many animals died out. This catastrophe probably also brought the human species of this era near to extinction; they could only survive in climatic islands. Ambrose suggests that this event triggered the last evolutionary phase in humans.

6. Cf. Wildgen (2003a, forthcoming 2004b) on the continuity versus discontinuity in linguistic processes and the symmetry breaking in evolutionary processes concerning language functions.

7. Heeschen (2001) points to two major functions of speech in archaic societies: On one side speech establishes a kind of fictional consensus which plasters over divergent interests and conflicts, on the other side it allows humans to go beyond the security-circle of a community, to address foreigners; the narrative deserves the first function, the aesthetic play or artifact prepares for the second one.

8. The comparison of living with Paleolithic populations has been criticized because living populations are heavily influenced by modern civilization and mostly analyzed in terms of them. Nevertheless, this evidence is the best we have because archeological findings before the appearance of art (before 40 ky BP) tell us nothing about the social organization, the religious beliefs and the ritual practices of these populations and even the first artifacts require proper interpretation in the light of existing ethnical entities (cf. Chapter 4).

Chapter 4

1. The thesis that Neanderthal men already showed such a kind of worship implying magical procedures, has been contested. Tattersall (2001) argues that only Homo sapiens, when he expanded to Europe (40 ky ago) had symbolic rituals which he correlates with a fully developed language.

2. This can be the sky line and characteristic points like a mountain peak or the sun, the stars. As the sun and the night sky are moving patterns due to the rotation of the earth, a stable frame can only be established if a biological clock tuned to diurnal motion of the earth is operative.

3. In Begun (2003) the Dryopithecus, which lived in Western and Central Europe between 13,5 and 8 my BP is seen as the basis, from which gorillas, chimpanzees and humans evolved. It had already a stable vertebral column preadapted for upright locomotion, long and very mobile arms and hands. These latter features were the precondition for efficient tool use and precise throwing.

4. Cf. Mottron (1987) for the link between gaze direction, attention and language development in an early stage of child development and Sinha (2003) for a correlation of rituals with evolutionary processes.

Chapter 5

1. In 2002 a team of archeologists found the lower jar of a modern man in the cave Petra cu Oase in south-west Rumania. This is the oldest bone of modern man found in Europe. It was dated to 35 ky BP. Cf. Proceedings of the National Academy of Sciences, 30.9.2003, p. 11231.

2. With rather negative connotations, Lorenz (1940) compares the evolution of recent men with the evolution of domestic animals. As in both cases many of the adaptations to natural ecologies are lost, he calls this "self-domestication of man". In the context of our argument we would rather say that the evolution of man enters a phase of self-reference. The ecology to which he has to be fitted (in a Darwinian sense) is more and more defined and shaped by man himself. Thus the process of Darwinian fitting becomes self-referential. This could theoretically have the consequence that the process would run to chaos and not only destroy the natural ecologies but also abolish all realistic adaptations to the world persisting outside human control (cf. Wildgen 1998b for the application of chaos-theory to semantics).

3. Anati (1991:17) refers to almost a million graphemes counted in Bhimbetka (India), in Lesotho 500 caves contain ca. a million graphemes, the same is true for Arnhemland (Australia), Tassilo-n-Ajjer (Algeria), the Sinai and Negev. In the Alps (from France to Austria) 16 areas with many places are distinguished. The Val Camonica in Italy contains alone 200,000 rock engravings; cf. also Priuli (1996; for Italy), and Sanchidrián (2001, for Spain and Portugal).

4. The first symbolic objects appeared 8,500 B.C. in Zagros (Iran); they distinguished four shapes: spheres, discs, cones, cylinders. Together with ornamental modifications twenty types were distinguished. The number of different types changed dramatically with the emergence of towns and more densely populated areas in the period 3,500 to 3,100 B.C.; it soon reached a total of 660 different types.

5. A recent notice in Antiquity, vol. 77:31 compares these signs with signs on bones from a common grave found in China and dated to 8,000 BP. It is still controversial if these signs are a precursor of Chinese writing.

Chapter 7

1. René Thom, in an article published in 1974, declared that linguistics is the paradigmatic morphological discipline, i.e., natural morphologies tend to be mapped into the system of linguistic categories and therefore the linguistic system is a guide to these morphologies. The term "morphology" means, in Thom's context, that the basic form-giving forces in nature and man tend to show up in a highly selective manner in the symbolic system. Thus the morphological principles underlying the evolution of language and symbolic thought should reappear in the linguistic system itself. One could interpret the program of George Lakoff (1987): What Categories Reveal about the Mind (part of the title of his book) as an informal answer to the question introduced by René Thom (first publication on the topic in 1968), because language can only be a window to the mind, if there is some evolutionary

continuity between the mind (which has a much longer evolutionary history) and actually existing languages. If languages just map historically recent cultural developments, they cannot reveal anything about the human mind (but a lot about cultural history as comparative linguists in the nineteenth century noted).

2. René Thom's hypotheses (published in 1968) that morphogenetic complexity in biological species and morphological complexity in languages are related implicitly prefigured the above hypothesis (cf. Thom 1972/1975) and Ballmer was aware of it. Thom's line of investigation was continued in Wildgen (1981, 1982a, 1985, 1999a). In the period between 1978 and 1984 Ballmer and Wildgen cooperated in several institutional contexts, e.g., they contributed to a lecture given by Hermann Haken at the Meeting of the DGfS (German Association of Linguistics) in Bielefeld in 1983.

3. Originally hands and feet were directly correlated in four-footed (or four-hand for monkeys) locomotion as the feet of horses, wolves and dogs are. In humans this coordination is only enforced by balance and the distribution of motor control. The conceptual links are used in idiomatic expressions like (German) *Hand und Fuß* haben (to be coherent, plausible). In Mandarin (Chinese) such idiomatic combinations are even more frequent and stand for: intimate brotherhood (*to be together like hand and foot*), to be in a hurry (*hands and feet are scrambled*), to use fraudulent means (*to make hand and foot*). I thank Peiling Cui for these examples.

Chapter 8

1. Even a range between 50 ky and 500 ky seemed possible, but less plausible (cf. Stoneking & Cann 1989). Meanwhile more genetic loci have been studied: Y chromosome, Xq13.3, β-Globin, ACE, LPL. The Y-chromosome which is transmitted from father to sons is the natural complement to the mitochondrial DNA transmitted from mothers to their children. Pääbo (1999:M14) summarizes: "However, the studies that have been performed tend to arrive at dates for the earliest variation of less than 200 ky years similar to that of mitochondrial DNA". The oldest skull attributed to Homo sapiens found recently has been dated to 160 ky BP.

2. There are some controversies on this topic related to the question of a multiregional origin of modern man or an origin in Africa. In the latter case the African type is called Homo ergaster by some authors and separated from the Homo erectus. Rightmire (1990) argues in favor of a proto-species Homo erectus. The oldest specimen was found in the Koobi Fora region (East Africa) and Rightmire says that: "it is likely to be more than 1.6 my old" (ibidem:191). The earliest Homo erectus found in Java is dated to less than 1 my (ibidem:193). Other authors consider the findings in Dmanisi (Georgia) in favor of a much earlier migration of Homo erectus to Europe and Asia (ca. 1,6 my BP).

3. Recent results in genetic comparison between humans and other primates show a 5.5-fold acceleration in the level of gene expression in the brain of humans (not in blood and liver) which is exceptional for mammals with a comparable overall genetic distance (primates were compared with rodents). Enard et al. (2002:341f.) say: "these results [...] supports the notion that changes in gene expression levels in the brain have been especially pronounced during recent human evolution". As Australopithecines were still rather ape-like, the change in expression level could have occurred in the stage of Homo habilis or Homo erectus/ergaster.

4. Chimpanzees may use a stone to open a nut; cf. Chapter 4 and current research in the group directed by Prof Boesch at the MPI "Evolutionary Anthropology" in Leipzig. Table 1 in Boesch and Tomasello (1998:593) classifies the "semiotic" behaviors in six chimpanzee populations. The group specific learned behaviors are also called a "culture".

5. Labov (1972) tried to adapt his empirical data to modified versions of a generative grammar, as Klein and Dittmar (1979) did. Developmental studies adopted the generative paradigm in its Principles & Parameter version (which in turn responded to comparative and developmental issues). Bickerton (1990:199f.) starts from eight modules of a current (Chomskian) model and he cooks it down to two principles: phrase structure (X-bar-theory) and verb-argument clusters. These two principles are then used to distinguish the protolanguage of Homo erectus and neanderthalensis which would be structurally limited insofar as neither complex phrases nor verb argument complexes could be mastered. I shall give an alternative formulation of these two features (cf. Bickerton 1990:189–197). In general, one should prefer formalisms stemming from dynamic system theory in all fields dealing with the dynamics of language, as they have a genuine dynamic dimension; cf. Wildgen (1982, 1985, 1994, and 1999a) for the elaboration of the dynamical paradigm in linguistics.

6. In the evolution of pongids the origin of the precision grip seems to be a critical transition which allowed "grasping predation of certain species of insects at the terminal ends of bushes and shrubs" and this "opened a niche for primate evolution" (Quiatt & Reynolds 1993:123). It had as consequence the "conversion of active behavior to crepuscular and diurnal phrases of activity" (ibidem).

7. Cf. Chapter 3 and Fischer and Hammerschmidt (2001) for a critical discussion and experiments with Barbary macaques. Thanks for a conversation on the topic with Catherine Crockford at the MPI-Evolutionary Anthropology in Leipzig.

8. A semantic space may be conceived as defined by a set of independent features, which are either polar oppositions or graded scales. Ideally a semantic space should be homologue to an imagined space, i.e., it should not have more than three dimensions. A very general notion without topological restrictions is used in "Mental space theory" by Fauconnier (1997). I suppose that his theoretical intuitions could be integrated with the phenomena discussed in this section, although it is not clear how the topologico-dynamic hierarchy of catastrophe theoretic semantics should fit the logical machinery he presupposes.

Chapter 9

1. Peirce was most of all concerned with questions of evolution, but his proposals (his "tychism") are very speculative and are Darwinian only insofar as he introduces chance systematically as a basic explanatory device. Any law of nature is for Peirce just a restriction

of probabilities; to explain is therefore to understand these restrictions and the conditions which have allowed them to gain force. Saussure is clearly a deterministic thinker and questions of evolution seem to be inaccessible. Cassirer assumes a natural symbolic outfit of animals which becomes gradually independent from its natural restrictions such that a category of artificial symbolism is developed in addition to natural symbolism. His ideas on language origins have been sketched in Tesak-Gutmannsbauer (2001); cf. also van Heusden (2003) and Wildgen (2003b) for Cassirer's contributions to biology and linguistics.

2. This element of his theory is linked to Bühler and the tradition of gestaltpsychology (mainly in Graz, cf. Meinong). Bühler (1933) reviews the historical development of "Ausdruckstheorie" discussing the physiognomic theories (e.g., Della Porta), Darwin's book "The expression of the emotions in animals and man" (Darwin 1972) and other authors of his time; cf. Chapter 3.

3. The basic difference between the proposals made by Cassirer and Luhmann concerns the generalized media: love and power/law, which are missing in Cassirer's list: both are based on an action of EGO, which is either selected by the experience of ALTER (love) or by his action (power/law). It is plausible for social interaction to consider both experience/perception and action as strongly correlated and at the same level of intentionality/consciousness. The generalized medium "truth" assembles Cassirer's three forms: myth, language, science, and Cassirer considers them to have (overlapping) ranges (cf. Table 9–1). The symbolic form "art" is separated in both systems, although Luhmann establishes a link to possession/money, which is absent in Cassirer's system. Cassirer instead points to the specific cognitive processes, which can produce esthetic values, a feature neglected by Luhmann.

Chapter 10

1. Such a hypothesis belongs systematically to the 17th century philosophico-theological occasionalism of Nicolas Malbranche (1638–1715). According to this view, God creates specific features of the world on specific occasions and thus enables man to participate in his eternal wisdom bit by bit.

2. Populations which were separated from those areas where major developments took place probably encountered difficulties of contact and exchange as soon as the geographical separation collapsed or was abolished. I assume that this was dramatic in the period of out-of-Africa migration and that the separation due to the worldwide migrations produced different lines of elaboration in symbolic means and languages.

References

Albertazzi, Liliana (Ed.). (2001). *The Dawn of Cognitive Science. Early European Contributors*. Dordrecht: Kleuwer.

Alinei, Mario (1996). *Origini delle lingue d'Europa, Vol. 1*: Le Teorie della continuità. Bologna: Il Mulino.

Alinei, Mario (2000). *Origini delle lingue d'Europa, Vol. 2*: Continuità del mesolithico all' età del ferro nelle principali aree etnolinguistiche. Bologna: Il Mulino.

Allott, Robin (1989). The Origin of Language: The General Problem. In Wind et al. (Ed., pp. 1–24).

Allott, Robin (1991). The Motor-Theory of Language. In Raffler-Engler et al. (Eds., pp. 123–157).

Allott, Robin (1992). The Motor-Theory of Language. Origin and Evolution. In Wind et al. (Eds., pp. 105–119).

Allott, Robin (1994). Motor Theory of Language Origin. The Diversity of Languages. In Wind et al. (Eds., pp. 125–160).

Anati, Emmanuel (1991). *Felsbilder. Wiege der Kunst und des Geistes*. Zürich: Bär.

Annual Report of the Max Planck Institute for Psycholinguistics (2001). Nijmegen: Max Planck Institute for Psycholinguistics.

Arbib, Michael A. (2002). Grounding the Mirror System Hypothesis for the Evolution of the Language Ready Brain. In Cangelosi & Parisi (Eds., pp. 229–240).

Bahn, Paul & André Rosenfeld (1991). *Rock Art and Prehistory*. Oxford: Oxbow Books.

Ballmer, Thomas T. (1982). *Biological Foundations of Linguistic Communication*. Amsterdam: Benjamins.

Ballmer, Thomas T. & Waltraud Brennenstuhl (1986). *Deutsche Verben. Eine sprachanalytische Untersuchung des Deutschen Wortschatzes*. Tübingen: Narr.

Ballmer, Thomas T. & Wolfgang Wildgen (Eds.) (1987). *Process Linguistics. Exploring the Processual Aspects of Language and Language Use, and the Methods of their Description*. Tübingen: Niemeyer.

Barham, Lawrence S. (2002). Systematic Pigment Use in the Middle Pleistocene of South-Central Africa. *Current Anthropology, 43*(1), 181–190.

Bateman, John & Wolfgang Wildgen (Eds.). (2002). *Sprachbewusstheit in Schule und Gesellschaft*. Frankfurt/Main: Lang.

Bechert, Johannes & Wolfgang Wildgen (1991). *Einführung in die Sprachkontaktforschung*. Darmstadt: Wissenschaftliche Buchgesellschaft.

Becker, Peter René (1993). *Werkzeuggebrauch im Tierreich. Wie Tiere hämmern, bohren, streichen*. Stuttgart: Hirzel.

Bell, Graham (1997). *Selection. The Mechanism of Evolution.* New York: Chapman and Hall.

Begun, David R. (2003). Das Zeitalter der Menschenaffen. *Spektrum der Wissenschaft,* December 2003, 58–66.

Beltran, Antonio et al. (1998). *Altamira.* Sigmaringen: Thorbecke.

Bichakjian, Bernard H. (2002). *Language in a Darwinian Perspective.* Bern: Lang.

Bickerton, Derek (1981). *Roots of language.* Ann Arbor: Karoma.

Bickerton, Derek (1990). *Language & Species.* Chicago: Chicago U.P.

Bickerton, Derek (2000). How Protolanguage Became Language. In Knight, Studdert-Kennedy, & Hurford (Eds., pp. 264–284).

Bickerton, Derek et al. (1984). The Language Bioprogram Hypothesis. *The Behavioral and Brain Sciences, 7,* 173–221.

Blackmore, Susan (1999). *The Meme Machine.* New York: Oxford U.P.

Boden, Margaret A. (1989). What is Creativity? In Mithen (Ed., 1998, pp. 23–60).

Boë, Louis-Jean, Shinji Maeda, & Jean-Louis Heim (1999). Neanderthal Man was not Morphologically Handicapped for Speech. *Evolution and Communication, 3,* 49–57.

Boër, Bart de (1999). Evolution and Self-Organisation of Vowel Systems. *Evolution of Communication, 3*(1), 79–102.

Boesch, Christophe (1993). Aspects of Transmission of Tool-use in Wild Chimpanzees. In Gibson & Ingold (Eds., pp. 171–183).

Boesch, Christophe & Michael Tomasello (1998). Chimpanzee and Human Cultures. *Current Anthropology, 39*(5), 591–614.

Bower, James M., Harvey Johnson, Jon M. Olley, John R. Prescott, Richard G. Roberts, Wilfred Shawcross, & Nigel A. Spooner (2003). New Ages for Human Occupation and Climatic Change at Lake Mungo, Australia. *Nature, 421,* February 2003, 837–840.

Bourdieu, Pierre (1970). *Zur Soziologie der symbolischen Formen.* Frankfurt: Suhrkamp.

Bradshaw, John L. (1997). *Human Evolution. A Neuropsychological Perspective* [cf. Chap. 5: Language and Communication]. Hove: Psychology Press.

Brandt, Michael (1992). *Gehirn und Sprache. Fassile Zeugnisse zum Ursprung des Menschen.* Berlin: Pascal.

Brandt, Per Aage (1995). *Morphologies of Meaning.* Aarhus: Aarhus U.P.

Bräuer, Günter (1992). Africa's place in the evolution of Homo sapiens. In Bräuer, G. & F. H. Smith (Eds.), *Continuity or Replacement. Controversies in Homo Sapiens Evolution* (pp. 83–98). Rotterdam: Balkema.

Brennenstuhl, Waltraud (1982). *Control and Ability. Towards a Biocybernetics of Language.* Amsterdam: Benjamins.

Brooks, Robert R. R. & Vishnu S. Wakankar (1976). *Stone Age Painting in India.* New Haven: Yale U.P.

Budil, Ivo (1994). A Functional Reconstruction of the Supralaryngeal Vocal Tract of the Fossil Hominid from Petralona. In Wind et al. (Eds., pp. 1–19).

Bühler, Karl (1933/1968). *Ausdruckstheorie. Das System an der Geschichte aufgezeigt.* [1st edition, Vienna (1933)] 2nd edition, Stuttgart: Fischer (1968).

Bühler, Karl (1934/1965). *Sprachtheorie. Die Darstellungsfunktion der Sprache.* [2nd edition (1965)]. Stuttgart: Fischer.

Bunney, Sarah et al. (Ed.). (1996). *The Cambridge Encyclopedia of Human Evolution.* Cambridge: Cambridge U.P.

Burtt, Edwin A. (Ed.). (1967). *The English Philosophers from Bacon to Mill* [Texts of Hobbes' Leviathan, 129–234]. The Modern Library. New York.

Calvin, William H. & Derek Bickerton (2000). *Lingua es Machina. Reconciling Darwin and Chomsky with the Human Brain.* Cambridge, MA: MIT Press.

Cangelosi, Angelo & Domenico Parisi (Eds.). (2002). *Simulating the Evolution of Language.* London: Springer.

Cangelosi, Angelo, Alberto Greco, & Stevan Harnad (2002). Symbol Grounding and the Symbolic Theft Hypothesis. In Cangelosi & Parisi (Eds., pp. 191–209).

Cassirer, Ernst (1923/1988). *Die Sprache. Philosophie der symbolischen Formen.* 1st vol. [first print 1923; English translation (1953). New Haven: Yale U.P., 9th print (1988)], Darmstadt: Wissenschaftliche Buchgesellschaft.

Cassirer, Ernst (1925/1987). *Das mythische Denke.* Philosophie der symbolischen Formen. 2nd vol. [first print 1925; 6th print (1987)], Darmstadt: Wissenschaftliche Buchgesellschaft. [English translation (1953). New Haven: Yale U.P.]

Cassirer, Ernst (1929/1982). *Phänomenologie der Erkenntnis.* Philosophie symbolischer Formen. 3rd vol. [first print 1929, 8th Edition (1982)]; Darmstadt: Wissenschaftliche Buchgesellschaft. [English translation (1957). New Haven: Yale U.P.]

Cassirer, Ernst (1944). *An Essay on Man. An Introduction to a Philosophy of Human Culture.* New Haven: Yale U.P.

Cassirer, Ernst (1946/1974). *The Myth of the State.* New Haven: Yale U.P. [first print 1946].

Cassirer, Ernst (1979). *Symbol, Myth, and Culture. Essays and Lectures of Ernst Cassirer 1935–1945* [Ed. by D. P. Verene]. New Haven: Yale U.P.

Cassirer, Ernst (1991). *Das Erkenntnisproblem in der Philosophie und Wissenschaft der neueren Zeit.* Vol. 4: Von Hegels Tod bis zur Gegenwart (1832–1932). Darmstadt: Wissenschaftliche Buchgesellschaft.

Cassirer, Ernst (1994). Der Begriff der symbolischen Form im Aufbau der Geisteswissenschaften. In Ernst Cassirer (Ed.), *Ideen, Wesen und Wirkung des Symbolbegriffs* (pp. 175–200). Darmstadt: Wissenschaftliche Buchgesellschaft.

Chauvet, Jean-Marie, Eliette Brunel Deschamps, & Christian Hillaire (1995). *La grotte Chauvet à Vallon-Pont-d'Arc.* Paris: Seuil.

Chen Zhao Fu (1989). *China. Prähistorische Felsbilder.* Zürich: Bär.

Chevalier-Skolnikoff, Suzanne (1973). Facial Expression of Emotion in Nonhuman Primates. In Ekman (Ed., pp. 11–89).

Chomsky, Noam (1986). *Knowledge of Language. Its Nature, Origin, and Use.* New York: Praeger Publishers.

Chomsky, Noam (1995). Bare Phrase Structure. In G. Webelknuth (Ed.), *Government and Binding Theory and the Minimalist Program* (pp. 383–439). Cambridge, MA: Blackwell.

Condillac, Etienne Bonnot de (1746/1973). *Essai sur l'origine des connaissances humaines.* Paris: Galilée [1st edition 1746].

Condillac, Etienne Bonnot de (1755/1987). *Traité des animaux.* Paris: Vrin [1st edition 1755].

Copernicus, Nicolaus (1990). *Das Neue Weltbild.* Drei Texte Commentariolus. Brief gegen Werner. De revolutionibus I (Latin-German). Hamburg: Meiner.

Coulmas, Florian (1992). *The Writing Systems of the World.* Oxford: Blackwell.

Croft, William (2000). *Explaining Language Change. An Evolutionary Approach.* London: Longman.

Daniel, Hal (1989). The Vestibular System and Language Acquisition. In Wind et al. (Ed., pp. 257–271).

Darwin, Charles (1872/1969). *The Expression of the Emotions in Man and Animals.* [Reprint, 1969]. Culture et Civilisation, Brussels [1st edition London 1872].

Darwin, Charles (1888). *The Descent of Man and Selection in Relation to Sex.* 2nd edition. London: Murray.

Davidson, Iain & William Noble (1993). Tools and Language in Human Evolution. In Gibson & Ingold (Eds., pp. 363–388).

Dawkins, Richard (1994). *Das egoistische Gen.* Heidelberg: Spektrum Verlag. (English original title: The Selfish Gene.)

Deacon, Terrence W. (1991). Brain-Language Coevolution. In Hawkins & Gell-Man (Eds., pp. 49–83).

Deacon, Terrence W. (1992). The Neural Circuitry Underlying Primate Calls and Human Language. In Wind et al. (Ed., pp. 121–162).

Deacon, Terrence W. (1996). Biological Aspects of Language. In Bunney (Ed., pp. 128–133).

Deacon, Terrence W. (1997). *The Symbolic Species: The Evolution of Language and Human Brain.* London: Penguin.

Dennett, Daniel C. (1995). *Darwin's Dangerous Ideas. Evolution and the Meaning of Life.* London: Penguin Press.

Descartes, René (1737/1966). *Discours de la méthode.* Paris: Flammarion [original edition 1737].

Die Evolution des Menschen (2000). [Dossier: *Spektrum der Wissenschaft*, 3/2000.] Heidelberg: Spektrum Verlag.

Dixon, Robert (1980). *The languages of Australia.* Cambridge: Cambridge U.P.

Donald, Merlin (1991). *Origins of the Modern Mind. Three Stages in the Evolution of Culture and Cognition.* Cambridge, MA: Harvard U.P.

Dretske, Fred L. (1981). *Knowledge and the Flow of Information.* Cambridge, MA: MIT-Press.

Dunbar, Robin (1992). Neocortex Size as a Constraint on Group Size in Primates. *Journal of Human Evolution, 20,* 469–493.

Dunbar, Robin (1996). *Grooming, Gossip, and the Evolution of Language.* Cambridge, MA: Harvard U.P.

Dunbar, Robin (1997). Groups, Gossip, and the Evolution of Language. In Schmitt et al. (Eds.), *New Aspects of Human Ethology* (pp. 77–89). New York: Plenum Press.

Dunbar, Robin (2002). *Human Evolutionary Psychology.* Princeton: Palgrave-Mac Millan.

Durham, William H. (1991). *Coevolution. Culture and Human Diversity.* Stanford: Stanford U.P.

Ebers, Edith & Franz Wollenick (1982). *Felsbilder der Alpen.* Hallein: Burgfried [2nd edition].

Eikmeyer Hans Jürgen & Hannes Rieser (Eds.). (1981). *Words, Worlds and Contexts. New Approaches to Word Semantics.* Berlin: de Gruyter.

Ekman, Paul (Ed.). (1973). *Darwin and Facial Expression.* New York: Academic Press.

Enard, W., P. Khaitowich, J. Klose, S. Zöllner, F. Heissig, P. Giavalisco, K. Nieselt-Struwe, E. Muchmore, A. Varki, R. Ravid, G. M. Doxiadis, R. E. Bontrop, S. Pääbo (2002). Intra- and Interspecific Variation in Primate Gene Expression Patterns. *Science, 296*(12), 340–343.

Falk, Dean (1993). Sex Differences in Visuospatial Skills: Implications for Hominid Evolution. In Gibson & Ingold (Eds., pp. 216–229).

Fauconnier, Gilles & Mark Turner (2002). *The Way We Think. Conceptual Blending and the Mind's Hidden Complexities.* New York: Basic Books.

Fauconnier, Gilles (1997). *Mappings in Thought and Language.* Cambridge: Cambridge U.P.

Fischer, Julia & Kurt Hammerschmidt (2001). Functional Referents and Acoustic Similarity Revisited: the Case of Barbary Macaque Alarm Calls. In *Animal Cognition, 4*, 29–35.

Földes-Papp, Karoly (1984). *Vom Felsbild zum Alphabet.* Die Geschichte der Schrift von ihren frühesten Vorstufen bis zur modernen lateinischen Schreibschrift. Stuttgart: Belser.

Foley, Robert (1991). Hominids, Humans, and Hunter-gatherers: an Evolutionary Perspective. In Tim Ingold, David Riches, & James Woodburn (Eds.), *Hunters and Gatherers: History, Evolution and Social Change* (Chap. 13, pp. 201–221). Berg: New York.

Foley, William (1997). *Anthropological Linguistics. An Introduction.* London: Blackwell.

Frank, Manfred (1992). Vom Lachen. Über Komik, Witz und Ironie. Überlegungen im Ausgang von der Frühromantik. In T. Vogel (Ed.), *Vom Lachen. Einem Phänomen auf der Spur.* Tübingen: Attempo.

Freeman, F. G. (1987). Altamira Revisited. First Steps in a New Investigation. In F. G. Freeman et al. (Eds.), *Altamira Revisited* (pp. 67–97). Chicago: Institute for Prehistoric Investigations.

Friedrich, Johannes (1966). *Geschichte der Schrift. Unter besonderer Berücksichtigung ihrer geistigen Entwicklung.* Heidelberg: Carl Winter.

Frisch, Karl von (1974). *Du und das Leben. Eine moderne Biologie für jedermann.* Vienna: Kremayer und Seriau.

Gamble, Clive (1986). *The Palaeolithic Settlement of Europe.* Cambridge: Cambridge U.P.

Gamble, Clive (1999). *The Palaeolithic Societies of Europe.* Cambridge: Cambridge U.P.

Gibson, James J. (1966). *The Senses as Perceptual Systems.* Boston: Houghten Mifflin.

Gibson, Eleanor J. (1988). Exploratory Behavior in the Development of Perceiving, Acting, and the Acquiring of Knowledge. *Annual Review of Psychology, 39*, 1–41.

Gibson, Kathleen R. (1983). Comparative Neurobehavioral Ontogeny and the Constructionist Approach to the Evolution of the Brain, Object Manipulation, and Language. In de Grolier (Ed., pp. 37–61).

Gibson, Kathleen R. & Tim Ingold (Eds.). (1993). *Tools, Language and Cognition in Human Evolution.* Cambridge: Cambridge U.P.

Grammer, Karl, Valentina Filova, & Martin Fieder (1997). The Communication Paradox and Possible Solutions. Towards a Radical Empiricism. In Schmitt et al. (Eds.), *New Aspects of Human Ethnology* (pp. 91–117). New York: Plenum Press.

Grolier, Eric de (1983). *Glossogenetics. The Origin and Evolution of Language.* London: Harwood Academic Publ.

Györi, Gabor (Ed.). (2001). *Language Evolution. Biological, Linguistic, and Philosophical Perspectives.* Frankfurt: Lang.

Habermas, Jürgen (1982). *Theorie des kommunikativen Handelns*, Vol. 2: Zur Kritik der funktionalistischen Vernunft. Frankfurt/M.: Suhrkamp.

Haken, Hermann & M. Stadler (Eds.). (1990). *Synergetics of Cognition*. Berlin: Springer.

Haken, Hermann (1996). *Principles of Brain Functioning. A Synergetic Approach to Brain Activity, Behavior and Cognition*. Berlin: Springer.

Halbritter, Kurt (1977). *Halbritters Waffenarsenal*. Munich: Hanser.

Harrap's Weis Mattutat (1981). *Dictionnaire Allemand-Français, Français-Allemand*. London.

Hauser, Marc D. (1996). *The Evolution of Communication*, [Bradford Book]. Cambridge, MA: MIT Press.

Hawkins, John A. & Murray Gell-Mann (Eds.). (1991). *The Evolution of Human Languages*, Santa Fe Institute Studies in the Sciences of Complexity. Redwood City: Addison-Wesley.

Heeschen, Volker (2001). The Narration "Instinct": Signalling Behaviour, Communication, and the Selective Value of Storytelling. In *Trabant and Ward* (pp. 179–195).

Heinroth, Oskar (1930). Über bestimmte Bewegungsweisen der Wirbeltiere. *Sitzungsberichte der Gesellschaft Naturforschender Freunde*, 333–343. Vienna.

Herder, Johann Gottfried (1770/1966). *Abhandlung über den Ursprung der Sprache*. Stuttgart: Reclam [1st edition 1770].

Heusden, Barend van (1999). The Emergence of Difference: Some Notes on the Evolution of Human Semiosis. *Semiotica. Special Issue on Biosemiotics, 127*(1/4), 631–646.

Heusden, B. van (2003). Cassirers Ariadnefaden – Anthropologie und Semiotik. In Sandkühler & Pätzold (Eds., pp. 11–147).

Hewes, Gordon W. (1977). Language Origin Theories. In Duane M. Rumbaugh (Ed.), *Language Learning in Chimpanzee* (pp. 2–53). The Lana Project. New York: Academic Press.

Hewes, Gordon W. (1989). The Upper Paleolithic Expansion of Supernaturalism and the Advent of Fully Developed Spoken Language. In Wind et al. (Ed., pp. 139–157).

Hockett, Charles, F. (1960). The Origin of Speech. *Scientific American, 203*, 88–96.

Hofbauer, Josef & Karl Sigmund (1984). *Evolutionstheorie und dynamische Systeme. Mathematische Aspekte der Selektion*. Berlin: Parey.

Holst, Erich von (1974). *Zentralnervensystem. Fünf Beiträge zur Verhaltensphysiologie*. München: dtv.

Hublin, Jean-Jacques (2002). Exploring Modernity: Background and Prospects in Paleoanthropology, Contribution to the Symposium: *Palaeontological and Archaeological Insights into Human Evolution*, June 2, 2002, Leipzig.

Humboldt, Wilhelm von (1963). *Werke*. In fünf Bänden, Vol. III: Schriften zur Sprachphilosophie. Darmstadt: Wiss. Buchgesellschaft.

Hurford, James R. (2000). Social Transmission Favours Linguistic Generalization. In Knight et al. (Ed., pp. 324–352).

Immelmann, Klaus (1979). *Einführung in die Verhaltensforschung* [2nd edition]. Berlin: Parey.

Jablonski, Nina G. (1998). *The Natural History of the Doucs and Snub-nosed Monkeys*. Singapore: World Scientific.

Jablonski, Nina G. & Leslie C. Aiello (Eds.). (1998). *The Origin and Diversification of Language*. San Francisco: Academy of Sciences.

Jackendoff, Ray (2002). *Foundations of Language. Brain, Meaning, Grammar, Evolution.* Oxford: Oxford U.P.

Jelinek, Jan (1975). *Das große Bilderlexikon des Menschen in der Vorzeit.* Bertelsmann: Munich.

Jerrison, Harry J. (1973). *Evolution of the Brain and Intelligence.* New York: Academic Press.

Jürgens, Uwe (1998). Affenlaute als Modell für nicht-verbale emotionale Lautäußerungen des Menschen – Untersuchungen zu deren zentralnervöser Steuerung. In Gundermann, Horst (Ed.), *Die Ausdruckswelt der Stimme.* 1. Stuttgarter Stimmtage (pp. 31–39). Heidelberg: Hüthig.

Kant, Emanuel (1790/1974). *Kritik der Urteilskraft.* Frankfurt/Main: Suhrkamp.

Kien, Jenny (1994). Developments in the Pongid and Human Motor Systems as Preadaptation for the Evolution of Human Language Ability. In Wind et al. (Ed., pp. 271–292).

Kirby, Simon (2000). Syntax Without Natural Selection: How Compositionality Emerges from Vocabulary in a Population of Learners. In Knight, Studdert-Kennedy, & Hurford (Eds., pp. 303–323).

Klein, Wolfgang & Norbert Dittmar (1979). *Developing Grammars.* Berlin: de Gruyter.

Knight, Chris, Michael Studdert-Kennedy, & James R. Hurford (Eds.). (2000). *The Evolutionary Emergence of Language.* Social Functions and the Origins of Linguistic Form (pp. 264–284). Cambridge: Cambridge U.P.

Köhler, Wolfgang (1921). Zur Psychologie der Chimpansen. *Psychologische Forschungen, 1*(2), 46.

Labov, William (1972). Contraction, Deletion, and Inherent Variability of the English Copula. In Wiliam Labov, *Language in the Inner City. Studies in the Black English Vernacular* (pp. 65–129). Philadelphia: University of Pennsylvania Press.

Labov, William (2001). *Principles of Linguistic Change, Vol. 2*: Social factors. Oxford: Blackwell.

Laitman, J. T., R. C. Heimbuch, & E. S. Crelin (1979). Developmental Change in a Basicrancial Line and its Relationship to the Upper Respiratory System in Living Primates. *American Journal of Anatomy, 152,* 467–483.

Lakoff, George (1987). *Women, Fire, and Dangerous Things. What Categories Reveal about the Mind.* Chicago: Chicago U.P.

Lakoff, George & Mark Johnson (1981). *Metaphors we Live by.* Chicago: Chicago U.P.

Laurendeau, M. & Pinard, A. (1961). *Causal Thinking in the Child.* New York: International U.P.

Le Petit Robert (1996). *Dictionnaire de la langue française.* CD-ROM, LIBRIS INTERACTIVE.

Leakey, Richard E. (1981). *Die Suche nach dem Menschen* (Engl. "The Making of Mankind"). Frankfurt/Main: Umschau Verlag.

Lenneberg, Eric H. (1967). *Biological Foundations of Language* (with appendices by Noam Chomsky & Otto Marx). New York: Wiley.

Leroi-Gourhan, André (1981). *Höhlenkunst in Frankreich.* Gladbach: Gustav-Lübbe Verlag.

Leroi-Gourhan, André (1992). *L'art pariétal.* Langage de la préhistoire. Grenoble: Jerôme Million.

Leslie, Alan M. (1987). Pretense and Representation: The Origins of "Theory of Mind". *Psychological Review, 4*, 412–426.

Lévi-Strauss, Claude (1962). *La Pensée sauvage.* Paris: Plon.

Levinson, Stephen C. (2001). *Space, Language and Cognition. Explorations in Cognitive Diversity.* Cambridge, MA: Cambridge U.P.

Lewin, Kurt (1936). *Principles of Topological Psychology.* New York: McGraw-Hill.

Leyton, Michael (2001). *A Generative Theory of Shape.* Berlin: Springer.

Liebermann, Philip (1989). The Origins of Some Aspects of Human Language and Cognition. In Paul Mellars & Chris Stringer (Eds.), *The Human Revolution. Behavioural and Biological Perspectives on the Origins of Modern Humans* (pp. 391–414). Edinburgh: Edinburgh U.P.

Livingstone, Frank B. (1983). Evolutionary Theory, Human Adaptations, and the Evolution of Language. In de Grolier (Ed., pp. 163–184).

López-Garcia, Angel (2002). *Fondamentos geneticos de lenguaje.* Madrid: Cátedra.

López-Garcia, Angel (2003). Species Building and Evolution in Biology and Linguistics. Paper presented at the "Institut für Deutsche Sprache" in Mannheim, Ms.

Lorenz, Konrad (1940). Durch Domestikation verursachte Störungen arteigenen Verhaltens. *Zeitschrift für Angewandte Psychologie und Charakterkunde, 59*, 1–81.

Lorenz, Konrad (1978). *Vergleichende Verhaltensforschung. Grundlagen der Ethnologie.* Vienna: Springer.

Lovejoy, O. (1982). Models of Human Evolution. *Science, 217*, 304–305.

Luhmann, Niklas (1975). Einführende Bemerkungen zu einer Theorie symbolisch generalisierter Kommunikationsmedien. In Niklas Luhmann (Ed.), *Soziologische Aufklärung. 2. Aufsätze zur Theorie der Gesellschaft* (pp. 170–192). Opladen: Westdeutscher Verlag.

MacNeillage, Peter F. (1998). The Frame/Content Theory of Evolution of Speech Production. *Behavioral and Brain Sciences, 21*, 499–546.

Marr, David (1982). *Vision.* San Francisco: Freeman.

Marshack, Alexander (1972). *The Roots of Civilization.* New York: McGraw Hill.

Martin, Alex (1998). Organization of Semantic Knowledge and the Origin of Words in the Brain. In Jablonski & Aiello (Eds., pp. 69–87).

Masali, Melchiorre, Silvana Borgognoni Tarli, & Margherita Maffei (1992). Auditory Ossicles and the Evolution of the Primate Ear: a Biometrical Approach. In Wind et al. (Ed., pp. 67–86).

Mauss, Marcel (1973). *Sociologie et Anthropologie.* Paris: Presses Universitaires de France.

Maynard Smith, John & Eörs Szathmáry (1995). *The Major Transitions in Evolution.* Oxford: Freeman.

McNeill, David (1992). *Hand and Mind: What Gestures Reveal About Thought.* Chicago: Chicago U.P.

Mellars, Paul (1998). Neanderthals, Modern Humans and the Archaeological Evidence for Language. In Jablonski & Aiello (Eds., pp. 89–115).

Mellars, Paul & Chris Stinger (1989). *The Human Revolution. Behavioural and Biological Perspectives on the Origins of Modern Humans.* Edinburgh: Edinburgh U.P.

Meyer, Laure (1993). *Englische Landschaftsmalerei von der Renaissance bis heute.* Paris: Terrail (translation from the French original).

Mithen, Steven (Ed.). (1998). *Creativity in Human Evolution and Prehistory.* London: Routledge.

Mithen, Steven (1998b). A Creative Explosion. Theory of Mind, Language and the Disembodied Mind in the Upper Palaeolithic. In Mithen (Ed., pp. 165–191).

Morford, Jill P. & Susan Goldin-Meadow (2001). Time and Again: Displaced Reference in the Communication of Linguistic Isolates. In Györi (Ed., pp. 173–197).

Mottron, Laurent (1987). Ein dynamisches Modell des normalen und des pathologischen Spracherwerbs. In W. Wildgen & L. Mottron (Eds., pp. 342–411).

Nersessian, Nancy J. (2002). The Cognitive Basis of Model-based Reasoning in Science. In Peter Carruthers, St. P. Stich, & M. Siegal (Eds.), *The Cognitive Basis of Science* (pp. 133–153). Cambridge: Cambridge U.P.

Oubré, Alondra Yvette (1997). *Instinct and Revelation. Reflections on the Origins of Numinous Perception.* Amsterdam: Gordon and Breach.

Pääbo, Svante (1999). Human Evolution. *Millennium Issue, TCB.TIBS.TIG,* M13–M16.

Pedretti, Carlo (Ed.) (1995). *Leonardo da Vinci. Libro di Pittura.* Codice Urbinate lat. 1270 Nella Biblioteca Vaticana (Trascrizione critica di Carlo Vecce). Florence: Giunti.

Peirce, Charles Sanders (1865/1986). Teleologische Logik. In Ch. S. Peirce (1986), *Semiotische Schriften,* Vol. 1 (pp. 105–106). Frankfurt/Main: Suhrkamp (MS 802, 1865).

Peirce, Charles Sanders (1991). *Naturordnung und Zeichenprozeß.* Frankfurt: Suhrkamp.

Petraglia, Michael D. & Ravi Korisettar (Eds.). (1998). *Early Human Behavior in Global Context. The Rise and Diversity of the Lower Palaeolithic Record.* London: Routledge.

Piaget, Jean (1926). *La représentation du monde chez l'enfant.* Paris: P.U.F.

Piaget, Jean & Bärbel Inhelder (1966). *L'image mental chez l'enfant.* Paris: P.U.F.

Pinker, Steven & P. Bloom (1990). Natural language and natural selection. *Behavioral and Brain Sciences, 13,* 507–508.

Piveteau, Jean (1991). *La main et l'hominisation.* Paris: Masson.

Pöppel, Ernst (1994). Temporal Mechanisms in Perception. *International Review of Neurobiology, 37,* 185–202.

Pöppel, Ernst (1997). A hierarchical model of temporal perception. *Trends in Cognitive Science, 1*(2), 56–61.

Priuli, Ausilio (1996). *Le più antiche manifestazioni spirituali.* Arte Rupestre. Paleoiconografia Camusa e delle Genti Alpine. Ivrea: Collana.

Provine, Robert R. (1995). Laughter Punctuates Speech: Linguistic, Social and Gender Contexts of Laughter. *Ethology, 95,* 291–298.

Provine, Robert R. & Kenneth R. Fischer (1989). Laughing, Smiling, and Talking: Relation to Sleeping and Social Context in Humans. *Ethology, 83,* 295–305.

Quiatt, Diane & Vernon Reynolds (1993). *Primate Behaviour. Information, Social Knowledge, and the Evolution of Culture.* Cambridge: Cambridge U.P.

Raffler-Engel, Walburga, Jan Wind, & Abraham Jonger (Eds.) (1991). *Studies in Language Origins, Vol. 3.* Amsterdam: Benjamins.

Ragir, Sonia (2001). Toward and Unverstanding of the Relationship between Bipedal Walking, Encephalization, and Language Origins. In Györi (Ed., pp. 73–100).

Rappenglück. Michael (1999). *Eine Himmelskarte aus der Eiszeit?* Frankfurt/Main: Lang.

Reynolds, Peter C. (1983). Ape Constructional Ability and the Origin of Linguistic Structure. In Grolier (Ed., pp. 185–200).

Rhotert, Hans (1956). Die Kunst der Altsteinzeit. In Weigert (Ed., pp. 9–52).

Riedl, Rupert (1980). *Biologie der Erkenntnis: die stammesgeschichtlichen Grundlagen der Vernunft* [in cooperation with Robert Kaspar]. Berlin: Parey.

Rightmire, C. Philip (1990). The Evolution of *Homo Erectus. Comparative Anatomical Studies of an Extinct Human Species.* Cambridge: Cambridge U.P.

Rizzolatti, Giacomo, Fadiga, L., Gallese, V., & Fogassi, L. (1995). Premotor Cortex and the Recognition of Motor Actions. *Cognitive Brain Research, 3,* 131–141.

Rizzolatti, Giacomo & Michael A. Arbib (1998). Language Within Our Grasp. *Trends in Neuroscience, 21*(5), 188–194.

Roudil, Jean-Louis (1995). Préhistoire de l'Ardèche. Soubès (Hérault): Conseil Général de l'Ardèche.

Sanchidrián, José Luis (2001). *Manual de arte preistorico.* Barcelona: Ariel.

Sandkühler, Hans Jörg & Detlev Pätzold (Eds.) (2003). *Kultur und Symbol. Die Philosophie Ernst Cassirers.* Stuttgart: Metzler.

Saussure, Ferdinand de (1916/1975). *Cours de linguistique générale.* Paris: Payot (1st publication 1916).

Schmandt-Besserat, Denise (1978). The Earliest Precursor of Writing. *Scientific American, June 1978* (reprinted in Wang, 1982 (Chap. 10): 81–89).

Shammi, P. & O. T. Stuss (1999). Humour Appreciation: A Role of the Right Frontal Lobe. *Brain, 122,* 657–666.

Sinha, Chris (2003). Biology, Culture and the Emergence and Elaboration of Symbolization, forthcoming in A. Saleemi, A. Gjedde, & O. S. Bohn (Eds.), *In Search for a Language for the Mind/Brain. Can the Multiple Perspective be Unified?* Download from: http://formes-symboliques.org/article.php3?id_article=34.

Smith, Noel W. (1992). *An Analysis of Ice Age Art. Its Psychology and Belief System.* New York: Lang.

Starck, Dietrich (1981). Stammesgeschichtliche Voraussetzungen der Entwicklung der menschlichen Sprache. *Nova Acta Leopoldina N.V. 54, Nr. 245,* 581–596.

Steels, Luc (2002). Grounding Symbols Through Evolutionary Language Games. In Cangelosi & Parisi (Eds., pp. 211–226).

Stein, Uli (1994). *Leicht Behämmert.* Erfindungen, die uns gerade noch fehlten. Oldenburg: Lappen.

Stoneking, Mark & Rebecca L. Cann (1989). African Origin of Human Mitochondrial DNA. In Mellars & Stringer (Eds., pp. 17–30).

Stopa, Roman (1981). Evolution der Sprache. *Nova Acta Leopoldina N.F.,* 345–375.

Studdert-Kennedy, Michael (2000). Evolutionary Implications of the Particulate Principle: Imitation and the Dissociation of Phonetic Form from Semantic Function. In Knight, Studdert-Kennedy, & Hurford (Eds., pp. 161–176).

Sylvester, David (1968). *Henry Moore. Catalogue of an Exhibition at the Tate Gallery,* 17 July to 22 September 1968. London: Lund: Humphries & Co.

Talmy, Leonard (1988). Force Dynamics in Language and Cognition. *Cognitive Science 12*(1), 49–100.

Tattersall, Ian (2001). How we Came to be Human. *Scientific American,* December 2001, 42–49.

Tembrok, Günter (1977). *Grundlagen des Tierverhaltens.* Braunschweig: Vieweg.

Tesak-Gutmannsbauer, Gerhild (2001). Ernst Cassirer on Language Origins. In Györi (Ed., pp. 263–267).

Thom, René (1972/1975). *Structural Stability and Morphogenesis,* Reading: Benjamins (translation from the French original 1972).

Thom, René (1974). La linguistique, discipline morphologique exemplaire. *Critique, 30*(1), 235–245.

Thom, René (1983). *Mathematical Models of Morphogenesis.* New York: Horwood (Wiley).

Thommen, Evelyne (1991). La genèse de la perception de l'intentionnalité dans le mouvement apparent. *Archives de Psychologie, 59,* 195–223.

Tomasello, Michael (1999). *The Cultural Origins of Human Cognition.* Cambridge, MA: Harvard UP.

Trabant, Jürgen & Sean Ward (Eds.). (2001). *New Essays on the Origin of Language.* Berlin: de Gruyter.

Vygotsky, Lev S. (1962). *Thought and Language* (translated from the Russian by E. Hanfmann & G. Vakar). Cambridge, MA: MIT Press.

Wang, William S. Y. (Ed.). (1982). *Human Communication. Language and its Biological Bases.* San Francisco: Freeman.

Webster's Encyclopedic Anabridged Dictionary of the English Language (1989). New York: Gramercy Books.

Weigert, Hans (Ed.). (1956). *Kleine Kunstgeschichte der Vorzeit und der Naturvölker.* Stuttgart: Kohlhammer.

Weiner, J. S. (1972). *Entstehungsgeschichte des Menschen.* Lausanne: Editions Rencontre.

Wenke, Robert J. (1999). *Patterns in Prehistory. Humankind's first Three Million Years.* Oxford: Oxford U.P.

Wickberg, Daniel (1998). *The Senses of Humor. Self and Laughter in Modern America.* Ithaca: Cornell U.P.

Wildgen, Wolfgang (1977a). *Differentielle Linguistik, Entwurf eines Modells zur Beschreibung und Messung semantischer und pragmatischer Variation.* Tübingen: Niemeyer.

Wildgen, Wolfgang (1977b). *Kommunikativer Stil und Sozialisation. Eine empirische Untersuchung.* Tübingen: Niemeyer.

Wildgen, Wolfgang (1981). Archetypal Dynamics in Word Semantics. An Application of Catastrophe Theory. In Eikmeyer & Rieser (Eds., pp. 234–296).

Wildgen, Wolfgang (1982a). *Catastrophe Theoretic Semantics. An Elaboration and Application of René Thom's Theory.* Amsterdam: Benjamins.

Wildgen, Wolfgang (1982b). Makroprozesse bei der Verwendung nominaler ad hoc-Komposita im Deutschen. *Deutsche Sprache, 3,* 237–257.

Wildgen, Wolfgang (1985). *Archetypensemantik. Grundlagen einer dynamischen Semantik auf der Basis der Katastrophentheorie.* Tübingen: Narr.

Wildgen, Wolfgang (1987). Dynamic Aspects of Nominal Composition. In Ballmer & Wildgen (Eds., pp. 128–162).

Wildgen, Wolfgang (1994). *Process, Image, and Meanings. A Realistic Model of the Meanings of Sentences and Narrative Texts.* Amsterdam: Benjamins.

Wildgen, Wolfgang (1996). How to Naturalize Semantics (in the spirit of Konrad Lorenz)? *Evolution and Cognition, 151*(2), 151–164.

Wildgen, Wolfgang (1998a). *Das kosmische Gedächtnis. Kosmologie, Semiotik und Gedächtnistheorie im Werke von Giordano Bruno (1548–1600).* Frankfurt: Lang.

Wildgen, Wolfgang (1998b). Chaos, Fractals and Dissipative Structures in Language. Or the End of Linguistic Structuralism. In Gabriel Altmann & Walter A. Koch (Eds.), *Systems. New Paradigms for the Human Sciences* (pp. 596–620). Berlin: de Gruyter.

Wildgen, Wolfgang (1998c). Selbstorganisationsprozesse in der Phonologie. In K. H. Wagner & W. Wildgen (Eds.), *Studien zur Phonologie, Grammatik, Sprachphilosophie und Semiotik* (pp. 123–137). BLIcK 6, Bremen: Bremen U.P.

Wildgen, Wolfgang (1999a). *De la grammaire au discours.* Une approche morphodynamique. Bern: Peter Lang.

Wildgen, Wolfgang (1999b). *Hand und Auge.* Eine Studie zur Repräsentation und Selbstrepräsentation (kognitive und semantische Aspekte). (Publications of the Center of Philosophical Foundation of Science, 21.) Bremen: Bremen U.P. (download from the homepage: http://www.fb10.uni-bremen.de/homepages/wildgen.htm).

Wildgen, Wolfgang (2001a). Représentations de l'animal sous l'aspect physiognomonique, éthique et politique (chez Della Porta, Bruno, Arcimboldo et Hobbes). *VISIO, 61,* 49–60.

Wildgen, Wolfgang (2001b). Kurt Lewin and the Rise of "Cognitive Sciences" in Germany: Cassirer, Bühler, Reichenbach. In Albertazzi (Ed., pp. 299–332).

Wildgen, Wolfgang (2001c). The Paleolithic Origins of Art, its Dynamic and Topological Aspects, and the Transition to Writing. Contribution to the Workshop on Semiotic Evolution & the Dynamics of Culture Groningen (NL), 23rd/24th November 2001; forthcoming 2004, in M. Bax, B. van Heusden, & W. Wildgen (Eds.), *Semiotic Evolution and the Dynamics of Culture.* Bern: Lang.

Wildgen, Wolfgang (2002). Dynamical Models of Predication. In *STUF* (*Sprachtypologie und Universalienforschunmg*), 4, 403–420.

Wildgen, Wolfgang (2003a). Die Repräsentation von Mensch, Tier (und Pflanze) und ihres Verhältnisses seit der Antike. In Silja Freudenberger & Hans Jörg Sandkühler (Eds.), *Repräsentation, Krise der Repräsentation, Paradigmenwechsel* (pp. 301–340). Frankfurt: Lang.

Wildgen, Wolfgang (2003b). Die Sprache – Cassirers Auseinandersetzung mit der zeitgenössischen Sprachwissenschaft und Sprachtheorie. In Sandkühler & Pätzold (Eds., pp. 171–201).

Wildgen, Wolfgang (2003c). L'evolució de les llengues: Continuïtat i catàstrofe. In *Mètode.* Universitat de València, 39 (special edition: Del crit a la paraula. Fonaments biològics del llenguatge), 73–75.

Wildgen, Wolfgang (forthcoming 2004a). Éléments narratifs et argumentatifs dans l'articulation de l'espace pictural. Transformations de l'Ultime Cène du XIIe au XXe siècle. Forthcoming in A. Beyaert & St. Caliandro (Eds.), *Espaces perçus, territoires imagés dans l'art.* Paris: l'Harmattan. (Download from: //www.fb10.uni-bremen.de/homepages/wildgen.htm)

Wildgen, Wolfgang (forthcoming 2004b). Le problème du continu/discontinu dans la sémiophysique de René Thom et l'évolution des langues, Contribution to: Journée d'Études, Université de Paris – Nanterre, 20th of June 2003; forthcoming in *Cahiers de praxématique.*

Wildgen, Wolfgang (forthcoming 2004c). The Dimensionality of Text and Picture and its Semiotic Consequences. In Alexander Mehler (Ed.), *Festschrift Rieger,* Part II. Berlin Springer.

Wildgen, Wolfgang & Laurent Mottron (1987). *Dynamische Sprachtheorie. Sprachbeschreibung und Spracheerklärung nach den Prinzipien der Selbstorganisation und der Morphogenese.* Bochum: Brockmeyer.

Wilkins, David P. (1996). Natural Tendencies of Semantic Change and the Search for Cognates. In Mark Durieux & Malcolm Ross (Eds.), *The Comparative Method Reviewed* (pp. 264–304). Oxford: Oxford U.P.

Wilton, Andrew (1982). William Turner. *Reisebilder.* Munich: Prestel. (English original (1982). *Turner Abroad.* London: British Museum Publication).

Wind, Jan (1989). The Evolutionary History of the Human Speech Organs. In Wind et al. (Ed., pp. 173–197).

Wind, Jan, Edward G. Pulleyblank, Eric de Groher, & Bernhard H. Bichakjian (Eds.). (1989). *Studies in Language Origins, Vol. 1.* Amsterdam: Benjamins.

Wind, Jan, B. Chiarelli, B. Bichakjian, A. Nocentini, & A. Jonker (Eds.). (1992). *Language Origins: A Multidisciplinary Approach.* Dordrecht: Kluwer.

Wind, Jan, Abraham Jonker, Robin Allott, & Leonard Rolfe (Eds.). (1994). *Studies in Language Origins, Vol. 3.* Amsterdam: Benjamins.

Wundt, Wilhelm Max (1863/1922). Vorlesungen über die Menschen- und Tierseele. Leipzig: Voss (7th augmented edition, 1922).

Wundt, Wilhelm Max (1911). *Völkerpsychologie: Eine Untersuchung der Entwicklungsgesetze von Sprache, Mythos und Sitte,* Vol. 2(2): Die Sprache. Leipzig: Engelmann (3rd augmented edition).

Yates, Frances A. (1966). *The Art of Memory.* London: Routhledge & Kegan.

Zwarts, Joost (1997). Vectors as Relative Positions: A compositional Semantics of Modified PPs. *Journal of Semantics 14,* 57–86.

Index of proper names

Subject index

Index of principles and hypotheses

In the series *Advances in Consciousness Research* the following titles have been published thus far or are scheduled for publication: